As We Are

AS WE ARE

Doubleday & Company, Inc., Garden City, New York

by Henry Brandon

1961

THIS IS A NOTE OF THANKS TO

H. V. Hodson, the editor of the *Sunday Times*, for his encouragement and advice and for making this series and, subsequently, this book possible

Iain Lang, the Foreign Editor of the *Sunday Times*, for being a patient critic

Walter Lippmann for his valuable comments and advice

Stewart Alsop for drawing the attention of Doubleday to these "Conversation Pieces"

Miss Ruth Thomas of the Thomas Transcription Service for the intelligent transcribing of the tapes

The interview with Walter Reuther is used by permission of North American Newspaper Alliance, Inc.

to the memory of

O. and I.B.

Contents

7

CONTENTS

Introduction

To speak about the American civilization is to enter into an endless conversation. It is so formidable a theme that I wonder whether I should have even mentioned it in the same breath with these "Conversation Pieces." But their main purpose is to throw light on some random facets of contemporary American civilization.

This is a hazardous undertaking, to say the least, and inevitably it is very incomplete. My original idea was to introduce to a British audience through the medium of the *Sunday Times* of London, whose correspondent in the United States I have been for over ten years, a number of interesting American personalities —strong individualists who have something pertinent to say about America, about American culture, about themselves and their interests.

That idea was inspired by my admiration for the stoicism and fascination with which Americans react to foreign criticism. Often they remind me of Indian fakirs lying on the pinpoints. They not only endure it, they actually enjoy it and take it seriously. I find this an endearing trait, and it is a pity that more nations do not behave in the same way.

What is the reason for that trait? Perhaps it is that America has been such a fast-developing civilization that its people need to look into mirrors held up by foreigners to see themselves as they are. Dr. Margaret Mead thinks it is because America was founded by people from various societies who want to compare their own culture with that of their countries of origin.

Now, for a change, I thought, Americans should explain themselves and their environment, especially as no country in the world is more misunderstood and more falsely interpreted than the United States. The Europeans' view of America is still very largely a catalogue of worn clichés. While this does not speak well for the reporting skill of foreign correspondents in America, I prefer to think that it is primarily the fault of Americans themselves. They have a curious liking for certain stereotypes and myths about their own society.

American capitalism, for instance, has undergone some radical changes. Yet it is still viewed with much suspicion in many parts of the world, chiefly because Americans are loath to admit that the United States has, in fact, become a welfare state. The United States has made an admirable adjustment of capitalism to modern conditions and today it has in many ways more advanced social legislation than some of the European semi-socialist states. A growing recognition of that fact is one reason why the world has become far more receptive toward American ideas.

Americans have also become more tolerant of noncommitted countries who do not wish to sign up on the dotted line. This reflects a greater realism and a maturer outlook. The notion that Americans can see things only in black and white is less true than it used to be.

Also it seems to me that American society is not so acquisitive as it once was. Although the stress on material comforts—money and success—are still very much in evidence, it is not quite what vulgar advertising methods would lead one to believe. In order to "keep up with the Joneses," for instance, it is no longer imperative to buy a new car every year or two. Indeed, a kind of pride is developing in being able to keep one's old car running longer. New yearnings for more "gracious living" have been awakened together with a growing taste for "the better things in life."

As the standards of life have risen, especially among the working classes and the lower middle classes, American society seems less restless. Various social groups have arrived at a plateau with their wants satisfied, and seem to desire a breather—to sit back for a while and enjoy their new level of life. Old symbols of class distinction fade away and new ones are created, but the class structure is becoming more and more blurred. What was once called the "American experiment," the gradual fusing of many racial, ethnic and religious groups with their varied traditions, habits and outlooks, has gone far enough to make Walt Whitman's phrase "a nation of nations" obsolete. The differences of background will, of course, linger for a long time and continue to create certain barriers, just as do differences of wealth.

But as the standards of life rise throughout American society, so ambitions, it seems to me, begin to pass beyond the mere desire for more material acquisitions. There is a new awareness that man does not live by consumer goods alone. To many observers this seems a negative sign, a flagging of the American spirit of adventure, the advent of decadence. But as long as people know what to do with their leisure, it may be a sign of growing maturity. The large sales of "paperbacks"—and there are many excellent ones among them—from the drugstore counter are a unique way of creating a mass appetite for books. The extraordinary popularity of long-playing records of serious music, the mushrooming of local theater groups, and the staggering attendances reported by art galleries and museums, are all signs of the times.

Between the wars men like Henry Ford, Charles Lindbergh, and Rudolph Valentino caught the imagination of the world. Today Leonard Bernstein, Arthur Miller, Walter Reuther, and Dr. Jonas Salk stimulate a new and different interest in American achievement.

Leonard Bernstein illustrates the changes in the tide of cultural influences. Anything that related to music—with the exception of jazz, of course—used to be imported from Europe. But Bernstein belongs to the new generation which does not feel so strongly indebted to Europe. American architects have added a new outer and inner spaciousness to architecture. American writers and playwrights have left their imprints on Europe for some time, but the influence of American painters is something new.

The most powerful impact the United States is having on Europe, however, is economic. The new European prosperity, originally stimulted by the Marshall Plan, is creating problems with which Americans have been wrestling for years, problems of mass education, of consumer credit, service and distribution. Will it infuse Europe with a similar materialism? Will it lead to the depreciation of old values? Will it mean a strengthening or a weakening of the sense of purpose in the West?

All this has fired European interest in America more than ever before. The world can no longer ignore the American civilization, as some would have wished, or be satisfied with worn-out notions about it. The old curiosity about the eccentricities and failures of American society, which Americans themselves tend to overdo, is being replaced by a deeper and broader interest in its character and its promise.

Perhaps these "Conversation Pieces" will help to satisfy some of this new interest. In order to make them fresh and to give them a relaxed conversational tone I decided to use a tape-recorder. I hoped that this method would give the reader a direct impression of the people I talked with, and, as much as possible, preserve the flavor of their personalities.

However, the use of the tape recorder narrowed the selection to the most readily articulate. Brilliant people often cannot do themselves justice when it comes to expressing their ideas. With fluent speakers my task was simple and easy. All I had to do was to act as a catalyst.

Arthur Koestler once remarked that the impulse of people to want to meet an author personally whose work they have admired is as unwise as wanting to meet a goose because one likes *pâté de foie gras*. None of the people I interviewed disappointed me. They were exceedingly co-operative, helpful, and hospitable. Men and women of integrity, they were endowed with a deep sensitivity to the joys and pains of American civilization. They reflected in their own way the vitality and insecurity, the optimism and frustration, the generosity and despair inherent in American life.

There was much disagreement among them as to whether an American culture has come into existence. Some said yes, others doubted it, still others saw an international culture emerging to which the United States was giving a lead or was making a substantial contribution. Some deprecated the standards and values of American culture, some defended them. Some complained that European critics tend to compare the best of their own culture with the worst of the American, others that Europe is adopting the worst features of American culture and is then complaining about it. It is my own feeling that with the growing saturation of the outer-man American society will be paying increasing attention to the needs of the inner-man, and that the resources of this unfinished society will be devoted more to the qualitative than the quantitative challenge of our times.

With the exception of Peter Ustinov, all are Americans. Dr. Wernher von Braun, the missile specialist, I consider an American for when a prying reporter once became too inquisitive about his German past he lost his patience and asked: "How long does it take to be considered an American in this country?" I included Peter Ustinov partly because he was too good to leave out merely for the sake of uniformity, partly because he is the personification of the cosmopolitan, and his views, I thought, would add to the stimulus and fun of the whole exercise.

The brief introductions I have written to each interview are not meant to be a searching analysis of either the person or his work. I wanted only to give the reader some sense of the atmosphere during the interview, some of my own reactions to the person and a minimum of facts to sharpen the focus. I hope they will help the reader to settle down more comfortably to the reading of these dialogues—which are, as Iain Lang, the Foreign Editor of the *Sunday Times*, put it, "True to tape."

As We Are

Who Are the Americans?

a conversation with

DR. MARGARET MEAD

Before I went to see Dr. Margaret Mead, the distinguished American anthropologist, I was advised to arm myself with a bulletproof vest . . . she is a sharp-shooter in any discussion, especially with men, I was told. I was therefore surprised to find her a warm, kind and easy, if determined, personality. She is nearing sixty, but she clearly has the vitality of a woman of forty. She looks short, in fact, very short—when she stands up, but seated one does not look down on her—only up. She speaks with a fluency, an assuredness that is impressive, almost breath-taking. And like any good teacher she uses her hands frequently to underline a thought. Some of my questions would have caused any less fluent thinker to hesitate or to stumble—she never did. Her seemingly effortless mental concentration, her facility in bringing some of the most complex problems swiftly down to earth were admirable.

After our session was over she surprised me by saying that at the outset of our conversation I had put her too much on the defensive. I was not sure whether she simply wanted to flatter me, whether she wanted to make me feel a man, or whether this was to soften the edge of some of her replies. Cornell Capa, who is not only a brilliant photographer, but also a student of people, later, however, confirmed that he had thought her a little nervous at the beginning. But with a photographer sitting crossed-legged in front of her, a tape recorder on the table, and me shooting complicated questions at her—who would not feel a little put off?

Our conversation took place in Dr. Mead's little, bohemian house in Greenwich Village in New York. The furniture was simple, almost frugal, its arrangement casual. There was no carpet and the slip-covers barely fitted. But once we had settled down in our chairs, I felt as comfortable and at ease as in an old shoe.

Some thirty years ago the word "culture" as anthropologists know it was simply not used by anybody—except, as Dr. Mead put it, "by a few people who knew anthropologists." But today there is a general recognition of cultural differences. The recognition that most of the behavior we used to think of as innate is learned, is very much more widespread than it was. And Dr. Mead in her books has greatly helped people to understand this word "culture" as anthropologists use it. Her studies include books about such primitive peoples as the savages of Samoa and New Guinea, such less primitive peoples as the Russians and the Americans, and such universal subjects as children, education, and sex, and their relation in modern society. Some of her books have hit the best-seller list. She teaches at Columbia University in New York and she is associate curator of ethnology at the American Museum of Natural History. She is unquestionably one of America's outstanding women.

BRANDON: Perhaps the most important question I can ask you as an anthropologist is whether you believe that American society or the American species is capable of world leadership. But to approach this question gradually I first want to quote from an American writer who in typical American self-critical fashion recently said that "American civilization is most sincerely dedicated to the isms of materialism, conformism, optimism, escapism, and Momism." First, what about the materialistic nature of the American?

MEAD: Perhaps I might start by quoting the comments of the natives of New Guinea that I went back to restudy in 1953—I studied them before in 1928 when they were real Stone Age savages . . . and the most possessive, acquisitive, competitive, materialistic group of savages that I had ever met among all the savages I know. They were exposed, during World War II, to about a million Americans. They said: "We learned from the

Americans that material things don't matter, that the only thing in the world that matters is a single human being. You can spend any amount of material goods to save the life of a single human being—now we have learned this, we want to have the kind of society that is organized around human beings instead of around property and things." If I quote this to an ordinary American audience, they have some idea what I'm talking about, but if I quote it to the professional intelligentsia, they gasp with amazement. The natives added: "The reason that Americans do *not* value material things too highly is because they have so many of them." There's been a great confusion between having many material things and being materialistic. Europeans feel that to prefer a bathtub to a garden is crass materialism. Americans don't set things up as between a bathtub and a garden, because a bathtub isn't a luxury in this country, it's a necessity. So from what I have seen and the discussions I have had in Europe—I think Americans are much *less* materialistic than Europeans, much less.

BRANDON: Still, the American economy really is built on persuading people to buy and buy more, and so you have a concentration here on acquiring material things rather than—

MEAD: Well now! How would you characterize other economies? What are they based on? Persuading people not to buy?

BRANDON: No, but the economy is not that dependent on whether everybody will own a washing machine or not.

MEAD: I know it isn't. And other countries have had rather serious production problems as a result, haven't they? Ours is an economy that is geared to a rising standard of living. We are geared to a notion that we could live better than we do—so no one settles down very comfortably and is satisfied with the way he lives. Whereas, of course, in many parts of Europe there are class-typed standards. If people reach them, they are contented and they don't want to go out to get more things.

BRANDON: Do you think conformism is an outstanding characteristic of the American scene?

MEAD: I think it's an outstanding characteristic of American life as looked at by Europeans. You see, they're not used to covering so much territory and finding anything that looks remotely like what was in another part of it; in a country of this size, which is, after all, under one government that has mass production and objects like drugstores and motorcars—how can you avoid apparent similarity? Another factor is that we're a country of immigrants, of people who came here as adults. They learn to be Americans from the outside in. They change their clothes before they can change their ideas. Their great effort is at least to look like other people before they can think and feel and talk like other people. Especially since World War II, there has been a tremendous hue and cry about conformism, or conformity, which is, I think, primarily because people are becoming more self-conscious. The young men who wanted to be successful businessmen always dressed like young men who wanted to be successful businessmen, but they were less conscious of it; there weren't articles in *Life* magazine about it and there weren't opinion polls about it, and so we've suddenly become conscious of many of the things that we are doing. We're told that we're doing things that other people are doing and this gives us a notion of great conformity.

BRANDON: You've spoken chiefly of outward conformism—I think, though, when Europeans refer to conformism, they also think of intellectual conformism.

MEAD: We have one of the most diverse educational systems in the world—hundreds and hundreds of school systems that pay no attention to each other. In Europe if you meet an educated man of your own class, you know what poetry he's read, so it's safe to quote it. But in this country you never know. So the whole gentle art of allusion, which means so much in civilized relationships in Europe, is missing in this country.

BRANDON: Let's take optimism and escapism together. Do you think that is a characteristic quality of Americans?

MEAD: I think Americans are optimistic, on the whole, although they can also respond rather quickly to what they regard as "bad news"—this is usually characterized as hysteria. So when we responded with a terrific fuss over Sputnik, which was a pessimistic response—it was very temporary—the minute we got a satellite up, people were likely to say: Now we've won . . . I think we're fundamentally optimistic, yes.

The word "escapism" means to me the sort of thing we talked

about in the twenties, when people wanted to go to the South Seas—things of that sort. But you could say there is a new form of escapism . . . and that is the escape into private life, which is so characteristic of the present age in this country and is also a characteristic of the Soviet Union: the escape into one's own little house and one's own garden and one's own children, and the small bit of life which one can make a success in and the concentration upon it, and the flight from larger issues.

BRANDON: What do you think is the reason for it?

MEAD: Partly the depression and war and the whole series of things that has happened in the last twenty years with a pressure on younger people, by older people who say: "Better get your happiness now, you can't tell what will happen." Also, a sense that the world's gotten so big and unmanageable that it's very hard for individuals to be able to influence it very much. Also a dread of disaster, because this country is—if not as conscious as we would like it to be—conscious of the dangers of nuclear warfare and the possibility of total destruction. It's almost as if they were trying to live a fifty-year life within ten or fifteen years.

BRANDON: Wouldn't you expect, then, that people would have a special incentive for participating in politics and government?

MEAD: If they thought they could influence events, yes. But we are told that whatever we do, we alone cannot determine our own fate any more. That is a new experience for Americans. It's discouraging for people who thought they were safely protected by two oceans and had only to make the correct choices to be perfectly safe.

BRANDON: You mentioned that the same is the case in Russia—

MEAD: Well, in Russia also—as nearly as we can tell—one always has to qualify—there is a great retreat to private life. The one association that is safe from criticism and from guilt by association is with one's own wife and children. So there seems to be also in Russia an increased emphasis on personal relations within the narrow family group, and a shrinking away from involvement in other sorts of things.

BRANDON: I read your treatise on the Soviet character and I thought some of your conclusions were very prophetic when it was written in 1951. You said there if the regime changes and the police power is loosened the country is likely to become stronger.

It's often been said that there's a good deal of similarity between Americans and Russians—

MEAD: I think there are certain similar characteristics. Russian farmers and American farmers appear to have got on very well together. The sense of belonging to a big country, and a country that belongs to the future, that makes for a similar kind of a national identity. The fact is that both the Soviet Union and the United States have had the job of continually making over the next generation. What the Soviet Union did at first was to make over the children of peasants and the children of other groups within the society; we had to take people who came to us from other societies. But in both cases this produces a kind of thinness of culture, and a kind of commitment to the future rather than to the past.

BRANDON: Well, how about "Momism"?

MEAD: That is a left-over idea from World War II. In World War II we conscripted boys that would not have left home under American circumstances that early. A lot of them were quite miserable at leaving home, and when they were examined by the psychiatrist, they blamed "Mom" for everything that had happened to them, which is quite correct because "Mom" in that period was the most responsible person for bringing up boys. Fathers of that era didn't take very much interest in their children and left a great deal to their wives, whether they were businessmen or immigrants. The immigrant was too busy learning how to make a living, and the businessman also tended to leave all the choices about children's education to his wife. So the mothers were responsible for what was good and what was bad, but with one of these characteristic overstatements, mothers were blamed for what was bad.

Now this is a type of upbringing that is disappearing in this country today. With greater leisure, far more participation of fathers now prevails in the home, but the word "Momism" still hangs around. What we're worried about at present is not the importance of the mother in the home, but the fact that fathers and mothers are so home-centered, which is quite a different problem from the problem of the thirties.

BRANDON: Well, James Thurber said to me the other day that he still thinks of America as a matriarchy.

MEAD: That is a feeling of people who have never seen a matriarchy and don't use the word very carefully. "Matriarchy" is a society in which women have the legal power, and America has never been a matriarchy; but America has been a society in which a great many of the things which, in Europe, were done by men are done by women—and vice versa. Women, for instance, don't play nearly as important a role in politics in this country as they do in England.

BRANDON: I think you said somewhere that the finer things in life are left to them.

MEAD: That's true. Women were supposed to be the custodians of ideals and they're supposed to be more interested in art and music than men are. And this tradition is still with us—it's muted somewhat, but it's still here.

BRANDON: Do you see a change in the function of the females in our society in this century—

MEAD: In the whole Western world?

BRANDON: Let's limit it to the United States.

MEAD: Well, there's very little happening in the United States that isn't happening to some degree in Western Europe and the United Kingdom now—an increase in education, continuing increase in education for females, continued expectation that they'll play a part in the economy, the gearing of the economy to the need for women to work . . . Now this may be done at a very simple level or at a high level, but it's being done everywhere. So asking women, who biologically are probably somewhat more content to stay close to home, to go out of their homes, which I think you can also say is balanced by the fact that we biologically ask men to come home every night and conceivably they were biologically more suited for roaming farther afield in every possible way—as hunters, as explorers—less willing to accept routine, more invigorated by episodic adventure, which modern life is asking them to give up . . . so that man and woman's roles are coming closer together.

BRANDON: You don't think that maybe we have passed the peak of the movement of equality for the woman?

MEAD: Well, I think this particular movement for the equality of women was localized in the West, has now become associated with a way of life in the West, and spreads to the East in quite a new way. I don't feel, however, that women in Moslem countries, in Asia, so much want the role that men had as they did in Europe—to the degree in the United States. They want the role that the Western women have now. But a style of life has been set up and it's certainly still spreading over the world. So it depends upon what you mean by "peak"—if we're only looking at ourselves, certainly there is no very obstreperous feminism today. But if we're looking at what is happening in the world, which I prefer to do, there is an enormous change in the position of women, it's spreading and spreading and spreading, with the United States and Western Europe at the hub.

BRANDON: Europeans often say that American women aren't feminine enough. Do you think that's one of the reasons for it?

MEAD: Well, I think definitions of femininity are exceedingly local and specialized. Men of each country are bought up to recognize one kind of femininity and not recognize another. So that many of the things that American men value in women very highly seem unfeminine to European men and vice versa; and if either one of them looked at the Japanese or the Indians, they'd find that their definitions of femininity had to take a considerable beating, and that all Western women seem unfeminine to the East and these are all matters of degree and definition.

BRANDON: Of course, European women have been very successfull with the American man during the war—surprisingly so—and I don't think that was purely because their own women were not there, not on the spot.

MEAD: Well, they weren't.

BRANDON: The other day a leading French political commentator was so struck by the concentration on the bosom in America that he thought it must have some peculiar repercussion even on politics!

MEAD: Hardly.

BRANDON: In the Renaissance there was a similar wave, of course.

MEAD: Well, there are a variety of points. If you look at fashion you find that fashion goes through cycles, and that if one part of the person is displayed another part is likely to be covered—they're always saving something up for the next fashion. And when you deal in appeals, public erotic appeals, which is what evening costume is, for instance, or bathing suits, they have to be so set up as to be both new and familiar. And there are a limited number of possibilities to work with in the world, and we have recently been working with bosoms. Now one can also develop deep psychoanalytic interpretations, which would stand up perhaps, but are only valuable if you compare several countries . . . and I think it's useful to compare the fact that in this country men want women to have traits that are easily seen by other people—their conquest, their date for the evening, their wife is recognized as having a sort of charm, physical charm, that's conspicuous. Whereas in England, for instance, they prefer to have the pearl buried deep in the oyster, something one discovers for oneself and doesn't flaunt quite as openly.

BRANDON: Europeans are often amazed at how self-critical Americans are—

MEAD: Well, we've always had to be self-conscious, you see, because we were a culture built by adults. But America was founded by people who came here with standards and style of another society and the moment they landed they started to compare—compare favorably and compare unfavorably—this new country with the old country.

Some wise European once remarked that Americans have substituted anthropology for history—the comparison of contemporary peoples for the time depth that Europeans rely on. This continual publication of what the teen-agers are thinking, what the parents of teen-agers are thinking, or who lives longest—and this is what you call self-criticism on the one hand, and conformity on the other. Anthropology then becomes a science especially congenial to Americans because it helps them highlight their own behavior. It takes it out of its extremely ethnocentric position, which we were more likely to get into than Europeans, simply because we lack the historical depth.

When Europeans think of the present period, they can always compare it with Agincourt or Runnymede or whatever . . . we haven't got this kind of background, and so we use comparisons among contemporary societies as our device to give ourselves some kind of depth. That's why Europeans wonder about the role of the social sciences in this country—especially anthropology—or the role of the psychiatrist.

The role of psychiatrist is primarily to give one a more disciplined awareness of what one's doing and inevitably in this country it's important to be aware, whereas in Europe it's been more important to absorb a tradition and live it. Europeans don't need to adjust so much. I think they also tend to reward more the person of the opposite extreme, who is sublimely unaware of what other people are doing and more wrapped up in his own dream or his own thinking. The English, for example, find self-consciousness exceedingly unappealing, as likely to interfere with the smooth execution of a life-long position . . . if you haven't got a life-long position, which is the American case, then you need something different.

BRANDON: And you don't think this country has more or less found it yet?

MEAD: No, I think this country has built in now the experience of wave after wave of immigrants who came as adults, and therefore learned about things out of books. We write books about everything—books about how to make a marriage a success, how to make friends, how to influence people, how to become an executive—this looks very comic to other countries, but when adults move into a society where they have not sat at their grandmother's knee and asked how to do something, they get a book . . . just as if they want to learn a new language, they don't learn it through lullabies, but through a book.

BRANDON: Another thing that is often baffling is the contrast between the pragmatic, practical approach and on the other hand a desperate clinging to certain shibboleths . . .

MEAD: I think if you contrast American culture with British culture—or shall we say English culture, perhaps—you'll find a greater blending of ideals and practicality in English culture, which has sometimes been called hypocrisy by, say, French critics. Whereas in the United States they tend to split apart into an explicit idealism, that sounds like the most extreme and mawkish sentimentalism or shibboleths, as you say, on the one hand—and

26

a statement of the practical, which sounds almost cynical in contrast.

BRANDON: American children are taught that the reward of success is love. I wonder if that isn't a basic fallacy that comes to haunt Americans later in life.

MEAD: Americans are taught that you should make good, do well in school, do well in any defined situation—and bring this success to your parents. These were the offerings that children brought to their parents in counterdistinction to what they bring them in some other countries where they bring docility, obedience, respect. Now in this country people have been taught—I think it works both ways—not only that you will be loved if you succeed, which for a child is true, but also that if you are loved it's a sign you have succeeded—you see, it's a circle. And so you get an evaluation of expressions of love from other people and more of a dependence on other people's judgment, and on signs of love.

BRANDON: One of the most frequent phrases one hears used is whether somebody is well-adjusted or not. In Europe nobody cares. Is this purely the influence of psychiatry here?

MEAD: No, I think it's deeper than psychiatry. If you go back even before psychiatry, you had always an enormous emphasis in this country on learning how to get on in a group. People were always conscious that they had to learn not how to behave as a single individual, but how to get on with the others and do the things that were expected by the outside world. Psychiatry has picked it up.

BRANDON: Now that we have dissected some of the characteristics of American society, do you think they add up to a nation that is capable of world leadership?

MEAD: In a sense that's almost a totally academic question. If we were looking for world leadership and the rest of the world had several candidates, then they might ask the question and decide to give leadership to this country or that. We're more or less trapped in a situation where at least a certain portion of world leadership has got to fall to the United States. So I think a more useful question is to say: What kind of world leadership is the United States capable of?

BRANDON: Well, how would you define that?

MEAD: I think we're far more capable of informal world leadership than formal world leadership. General attitudes in this country toward government—toward our Federal government and the normal distribution between voluntary activity and governmental activity—mean that we're far more able to be friendly, co-operative, and respectful of the rights and capacities of other countries in a private capacity than we are in a public capacity.

One of the difficulties at present is that so many other countries are organized so that things go through government—and that we've been asked to organize more things through government than we have the experience or preference for. This is especially true of the new countries that are doing planning on a national scale. When we act in our public personality, we are, in a sense, acting not as ourselves because the Federal government is our Uncle rather than ourselves.

BRANDON: As you have given some thought to the characteristics of Russian society, have you any ideas whether ultimately the Russians, being white, will side with Western civilization in an ultimate struggle with the yellow races?

MEAD: Racial equality is one point that has been deeply accepted in the Soviet Union and is very consonant with Russian culture, because the Russians have never suffered from the same degree of arrogance that most of the other Europeans have. They have a long history of friendly relationships with Mongolian peoples of their own empire. I think the only possibility would be if African communism, or Asiatic communism, used race as a shibboleth, which it might very easily, because there you have people with a long history of indignity at the hands of Europeans. It's been very easy for Chinese Communists to talk about the "running white dogs of Chiang Kai-shek" and make a racial point and a political point at the same time. It's conceivable that in some sort of internal struggle among different Communist countries, the other countries might attempt to use race, but I think it's quite inconceivable that the Russians would as we know them at present. The Russians believe that a Communist may have to use a most repugnant means to attain great ends—that is, of course, a general principle of Russian communism—so that one can, in fancy, imagine them with deep regret having to decide on some thoroughly loathsome racial policy. But it doesn't seem to me likely, and I don't think anybody else better count on it.

BRANDON: Their recent accomplishments—in the technical field particularly—are obviously doing a lot to their ego. I was wondering where this might lead?

MEAD: The Russians have passed the period when they felt tremendously behind the West. In fact, the Russians seem now to be reasonably assured of their superiority. This may lead to a period of "big-headedness," of conceit, which may have all sorts of repercussions. It may mean a slackening of effort, which they will have to deal with, it might mean a great degree of recklessness. In traditional Russian literature the conceited man is a man without judgment. So that the chastening effect of technological inferiority, when it's removed, might leave us with a Russia that was an even less comfortable sharer of the globe than the present Russia.

BRANDON: We have in this century opened up this frightful Pandora's box of nuclear fission. Do you think man will be able to control it?

MEAD: Any estimate that one makes only expresses either the feeling of confidence or pessimism. I replied in California the other day (I was speaking at a radio interview) to the question: What do you think our chances are of getting through? About fifty-fifty. The interlocutor replied: Fifty-fifty? That's all right!

I do think there's a very serious danger that we won't get through. The readings of history and anthropology in general give us no reason to believe that societies have built-in self-preservative systems. And, therefore, we can't say that man will be sensible enough not to destroy himself. He never has been sensible enough not to destroy himself, but he lived in small groups so that when he destroyed himself, he didn't destroy everybody—and that was the only difference. So I don't think the danger can be overemphasized, and the necessity for attempts to find new inventions for the conduct of the world cannot possibly be overemphasized.

BRANDON: Are you thinking of disarmament or world government or—

MEAD: I don't think any of the plans proposed today will be enough. Diversion of people's energies into constructive directions that they really believe in and are interested in, would certainly be one part of the picture—to move from fear to activity—that's the major function of trips to the moon at present. No matter how much people try to convert trips to the moon into military activities, they aren't very military; but they are a sort of activity that can focus the interest and energy and excitement of all peoples.

But we also need a good many specific, political inventions inside countries. It's a lack of political responsibility inside the countries that makes it possible for us to fear that leaders will precipitate war. This is our special task in this country which we share with all the peoples of the world.

None of us know how to run cities. We don't know how to run large aggregations of people. We don't know how to make the average citizen in a country of this size take responsibility. We don't know it here and they don't know it in the Soviet Union. The Soviet Union uses the secret police and every form of suppression, because they are afraid of ignorance and misdirected energies of the mass of the people. The methods that we use here are not so much methods as lack of methods, in which we let delinquency and crime and alcoholism and political corruption build up and corrode our capacities to behave as a people.

BRANDON: Do you think it's more a question of government rather than a question of family responsibility?

MEAD: I don't think there's the slightest use of talking about family responsibility. How do you get to "The Family"? I think it's community and national responsibility to create the kind of conditions in which the family can fulfill its role. But to sit and lecture "The Family" and tell "The Family" what to do, which we hear all the time, is, you know, like going out and preaching to the fishes.

BRANDON: But aren't all these efforts to go to the moon not another form of escapism?

MEAD: I don't think it's escapism at all; it's an area in which people's imagination can be caught and in which they can have a chance to participate. Here, of course, I'm also speaking as an American. The idea of a new bit of space is exceedingly attractive to our people who have always been interested in what they could do with new space. Space appeals to me in somewhat the same sense as the Pacific Ocean does—that we may be able, in time, to have small space colonies, where we have great possibilities of variation.

BRANDON: Is there much discussion among anthropologists these days about what might happen to their science if other species were discovered up in space?

MEAD: I think the discussion among anthropologists is more of the problem of space colonization and possible variations in human culture that we could artificially produce. As the world closes in and we have so much communication among ourselves our possibilities for variation are diminishing. So space offers new possibilities for variation in culture. You see, if you isolate a group of people, then over a period of time their language will change, and they will develop new styles, a different culture. Now the stock in trade of anthropologists are the differences between the cultures of small primitive people, who are left in the jungle or on an island somewhere and didn't learn the things the rest of us learned. Pretty soon the whole world is going to be exposed to the things the rest of us are being exposed to and this source of variation is going to disappear. Even without space, we may have to create new kinds of groups where specially gifted people are left alone for a while, left in ignorance of what is going on in other parts of the world—the sort of thing that happens in wartime when there are barriers between groups and they try different solutions to the same problem; then they come together again and you get a spurt of advancement.

BRANDON: You mean people would be left isolated on a planet—?

MEAD: Or in space colonies . . . The importance of space primarily at present is the effect it will have on the people on earth and their imagination. The mere notion that there may be other creatures on the planets and that we're going to look for them—it doesn't increase the probability of their being there, but it changes our attitude.

Even ten years ago when one talked about the human race, one was being broad and generous and inclusive and free from all prejudice, identifying oneself with one's entire species . . . this was a very broad gesture. Today when one talks about the whole human race, one feels narrow rather than broad.

BRANDON: It's always intriguing to project one's mind forward—if you projected your mind, say, five hundred or a thousand years forward—what kind of place do you think twentieth-century man would have in evolutionary history?

MEAD: Well, this depends so much—not on what we do, but what comes afterward. I think we are in the most crucial period since, perhaps, the discovery of fire. And if one considers that the original people who discovered fire and started moving north with it—if they had let that fire go out, man might have perished with them for all we know. The future of man as a developed species may have depended upon very few people and a very few accidents.

Now we again have hit a period where the future of the whole species depends upon what happens in this period. Whether people five hundred years from now will realize that they owe their being here, if they are here, to the choices that we've made—whether they'll be able to judge whether we accidentally found the solutions or had become self-conscious enough to be able to seek them, indicating that the age of social invention had actually begun (just as the age of technical invention began earlier)—that's the sort of question I've asked, but I can't project it any more sharply.

If we go on now into the use of solar energy to a period of "free power," this will be a change whose magnitude we are unable even to imagine. But I think we are failing to realize the resiliency and the possibilities of spontaneity and, moreover, responsibility in human beings. And a great deal of the fear that you find in science fiction is based on a failure to realize how far man has come by his own efforts, and how much it is possible to improve any single facet of man's behavior by social invention. The great advances in the next fifty years, if we survive, are not going to be in technical inventions; they're going to be social inventions. I think we should concentrate our attention on increasing our knowledge about how people learn and change, how it's possible even for adults to change, especially how it's possible to change adults in their sixties—you see, there will be no possibility of depending upon the education of the children to get us out of this mess—we've got to get out of this long before the children are grown up.

We will learn the new conditions under which adults learn—and we have made a good research beginning—and we will learn ways of teaching adults, entirely new ways of looking at things, of doing things. This is a crying need at present. Of course, we don't know how to do these things—we're stumbling around with ineffective technical assistance in underdeveloped countries—we don't know what kind of competent help to give a country like Indonesia in its effort to knit itself into a new nationhood. We don't know how to work out communication between one group of people and another; we don't know how to govern the relationships between public opinion and public pronouncement; we don't know the answer to such questions as when there is a juvenile gang war in New York City, should the newspapers play it up or down? Now these are the things that by some sort of really concerted effort we must learn very quickly.

Therefore what we need now are human sciences—to educate people how to live in this new world and how to develop social inventions that will make it possible for us to survive. This isn't a technical problem. All that these technical inventions will do is to lead to more and more deterrents, more and more destruction.

The American Quest for Culture

a conversation with

PETER USTINOV

When I met Peter Ustinov in Washington on tour with his play
Romanoff and Juliet, I had not seen him since the early days of
his career when he helped to make the London audiences at the
Player's Theater, then in a basement off Piccadilly, forget that
V-bombs were exploding outside. He was nineteen then and
outwardly he has not much changed. He always reminded me
of a king-size, good-natured Teddy bear. And he still does. His
claws have grown a little sharper, his beard is fuzzier, but its
main function still seems to be to add age to his boyish face.
There is also still the same contagious joie de vivre, his good-
natured coziness, his readiness to entertain people at any time,
his waddling walk, his graceful bulkiness.

Peter Ustinov, once a boy wonder, must now be considered
something of a renaissance man. In the age of the specialist, this
is not an easy cross to bear. In many ways his dilemmas are
similar to Leonard Bernstein's. He, too, is a many-sided genius, not
quite certain what he is best at. But Peter, I think, bears his
dilemma more lightly. He also knows what he likes doing best.
It is writing rather than acting, but it is the latter probably that
earns the major part of his upkeep. Also he is not as intense as
Bernstein. He has the advantage that it is easier for him to tap
his varied talents almost simultaneously. He writes his plays, di-
rects them and plays in them; in between he finds time to write
short stories and to appear on television or in films.

He moves from one medium to the other almost effortlessly.

He has in him an infinite capacity for versatility, for adaptation. He is, in fact, so adjustable that he can appeal to almost any audience. One evening he impersonates a grotesque Nazi general on television, a performance that comes close to slap-stick, and the next he appears as Danton or Dr. Johnson in a serious and brilliant character study. In his own plays there is usually enough wit and sophistication to satisfy the intellectual theater-goer, but also enough plain fun to make for a broader appeal. His range, if he tried, would not be limited to Anglo-Saxon audiences. He could entertain French, German, Italian, Russian audiences with equal facility. Before my tape recorder he was the most relaxed and fluent performer of all.

He is something of a cosmopolitan Will Rogers. His power of observation and his understanding for the weaknesses and peculiarities of various nations make him a perceptive and amusing social critic. But however devastating his comment or his parody, however much it touches on sensitive nerves, it is never malicious. At worst it is irreverent. One of his great assets is a sensitive ear, tuned to capture the nuances of accents and dialects. His cosmopolitan background, of course, helps and so does his command of a half-dozen languages. His father was a German diplomat, his mother was French, but originally his family came from Russia. Peter himself was born and educated in England.

He was hardly twenty when his first play was shown in London's West End. Since then he has written more than a dozen plays. Two, The Love of Four Colonels and Romanoff and Juliet, were produced in the United States, but it was probably his success on television that made his name in America. Apart from his manifold talents, one important ingredient of his success is his incredible mental and physical vitality. He could not otherwise stand his own breath-taking pace.

For twenty-four hours in Washington, I was able to follow him personally—and I must add, barely. What occurred may not be typical, but here it is. That day he played a matinee and an evening performance in his Romanoff and Juliet. After the play, he came to my house for a supper party. Without any prodding, with little food and not much alcohol, he soon began telling some of his funny character stories in a dozen different accents. He returned *to his hotel after two* A.M. *with his wife, Suzanne, by then showing signs of fatigue. Next morning, when we met again for lunch, I apologized for having kept him up so late, but he only grunted modestly: "When I got back to the hotel I had time enough to finish one of my short stories for* The Atlantic Monthly." *That morning he also presented me with a sketch of his own conception of an international gallery of dogs. Caricatures are a hobby of his.*

His early successes have not spoiled him. James Agate of the Sunday Times, *once the pundit among English drama critics, considered Ustinov "the greatest master of stagecraft now writing in this country." He was then twenty-two. Success and praise and some failures over the years have made him warmer, wiser, gentler, and more generous. He is still a "young man" in his late thirties, but he does not get "angry." His is a world full of fun and dreams. He likes to parody it, but not really come to grips with it, though there is always an undertone of seriousness. But parody in the theater is easily perishable, even with a Bernard Shaw, and that is perhaps one reason why so much he has written so far has been transitory—but then he has almost a lifetime still ahead of him.*

BRANDON: *Romanoff and Juliet* has been such an extraordinary success in the United States, I wonder if you think that Kipling's remark that "There is not enough Romeo and too much balcony in the United States" still has some justification.

USTINOV: I think he knew a completely different United States from the one we know now. I think it's changed a great deal. Before we came here I was warned by many Americans that this country would not be able to stomach satire in which it was personally involved. And I'm delighted to see that that's not so. I think they've got beyond the "too much balcony" stage. I think they're in quest of romance. Their great love for Paris is indicative. I always feel that their real ambition so far as Paris is concerned is to rescue Paris from the French.

BRANDON: You mean, transplant it . . .

USTINOV: No, I mean to them it represents Toulouse-Lautrec and Renoir and things they have on their walls, and they're rather

The American Quest for Culture

annoyed when they get to Paris to find that everybody talks French and, in point of fact, is French . . .

BRANDON: You don't think that Paris has a different attraction for Americans? It's always had the reputation here of being a naughty city.

USTINOV: Oh yes, but I think that the vogue of French Impressionist painting especially has done a lot for France. Naughtiness has, too, because their films, of course, get by and are not censored —simply on the basis that they're French; if they were in any other language they would be. A friend of mind did a television series which was to be called *My French Wife*, but the powers-that-be decided that that title was too naughty and it was called *My American Husband*.

BRANDON: You think that Americans now are in quest of romance?

USTINOV: What makes America so very different from England is its size. In England you travel from Liverpool to London in a train, and there are eight people in your compartment and they don't talk to each other; it's a way of wishing the country were bigger than it is; that's also why an Englishman's home is his castle; it's because the Englishman can't have a castle. He'll willingly greet his neighbors in the street but on a Sunday, sitting in his backyard, four feet away from his neighbor, they will pretend not to see each other. That has given birth to a kind of reserve in which your privacy is carried about with you like a suit of clothes. Whereas in America there's tremendous "togetherness" and the front door is nearly always ajar, and somebody pokes their head through it and says: "Anyone home? Can we borrow your mixer?" It's a hangover, I think, from the pioneer days when neighbors were desperately needed as someone to talk to.

Americans are very sensible now of criticisms that are leveled at them, especially that of being commercially minded. I think that's rather out-of-date. Nobody owning a country this size which is *still*, to a great extent, unexploited quite knows what is under the soil they buy; you might strike anything by digging. It's quite natural to be commercially minded in a country where such things are possible. If you *know* that you've got nothing but a nationalized mine two miles away, you're liable to be more

37

spiritual perhaps. The Americans have reacted against this criticism, which they see often in European caricatures and in European plays and writings, and have now gone overboard for culture.

BRANDON: Do you think there is an American culture?

USTINOV: There obviously is. I think they're still looking for the great American novel and the great American symphony and the great American opera . . . It's very possible that these things have already been written, but haven't been recognized as being of any importance at all. They are obviously trying very hard and *consciously*, which is not the right way to go about it, yet it's human. But very often it has a kind of organ-loft pomposity, which reveals the intentions of striving toward a kind of Roman-Empire greatness, instead of waiting to mature in a "Greeker" way.

BRANDON: Well, you say that some great work may have already been written in different fields and nobody has recognized it. Do you think that's because it may not be commercially salable, and therefore has not been recognized?

USTINOV: That's possible anywhere. We may at the moment be overestimating a work like *Doctor Zhivago* just because the Soviet government insists on underestimating it. In any case that's a good sign because the works of *all* great men are never finally assessed; they're always on a kind of intellectual stock exchange and one can almost look up the points gain or loss in the morning. Bach, at the moment, is suffering a slight reverse at the hands of Vivaldi who is being discovered madly . . . endless Italian chamber groups are performing unknown concerto after unknown concerto; the "V" section in any gramaphone catalog is becoming nearly as long as the "B" section. That's a very healthy thing.

BRANDON: You really mean that powerful expressions of typical American culture are not yet really too noticeable, but there's a great interest in culture generally.

USTINOV: America has exerted a great influence on us all, and consequently one can talk of American culture. For example, the so-called "angry young men" in England, I think, are basically extremely jealous of American vitality and of American freedom of thought, which perhaps is not possible in a country which has made a God of stability for so long. It's very, very difficult to push against the British status quo, because the machine of government is so full of safety valves, put there by experience, that nobody gets really angry; they tolerate the angriest of us with a kind of headmasterish benignity. Whereas these "angry young men"—I hate the phrase and I don't really think they exist as a group—come over here and go to Harlem and start bouncing long before the average American would be captured by a rhythm.

BRANDON: The extraordinary difference between the angry young man in England and the young man here, then (they're not very angry here), is that here they want above all security and stability. That is one of the basic changes in the American outlook since the war.

USTINOV: Yes, but that is not realized by those who live their particular cloistered kind of life in England. And I don't think that England is really very conducive to creative work in the arts, although she's very rewarding in many ways. Also the raw material isn't of the same spectacular quality. It doesn't mean that it can't be done, but if you're going to write a play about the average English people—they're not the most expressive of people. They've got an extremely rich vocabulary at their disposal of which they use, I should think, about a tenth of the words that they know are in current use. The language now is riddled with clichés. All this nonsense about the weather, which one is forced to indulge in when one first meets somebody in the morning or goes into a tobacconist's shop. And if there is a family drama, they're not very explicit about why they're going to leave their wives or husbands. That makes them more suitable for certain kinds of comedy than drama. Whereas here, with this immense admixture of blood and the fact that the language is spoken differently by so many minority groups, means that you can get a very salty kind of false poetry into anything that you write in American. Many American plays use these minorities to a very great extent. In Tennessee Williams you'll find Polish truck drivers, New Orleans French types; Clifford Odets has largely exploited the Jewish community of New York. But there's always a grandmother who has a very peculiar usage of English, which gives it a tremendous flavor. The condiments are very much stronger over here.

BRANDON: Do you find that the atmosphere has inspired you here—creatively?

USTINOV: Yes, I do. I've always thought that travel is an integral part of education. It's very refreshing for somebody who has grown up in the rather cloistered atmosphere of Europe, of England especially, to go out—not only to the United States, but to Canada, for instance, which is, I suppose, very much what the United States must have been like fifty years ago, except that it already has all the modern conveniences. But it's a tremendous challenge to be in a country where everything is yet to be done, and I think that is an aspect which many English tend to lose. They didn't in the old days when they had an empire to travel in; when they were busy doing the things that had to be done. I get the feeling that England is very often a little bit parochial nowadays, and I think that's regrettable.

BRANDON: Growth here is so much more noticeable because it's going on at such a fast clip.

USTINOV: Yes, and the culture of the country is like a quicksand; it's not only growing very fast but it's growing out of so many different elements. You get large German communities and large Polish communities who still have very many different traditions in Europe, but when they're over here they're all perfectly American by now and, in point of fact, I would have said that an American culture—the American way of living (I don't mean the same thing they say when they talk about "the American way of life")—the American way of living has grown extremely quickly.

BRANDON: What do you mean by "the American way of living"?

USTINOV: The American way of eating and sleeping and looking at television, of getting their boys to deliver newspapers during their holidays, a more useful education than to be an average Boy Scout sitting on some wet leaves in Windsor Forest and doing Indian signs. You know, I think it's a much more practical preparation for what is to face you afterward. Not all of us can end up as brigadier generals in the jungle and benefit from our Boy Scout training in Windsor Park.

BRANDON: One American friend of mine who recently spent a

year in England came back worried that England was adopting the worst parts of American culture and vulgarizing them at that. In America, he also said, when children watch too much television the parents worry about what the results may be, but in England they are allowed to watch television and nobody worries.

USTINOV: Yes, but there's much less television for them to watch. They're still governed there by certain hours; television isn't a round-the-clock thing in England. Whereas over here the late-late show seems to overlap the early-early show by several minutes.

BRANDON: Do you find the audiences here laughing at the same things?

USTINOV: Yes, surprisingly similar. For pretty obvious reasons the English audience has a greater sense of irony; at the same time the American audience has a greater sense of fantasy. At the end of my play I have a line in which I say to the young lovers, "You invented everything, including the country which is yours," which never fails to affect an American audience; whereas in England there was always dead silence.

BRANDON: Do you find audiences more responsive here or in England?

USTINOV: I would say that certain towns have been particularly responsive. I would say that Edinburgh was perhaps even more responsive than London; Toronto was probably more responsive than New York; and certain nights, even in a place like Cincinnati, which is in the traditional Middle West—an isolationist background, I presume—the reaction was extremely violent and happy and uninhibited. And because they don't get much theater, one has a little bit the same feeling of freshness as one did during the war when one was playing to the troops who hadn't seen the theater for a long time and therefore looked at it with very fresh eyes; and one got a reaction— and I'm not being at all patronizing when I say this—tremendously invigorating, and not at all devoid of subtlety.

BRANDON: What do you think is the difference between American and English humor, now that you've had a chance of sensing it on both sides of the Atlantic?

USTINOV: I have always thought the English have a great capacity of laughing at themselves—they have said so themselves. I'm not sure it isn't just in order to forestall anybody who might want to laugh at them; there seems a degree of tact and it's a kind of defense mechanism in the English. It's like when I was watching a member of some West African Student Union talking near Marble Arch and he was running the English down on a Sunday. There was a large crowd around him, and a couple of policemen, who weren't listening—and he was saying the most frightful things about the English. But there was dead silence until it became too much for an old colonel, an old military man with a white mustache, who said: "Wherever you travel in the wide world, you won't find a more upright man than your average Englishman," and the crowd turned on him and said: "Shut up! Let the man say what he wants to." I think they were angry with the colonel because he'd showed his hand. And I think that the English are basically very passionate and very romantic and energetic people, who have controlled themselves almost too well; and that is why they have the reputation in history of being *perfide Albion*. They're so determined to control themselves and to be prepared for disaster the whole time, they're never surprised when disaster comes; they're at their finest then. At the same time some foreign countries may think that they don't make the best of the periods in between disasters.

BRANDON: And the Americans?

USTINOV: The Americans, on the other hand, are determined to be open. That's what makes some of their diplomacy so touching. When you get these businessmen who are ambassadors and who run their embassies as businesses and say: "Let's get round the table and kick this thing around. Can't we come to terms?"—they seem to the English and to many Europeans to be rather naïve. The American expression is one of extreme openness, and a willingness for there to be no defense. If you attack the Americans, I don't think they'll get very indignant, because they'll wish to see whether there's any truth in what you're saying, and even if they don't laugh at themselves they're very willing to laugh at each other. I find that also very refreshing, because the methods which govern behavior are less established here really, and are just guided by a sense of self-criticism which the Soviets might envy. This tremendous openness to other ideas is due to the thought that there might be something in that which they could use to improve themselves. And then they tend to take what criticisms one has too seriously and to try to put things into effect which were not meant to engender such a response.

BRANDON: Your plays, for instance, *The Love of Four Colonels* and *Romanoff and Juliet* were chiefly written—I mean, as far as the American characters go—on the basis of your impressions of Americans abroad.

USTINOV: Yes, inevitably.

BRANDON: Have your impressions changed now that you have spent a year here?

USTINOV: No, not very much. I would now be in a position perhaps, with luck, to write something a little more profound about them, but in the kind of plays which I was writing there, which I did deliberately in order to bring a little excitement as I "figured" it, as they say, back into the theater, in those plays I wanted to revert to the eighteenth century but with modern characters, to reinvolve the audience, to have the possibility of asides at any moment, in order to break down that fourth wall which, to my mind, had outlived its usefulness in the theater. It was brought in at a time when it was very necessary in order to stop a stilted way of acting and writing. But by now the tendency, which it started, has done better by movies and television, because you don't have to pretend it's a house any more on the television and the movies—you can get a real house. So if it's realism you want, I think that those other two media do it better. The theater—in order to survive—must do something which is impossible for the other two. And what advantages has it got? It has a living audience, and therefore, there's no use pretending that audience isn't there; it's much better to make use of it and to make them experience some kind of communal excitement which can only be felt in the theater, or the football match, or the bull ring.

BRANDON: Well, what fields does this leave for the theater?

USTINOV: Well, I just don't believe that naturalistic plays have any future any more. I'm tired of having my eye pressed to a keyhole through which I really don't want to look. I'd much prefer to know that it's a play and to involve the audience.

There are more and more plays written with commentators or with asides and with round stages in which people are acting in the middle of the audience. You can never get as excited in that way in front of a television set because the telephone rings and about the time you come back to it you've lost something; in the theater you're caught in your row, and unless you're very keen to get out, you can't.

BRANDON: Well then, you really think that Arthur Miller and Tennessee Williams should write for the cinema rather than for the theater.

USTINOV: Oh, I wouldn't dream of imposing my personal creed on anybody else because that's foolish, but I think that's what will happen. I think the musicals are pointing the way, too. They're in a kind of way neo-classical. They're a reversion to a kind of theater that is gone, but they're very fresh, they have asides; they're therefore the enjoyment of the public and, if they're good, they bring a little magic back into the theater, which has become drab even if it's spiritually exciting.

BRANDON: Not long ago Arthur Miller wrote that American playwrights deal almost exclusively with the effects and not with the ultimate causes, that American plays imply that where the parents stand the world ends, and where the son stands is where the world should begin. But he cannot because he's either made impotent or he revolts, or more often he runs away. He admits they are important social plays, but in his view they fail to grasp the total social problem. This is one of those very severe American self-criticisms.

USTINOV: Yes, but this, mind you, breeds not only men who say what they think and men who are temperamentally bulldozers, but it also breeds martyrs to an enormous extent. I have a feeling that in the McCarthy Period, it was made easier for the McCarthys by the fact that there were so many martyrs wishing to be Joan of Arcs, and wishing to make *more* out of the tragedy of their cases than was really necessary. If the counterattack to that had been a little more humorous the investigation would have been made to seem more ridiculous sooner.

The tendency to try and build up a great American tradition of some sort is a slightly Victorian organ-loft mentality, an attempt

44

to produce majesty prematurely. I don't think that Americans should be so keen to drink their wine before it's ready.

I think what is missing is the kind of maturity that comes inevitably, and which may be here if they weren't trying to force it. Also, I think there's a lack of sensitivity involved in what Miller says. You can say the same thing about Chekhov, that he was dealing only with a cross-section of weary landlords on the point of bankruptcy. But as soon as the revolution broke out these things were accepted, or just before the revolution, as very valid symbols of social criticism. In fact, they moved the audiences to tears because they recognized the truth of just these tiny little gems.

It's part of that tendency to consider that perhaps Maupassant would have been more important if he had written novels instead of short stories, which I completely deny. A Maupassant story will make you think personally, it will stimulate you, or me, *more* than if it had been a long, ponderous work with the same content. It's part of the tendency, which is again a search for greatness, which thinks that a symphony must necessarily be a greater work than a sonata, or a tragedy must necessarily be a greater work than a comedy. This is something which is obsessing us all now. The French now even consider a drama often more valid than a comedy, and it's certainly ironic considering that certainly their greatest playwright is Moliére. It's reached such a pitch of lack of comprehension that perhaps a bad tragedy could be considered slightly more honorable than bad comedy.

BRANDON: Probably the most typically American expression is the musical comedy.

USTINOV: Certainly it is. After all, a writer is there to stimulate and to start trends of thought in the reader. He is there to ask questions. That was Shakespeare's greatness: he never answered any questions. He said "To be or not to be" and then gave no solutions. That sort of thing starts a whole lot of balls rolling in the mind and it starts one thinking of them. This catholic span of his is a tremendous irritation because, of course, it's very cold in his shadow and that's what happened to the English theater—saved, I suppose, to some extent by the critics who tended to think that although Shakespeare was the greatest of our writers, Pinero was probably the best and should be emulated.

BRANDON: Miller in what he said reflected the German influence here.

USTINOV: The German influence here is enormous. There is, for instance, a resemblance between America and Germany in the strange civic pride of this decentralized country. Cincinnati, in a civic sense, is a town like Mainz [Germany], in which they're so keen on their own local orchestra. A committee of ladies wants to make it as good as the Boston or Philadelphia orchestra within five years. They don't realize the ladies in Detroit have the same sinister scheme over their museum.

It makes it very interesting to travel in America because although the architecture is all terribly similar, when you come into a town you find that you're on another team and that they're hatching very different plots. Usually the men travel in the background and confidentially the man will say to you: "Well, my wife is behind this orchestra. I hate music, I prefer golf, but I have to be here because, well, we're very close to each other, Mrs. Smith and I . . ." I find that very touching.

BRANDON: Among Germans, too, there is also a desire for solutions.

USTINOV: Absolutely. I once said and it's not quite true—but I thought it was true enough—that in order to reach the truth the French subtract, the Germans add, and the English change the subject.

BRANDON: The middle class is getting stronger in this country every day. And the middle class really likes to be soothed. Have you any feeling how this is influencing art here, creative art?

USTINOV: This is a country which can be swayed by publicity. By the same token, immediately they become conscious of anything, they shy against it. That's why, I think, it's a country of vogues and changing fashions the whole time. Immediately they became conscious of the fact that everybody thought they were too commercial, they embraced the artistic with such vigor that it became almost farcical. Or they became conscious of the fact that people were laughing at them in a way for transporting Venetian palaces and getting them set up in Detroit. They no longer do this; they just get the contents of the Venetian palaces and lay them out more brilliantly than in any European museum. There is now this rumor about, which they all feel and talk about, that conformity is the present bugbear which must be escaped from, just as bad breath must be escaped from.

Gradually the Americans will decide *not* to conform any more. I think one can see the tendency in the sudden sale of European cars. I don't think this has anything to do with the ease of shopping or parking a car; it's got to do with a sudden nostalgia for finding hand-made things from remote parts of the world. There are aspects of New York in all American towns that I've been in, which didn't exist when I was here eleven years ago: shops devoted entirely to imported Siamese sandals, or various commodities from distant parts of the world. I remember in the old days, if you went into a shop to buy your wife something, they would try to help you because, after all, you shouldn't know too much about what women like to wear, by saying: "We're selling a lot of these." But I've heard less and less of that. Nowadays they would say: "These have just come in from Florence, Italy, and they are the latest." It's a very perceptible trend toward the custom-made goods.

BRANDON: On my first visit to this country, for instance, some fifteen years ago, many theaters were turned into cinemas. Then about five years later, more theaters were turned into television studios. Now you will find that movie houses are being reconverted to theaters again.

USTINOV: Don't you think that goes by the same token as "imported"—a sudden reversion to a luxury article, which not everybody goes to. Suddenly the movies became too popular, and, in a certain sense, television was a revenge of the theater on the movies.

BRANDON: But plays like *Ulysses in Nighttown* or *Waiting for Godot* have been running here in off-Broadway theaters for weeks!

USTINOV: Sure, I think Americans are very frightened about this overmechanical development. At the end of the road on which we're traveling, one ought to be able to take a holiday without ever leaving home. One will ring up the travel agency and have a panorama of where one is supposed to be projected . . . and one will bask in artificial sun. I mean, this is ridiculous but

47

everything is going in that direction eventually. I think that the fear of over mechanical life also has led to this do-it-yourself business, the going back to the pioneer, of making your own 90-foot sailboat in your backyard. You know? It's all indicative, too.

I remember having been chosen as "Stage Father of the Year" at a big dinner in New York, and we were all given Father's Ten Commandments. One of them was: "Be a pal to your son—share his adventures!" It's an invitation to be young again and to realize that what we made of this country we made ourselves, with our own hands. And let us not trust realty operators too much and construction engineers. It will be bad for us eventually if we turn too many switches without knowing the exact process by which that luxury of light or heat is conveyed back to us again.

BRANDON: You really mean that the psychiatrist is the savior of this country, because it's all by analysis that these inherent dangers are being uncovered and talked and written about.

USTINOV: I think that's ironic, but it's very possible, because a lot of fun's been made of the psychiatrist and everybody being analyzed. But they're certainly very conscious of the dangers of everything they do.

BRANDON: Do you think Mr. Dulles was?

USTINOV: No, there is a weakness, I think, in drawing your executives from business and law offices because there is an inimitable tendency to continue running everything as though it's a law office, or a business, which it isn't.

BRANDON: Do you mean that the human factors are disregarded?

USTINOV: How shall I put this—that I'd probably feel safer with a judge than with a lawyer, because a lawyer is used to pleading, to distorting. Lawyers and politicians are all people who are adept at presenting what they consider to be the truth in an attractive way. And I'm not sure . . . it seems to me that a lawyer's opinion plays a very odd part in life altogether. They've started every revolution. In the French Revolution they were all lawyers, except one, and he was no good. But I think that came out of close proximity to injustice.

BRANDON: You remember Helen Hayes once talking critically

about British acting. How do you feel about American actors
and American actresses?

USTINOV: Well, they're trained in a completely different way to
ours. In small parts our actors have a much wider span; they're
trained to play more different kinds of parts. The American actors
tend to be realistic, or else tend to have the comic effects which
are associated with a lot of broader kind of comedy than we're
used to, and it's sometimes a little bit difficult for them to strike
a note in between. But on the other hand, they're so eager to
learn and they're so eager to improve themselves. This often leads,
incidentally, to bad results because they become tremendously
theoretical, and the end result is trying to make love to someone
while reading a handbook on how it's done.

In the case of acting, the result it has is to make you
conscious of something which should, by now, be instinctive.
And that is always bad, because then you start expressing something, which satisfies you enormously and satisfies nobody else,
because nobody knows what you're doing. In other words, to my
mind, acting is the imitation of the imaginary. But they believe
very often in different processes. They believe in doing things
consciously and then making a habit of doing things consciously,
and it's really a fretful and annoying procedure, which I think
has harmed a great many actors.

The cultivation of the instinct is the most important thing in
acting, and it's quite possible to do it by force of habit; you
begin to know, in an abstract sense, which is very difficult to put
in words, exactly what is the right thing to do at that moment.
Immediately you try to put it into words, you destroy it; and that
is precisely what they do.

Acting must be like driving a very fast car. Racing drivers will
tell you that they don't grip the steering wheel; the only time
they do that is to correct the car, not to drive it. Acting is the
same thing because it deals with very quick reflexes. It's like a
game in tennis, after a very fierce exchange, when you don't
understand how the players manage to get the ball back, one of
them lobs and the other one puts it in the net because he's got
time to think. Precisely the same thing is true of acting. The
whole process of acting is that the intelligence must be there to

correct the instinct. The theory of trying to reverse that process is to make the instinct push the intelligence from behind and, of course, the intelligence reacts with jarring results for the spectator.

BRANDON: How do you like working on television here?

USTINOV: Oh, television anywhere is very, very similar. It's a very strange technique; it's a very dangerous technique; and it's a very rewarding technique in many ways. It has its advantages in that maybe there is a play, a classic, something of that sort, that you've always dreamed of doing but would hate to get stuck with for a long run. You can do that for one night and give yourself great satisfaction for having done it. At the same time, you can attract toward that a very good cast, because there are many people who are willing to do one performance, well paid, who wouldn't be willing to do it for a long time. At the same time, just technically, it's a very curious medium.

I think one sees that also in the politicians, who know its danger. Their attitude toward it is colored, or seems to be to me, by the fact that they know that as they're talking fifteen million people are listening to them. But at the same time they tend to forget that that fifteen million is not sitting in serried ranks but in their own rooms in units of one, two, and three. And, therefore, I find nothing more enervating than to turn on a television set and find the man is addressing the nation at a range of about two yards, and is looking you straight in the eye and talking to you really as though you were a child, because he estimates the level of fifteen million people rather low.

The whole approach in television must be rather bland. It must be so relaxed that anything can happen and yet nothing very violent will. It's like overhearing; it's halfway between an entertainment and a lullaby at that time of evening.

BRANDON: Have you ever tried anything political on television?

USTINOV: Oh, it's quite possible. One is more in trouble if one tries to talk about the motorcar when one is doing a program which is sponsored by a line of buses; or if one talks about "Mmm, this coffee's good," on a program which is sponsored by a tea corporation. It's full of surprises of that sort which one doesn't realize.

BRANDON: But you've had a number of exceedingly successful performances on television and you have become a celebrity in this country now. Don't you think it is more because of your television performances than because of your play?

USTINOV: Well, what people do here and what they don't do anywhere else is to link the two. I don't really think that in England, or in France, if you gave a very good performance on television, their first reaction would be: Oh, we hope he appears on television again. Whereas here, they connect that with the person that is appearing at the theater and it has a very definite effect on the box office.

BRANDON: Why do you think there is so little political satire here?

USTINOV: There was a time when all those films—like *Mr. Deeds Goes to Town*, and *Mr. Smith Goes to Washington*, I think it was called—were very popular, the great Frank Capra era. There were even elements of a sort of political satire in a play like *Born Yesterday*, in which a gangster comes to Washington in order to get some contract or other. And Arthur Miller in *All My Sons* had a vaguely—not even vaguely—political theme.

BRANDON: I think political satire has not the same freedom it had in Will Rogers' days—though Mort Sahl seems to be making a successful effort to revive it.

USTINOV: This has something to do with the fact that there is a wide span of political opinion in Europe. It is natural that if you had, let's say, a large suitcase to go to the weekend with, you are rather careless about what you put into it; but if you had a small suitcase with the same amount of stuff to go in it, there are bound to be ten or twelve more different opinions about how to put the clothes in. And that's why we have a much wider span of political opinion in a smaller country. There is also much more difference between our political parties. The difference in this country is a much more subtle one. Also it seems to me that this is fundamentally a wealthy country, tremendously wealthy country, so that corruption, if it occurs, never seems to do anybody a great deal of harm. Somebody may get rich, but not many people get poor because of it.

BRANDON: Do you think humor has a future here?

USTINOV: I think humor must have a future anywhere. It has a great future here and that's the most helpful and marvelous and invigorating sign because as soon as a nation gets into any sort of difficulties, the first indication that this is happening is that it loses its sense of humor. Everybody could have been sure that there would be a war with Germany the moment they started arresting comedians for references to Goering's size or Goebbels' size in night clubs. Humor is probably the most indicative safety valve in any nation.

The Hectic, the Lonely, and the Athletic

a conversation with

LEONARD BERNSTEIN

After Leonard Bernstein's debut with the New York Philharmonic Orchestra as its regular conductor, the critics were lukewarm and cautious. The following night, after his second concert, I asked "Lennie" as he is called affectionately by his friends, how he felt about these reviews. "Music critics," he said, without showing the slightest disappointment or rancor, "are cautious by nature and they are bound to be even more so in my particular case. You must realize that I have at least three strikes against me: I am only forty years old, I have written music for Broadway which is a sin for somebody aspiring to be a conductor of serious music, and I am the first American-born conductor in charge of the New York Philharmonic."

In the world of music, with its ingrained European traditions, it is not easy to be an authentic American. But Leonard Bernstein certainly is one. Yehudi Menuhin, for instance, is American-born too, but, as his wife said to me the other day, in Europe they consider him a European, in the Soviet Union a Russian, in Israel a Jew. Bernstein is different. Unlike any other musician he epitomizes the new generation that does not look to Europe for inspiration, but that has brought something new to Europe.

He grew up in the thirties when jazz for the first time began to be thought of as serious music, and his sense of rhythm comes from jazz, it pervades his body and soul. He has therefore, in spite of his broad musical education, not quite the same feel for Beethoven as he has, say, for Shostakovich. He has another very

53

American quality too, a sense of showmanship. Not the Madison Avenue kind. It is nothing contrived, nothing cheap, nothing commercial. It comes naturally to him. It is instinctive.

Bernstein is a man of many talents and accomplishments and like most geniuses of great versatility he is uncertain what he is best at and what he wants to do most. He is a resourceful composer. As such he has two symphonies to his credit, he has written the music to the wildly successful musical West Side Story, *a musical comedy* Wonderful Town, *to a satirical operetta* Candide, *and to a ballet* Fancy Free, *to mention only his most important works. He is also a fine pianist, an inspiring conductor and a brilliantly articulate educator. His ability to fire others with his passion for music is one of his great virtuosities, whether it is in the concert hall or on television, and it is part of his success. His television lectures on "The Art of Conducting," on "What is Jazz," on Bach, on musical comedy, on opera were all superb examples of translating the art of music into language that anybody can understand. His intensity, his velvety voice and his handsomeness all add to the magic, the fascination, the excitement that he creates, that gives everybody the feeling of participating with him in a great adventure.*

Our conversation took place in his private apartment opposite Carnegie Hall. He had just returned from a strenuous recording session and he needed a respite. We settled down in the deep, brown-satin upholstered chairs and he started by asking me questions about disarmament. It was quite clear that he did not only read music but that he is also deeply interested in current affairs. He has clearly kept up the all-round education he got at Harvard University. Our tape recording was only once interrupted when his two little daughters entered the room. They wanted to hear their father's voice on tape and so we did a brief playback for them. Then they departed satisfied and happy. After it was all over he seemed completely relaxed, the heavy day had disappeared from his brow and he asked me to stay on a little longer, sat down at the piano and began to play.

Leonard Bernstein lives between two musical worlds: the traditional one and the modern. This creates obvious dilemmas, frustrations, and certain limitations. But it also means a richer world. *It enables him to personify the change in the cultural tide. He is the American who has no inferiority complex about Europe, he is aware that he, the American of this new generation in music, is giving the Old World something new, something inspiring, something authentically American. And among Americans he has helped to create more interest in serious music than any other individual.*

BRANDON: A reader of the *Sunday Times*, replying to a favorable review of *West Side Story*, complained that it glorifies evil—juvenile delinquency—because it does not apply the Hollywood formula that the good triumph and the bad are punished.

BERNSTEIN: No glorification of these juvenile delinquents was intended. What we intended was a great love story, albeit an adolescent one, set against the background of violence and horror and deliquency which ultimately destroys the love and physically destroys one of the lovers. Not a story of hate with an incidental love story.

BRANDON: What made you select gang warfare as background?

BERNSTEIN: Originally our idea had nothing to do with gang warfare. The idea was to have a love story—a Romeo and Juliet situation played against a background of hostility and contemporary problems—only the Juliet was a Jewish girl and Romeo was an Italian boy, and it was kind of in the slums during the Passover-Easter period when feelings were running very high. We dropped this idea because it turned out to be rather stale; and because that particular aspect of slum life had changed.

Then Arthur Laurents and I happened to meet in Hollywood on different errands. The great migration of Puerto Ricans to New York was then in first flower and the hostilities were just impinging themselves on our consciousness as New Yorkers. We were suddenly terribly excited about the original idea because this was something we were actually living through.

BRANDON: Why do you think Americans select such sordid backgrounds for their musicals?

BERNSTEIN: They don't—really.

BRANDON: Well, take *Carousel, Guys and Dolls, The Pajama Game.*

BERNSTEIN: That isn't fair because *Carousel* is a Hungarian play which has been transferred to the Maine coast. So that's not even an American subject. And the interest of *Guys and Dolls* is not its sordidness at all, but the glory of these Damon Runyon characters. If he hadn't glorified them in the first place, then they couldn't be put on the stage. *Guys and Dolls* doesn't try to make sociological dicta about life in America. As for *Pajama Game*, I find it not sordid but rather a dreary milieu—a pajama factory in the Midwest.

BRANDON: What I mean is that they are subjects that you would not normally think of as a background for a musical.

BERNSTEIN: Well it never used to be that way—obviously. A musical always had to be something that you never had to pay attention to. But the musical theater in America is growing up very fast. As a matter of fact, the musical theater in America is one of the aspects of American art, if I may use this big three-letter word, which is forging ahead faster than almost any other, at least of performance art. And because of that it strikes out in all kinds of new directions.

The musicals that I see when I'm in London are still more or less standard, trifling in subject matter. During my last visit in London I saw one which was certainly not like an American musical—it dealt with no subject of any weight—Julian Slade's *Free As Air.* But even that has caught some of the disease from American musicals. The whole story is zany—it's a delightful show —but there is something in this girl's running away from civilization and trying to find peace in contemplating the sea and breathing clean air which smacks of an influence from America. I'm sure that a few years ago you wouldn't find elements like that in the typical English musical.

You happened to pick certain musicals which do deal with odd and weighty subjects. But 90 per cent of all our musicals are still frothy ones. They're not brain-crackers by any means nor do they try to be heartcrackers, and if you go from *Li'l Abner* to *Happy Hunting* to *Jamaica,* you will not tax your mentality very much. *West Side Story* is an exception, not the rule at all.

The Hectic, the Lonely, and the Athletic

BRANDON: In England, where it originated, the musical seems to stagnate; but here it is fresh, creative, vigorous—as you said, a new expression of American art. Why do you think this is?

BERNSTEIN: Well, the answer to that depends on whether you hold a deterministic view of history or not. Are you a Hegelian? If you are, then you simply accept that every form has its time and its place and that every cultural wave is influenced by other waves in the great ocean. After all, why should there have been such a great period of architecture in Greece at one particular moment and there isn't any good period of architecture in Greece now?

It is certainly true that England presented us with the musical and that all our early musicals were blatant imitations of the English techniques, which reached a fantastic high with Gilbert and Sullivan. But when we began to grow as a place of our own, we began to develop our own little cultural wave. England had already hit the top of her cultural wave in this and from then on it was a kind of decline, not without its minor glories but still a decline.

BRANDON: I think that some time ago you said that the musical may provide the transition to serious music in America.

BERNSTEIN: Yes, well I have the feeling that the form is growing in such a vital way that it may wind up—and I hope it does—in some kind of American musical-theatrical form which I hesitate to call opera, but that's the only word I can find for it at the moment, which would treat the English or rather American language in a natural way so that you could do serious things through music and say serious things through music in the theater without sounding like a translation from *Aida*. We are doing that in our musical shows.

In addition to that, dancing has achieved great importance. In *West Side Story* much of the story is told in dance and much of the emotional content is in dance. And this peculiar amalgamation of dance with some American rhymed speech, let's say, has combined in a concoction which is different. This is very hard to describe but anybody who goes to a good American musical senses it right away.

BRANDON: Yes, I think the variety of languages, cultures that are mixed in the American scene must have something to do with it.

BERNSTEIN: Well, a great deal of the language in *West Side Story*, for example, is affected by the talk of jazz people and jive talk, which is basically Negro, and by the talk of Puerto Ricans. The way they speak English has lent this book a beautiful poetic quality, which it couldn't otherwise have because you can't sit down and write poetry in a realistic play about delinquents.

BRANDON: Do you think there's anything basically distinctive about American music as compared to modern music in other countries?

BERNSTEIN: Yes, I do. I really do. There are two kinds of so-called American music. One is—I take it you're speaking of serious music now? . . .

BRANDON: Yes.

BERNSTEIN: One is an American music which is deliberate, which is self-consciously nationalistic and as a result hardly ever works. Gershwin was an exception to that. And then there is the unconscious kind, which works in proportion to the talent of the composer, but is much more meaningful in that the jazz influences and whatever other influences we have infect the music. In the final result these influences appear in a much more subtle way, so that the music doesn't scream: "Listen to me! Look how American I am." It just is American because that's the way it had to come out.

Jazz is certainly the chief of these influences and there are others. There's a certain kind of loneliness that inhabits a lot of American music and a kind of athleticism which is different from British athleticism, and there is a certain kind of urban melancholia— it's awfully hard to pinpoint these things. You feel them when you hear them. And there's a feeling very often of big spaces in American music. I think the hectic quality, the lonely quality and the athletic quality are the three main qualities.

BRANDON: You're such a gifted musician, you're a composer, a pianist, a conductor, and a teacher. Which one gives you the greatest satisfaction?

BERNSTEIN: Well, if I knew, then I would do that exclusively. Because there is nothing I would like better than to be able to concentrate on one thing. But I can't! Everything to do with music excites me. And music is my world—that's where I live.

BRANDON: Do you prefer to conduct modern or classical music?

BERNSTEIN: No, I'm very promiscuous about music. I have no preferences—literally no preferences. Isn't that awful? I just like *good* music better than bad, and the better it is the more I like it, whether it is by Vivaldi or Bartók.

BRANDON: I prefer a poem with rhyme and rhythm to one without, and it probably also influences my taste in music.

BERNSTEIN: Well, I don't think any poet would ever admit that his poem didn't have rhythm. You can find them without rhyme but then they have other kinds of rhythm.

With modern music you don't feel easy because it's a new kind of language. You depend too much on symmetry and on the old formal rudiments of composition, which have been protested against and revolted against for half a century now. And maybe that's all wrong—maybe we'll find that we just have to go back to writing equal phrases and C major triads and all the rest of it again. Maybe that's what music is really all about.

But for the moment we are living in a time when most composers are busy trying to find new ways of writing music, new musical things to say.

BRANDON: The other day in an interview in *Encounter* Stravinsky said: "Today harmonic novelty is at an end. As a medium of musical construction, harmony offers no further resources in which to inquire and from which to seek profit." Do you agree?

BERNSTEIN: He's absolutely right. The word I quarrel with is "profit." I still believe—and *very* strongly—that one can still derive what I think Stravinsky means by "profit" from a C major chord, if one has something to say. In other words, one can use harmony with all its resources, even though I agree with him that these resources are exhausted in terms of trying to find new materials.

But there *are* ways—I know there are ways—of using these materials in a new way. Because, you see, it's like saying that the words of a language are finished. There can't be any new words. We have all the words we need except technical words for new inventions. And therefore nothing new can be said in that language. But that's not true. Somebody can come along with the word "bread" and the word "lamp" and make something new out of it.

What Stravinsky had in mind with that paragraph is another way of looking at the construction of music. Music, in the great line from Mozart to Mahler, has depended upon the notion of a melody accompanied by chords, which are called harmony, with the addition of occasional counterpoint—that is, other subordinate melodies along with the principal melody. And color, in terms of orchestration, and various combinations of sound. And rhythmic ingenuity. But basically the notion of music is a tune and its accompaniment.

Stravinsky doesn't write tunes, except now and then in ballets and such. But his fundamental approach is what is known as "motivic" and his fundamental technique is what is known as "serial." The serial technique is based on the succession of a number of notes—which do not necessarily mean a melody in the old sense with an accompaniment—which series is then manipulated in a variety of ways to produce a composition.

And by "motivic" you would mean using motives rather than long themes or long, romantic melodies. And this produces a kind of music which is not so immediate as old music and not so easy to follow, but it is different. The very fact that so many composers are composing this way now *must* mean that there is something to it. If they are all proved wrong eventually, well then, they're proved wrong.

BRANDON: You spoke of the flowering from Mozart to Mahler, and you implied that there was progress.

BERNSTEIN: Well, there was a great development of the sonata from beginning just before Mozart and culminating in the gigantic works of Mahler. Perhaps the high point of this was Beethoven; many people would say that everything that followed Beethoven—like Brahms and Schumann—was already the decline. That's a highly puristic point of view. Many people feel that Beethoven was just a step along the way and that it reached its ultimate in Bruckner and Mahler and then exploded—finished. But there is a definite line of symphonic development.

BRANDON: But what about atonality—the era of Schönberg?

BERNSTEIN: Schönberg followed that period. Atonality came out of the decline of this great rise in German music. That is, once the pieces became so expressive and so huge and so full of development and complexity, then something new had to be found. Atonality was a desperate attempt to find something new. It had to happen. It had to happen because with Wagner tonality had been stretched to the breaking point. *Tristan* has places which begin to sound almost atonal, although he never does give up the center of the tonality. And the logical next step was to dispense with it altogether. We are still in the struggling transition period started by Schönberg at the beginning of this century. We are trying to find a meaningful, expressive music without tonality. It's a tough fight to keep tonality and not sound like what everybody else has written before.

BRANDON: Whom would you count among the foremost American "fighters"—if you put it that way?

BERNSTEIN: Well, among them are Aaron Copland and Roy Harris and Roger Sessions and William Schuman and so on. But there are many, many composers in America—and mostly the younger ones—who are following the Schönbergian ways. Now there seems to be taking place a *rapprochement* of these two camps—the camp headed by Stravinsky and the camp headed by Schönberg. Now they are borrowing from each other.

In other words, the atonal composers are writing more moderately—not quite so neurotically as they were before; and the tonal composers are using tone rows and serial techniques which they have borrowed from the atonal composers. Any maybe out of this coming together of the two camps will come the real, basic music of our century.

BRANDON: Do you see this sort of development among modern composers in England?

BERNSTEIN: Exactly the same division into those two camps and the same *rapprochement* between the two camps is happening in England and France, and in Germany.

England writes more symphonies than we do per capita, because they are still closer to the German tradition than we are. And they're still surrounded by the aura of Elgar and Vaughan Williams, who were essentially symphonists in the German tradition. But there are more and more symphonies being written in England now by young composers, which are tonally free or atonal, or which use serial techniques and so on.

BRANDON: You wrote the other day in *The Atlantic Monthly* that you discern four levels of meaning in music: narrative literary meaning as in *Till Eulenspiegel* and *The Sorcerer's Apprentice*; atmospheric pictorial meanings as in *La Mer* and *Pictures at an Exhibition*; effective reactive meanings such as triumph, pain, wistfulness, regret, cheerfulness, melancholy . . .

BERNSTEIN: Goodness, did I write all that?

BRANDON: . . . typical of nineteenth-century romanticism; and purely musical meanings. And then you said that only the fourth is the really important one. I was wondering whether you are not almost saying that neither the good novel nor poem nor drama is important; what matters is Fowler's *English Usage*.

BERNSTEIN: Oh, when you speak of a novel or a poem or a drama —well not a poem necessarily, but when you speak of something done with words in general—you are speaking of forms which use a medium that is transparent. In other words, "words" are mainly important for what they mean. The word "lamp" means just that and you can use it in various contexts, but it will always mean lamp. But an F sharp means absolutely nothing except in context. So that musical meanings are necessarily abstract.

There is a great meaning in the way an E flat relates to an F sharp, which has nothing to do with sorcerers or anything else; it has to do with that E flat and that F sharp and the way it affects the human ear.

Musicians are working with an abstract medium. It's the difference between objective and nonobjective painters. An objective painter will say: What is the point of painting? The point is to represent things as you see them. He will say that all these other people who paint lines and circles and blobs are fakers.

Now those fake people will say: No, we are closer to music. We're doing more what the musician does, which is to take the abstract elements of his medium and make meaning out of them. And on either side of these two painting schools, you will find on the objective side the extreme is the writer, who has settled down with meaningful words because his medium is all meanings, representational meanings. And on the other extreme—next to the abstract painter—is the musician, because music means absolutely nothing except musically.

Now there are all kinds of variations and gradations—there are lots of literary people who have tried to use words in a nonobjective way, like Gertrude Stein and Joyce, and this has affected a great deal of modern poetry—Cummings, the surrealists—and it has also affected the other extreme of musicians in a way which makes them try to write music that has extra-musical meanings. That's the origin of the whole plot to make the opening of Beethoven's Fifth mean V for Victory . . . and that makes the symphony twice as popular because the first four notes stand for V.

But that's nonsense! V has nothing to do with those first four notes—all they are is three Gs and an E flat and a certain rhythm and sonority and tempo, which produce an extraordinary effect on the hearer. Music can excite visions in you of leading an army to battle or of sleeping with the girl you love, anything you want, but it's still three Gs and an E flat which don't mean anything. You can *make* them mean anything you want . . . You can say those three Gs and an E flat have something of rage and power and dynamism about them, but that's all vague talk. What do rage and power and dynamism mean? They mean nothing compared to the effect of those notes. The notes are important, that's what I mean by musical meaning.

It may not create any reaction in you, but it has a meaning for you no matter how much you try to avoid it. Words *mean* things. They are representational and that's the whole trouble; that's why literary people can never understand how a musician works and why very often musicians are so inarticulate.

Nightmare: Goya Gets a Guggenheim

a conversation with

BEN SHAHN

When I failed to recognize Ben Shahn at the Princeton Junction railway station, it was probably because I expected him to look differently. On first sight Shahn looks more like a prosperous farmer. He is tall and broad-set, his face is round, his complexion as if he fed on milk rather than, say, whiskey. And in addition his grayish, drooping mustache gives him the air of an old Russian muzhik rather than that of a painter. Certainly as I glanced searchingly across the platform he did not seem like a man who likes to choose stark, even morbid subjects.

It took us about half an hour before we reached his house, just outside the small town of Roosevelt, New Jersey. In the past it was always I who tried his best to relax my victim before leading him to the tape recorder. But during our drive from Princeton Junction it was Shahn who in his own compassionate way tried to make me feel relaxed. He told me about his recent trip to Europe, his experiences in London, and his life in Roosevelt.

We walked briefly through his house and then out into the garden where he had his studio. I first browsed through some of his sketches and photographs of paintings which had either been already sold or were still with his dealer. He told me about his family and finally we settled down. Our conversation, with a short interruption for lunch, continued until late in the afternoon. It lasted much longer than I had planned for, and as a consequence I ran out of tape. I saw myself already robbed of part of the fruits of this expedition when Shahn remembered that his older daugh-

64

ter, who was learning to sing, had only recently been given a tape recorder to enable her to hear herself. It saved the day.

Ben Shahn came to the United States at the age of eight from Russia. His artistic career began as a lithographer's apprentice. He said he made enough to help him through night school. And it is clearly this training that has continued to dominate much of his style. What inspires him in his work as an artist are the hopes and dreams, fears and tragedies of other people, and it was Ben Shahn's social consciousness, or as he prefers to call it "moral conscious-ness," his driving need to comment on human nature against the background of the contemporary scene, that made him resist the tide of abstractionism that has come to dominate American paint-ing. He finds himself, therefore, in a somewhat lonely position, reminiscent of Hogarth and Daumier, whose great satirical tradi-tion he follows.

Just as Leonard Bernstein has the rare gift of discussing music in language easily understandable to the layman, so Shahn has a similar gift of articulating his thoughts about the art of painting in all its aspects. He can recapture what inspired him to paint certain paintings and to define the ideas behind them. It is there-fore not surprising that he was the first painter to be invited by Harvard University to deliver the Charles Elliott Norton lectures, which have since been published in book form under the title The Shape of Content.

His works hang in many museums and private collections and in spite, or perhaps because, of his refusal to follow the sheep into abstractionism, his paintings have been fetching high prices and high praise. In 1947 he had a one-man show at the Museum of Modern Art and in 1954, together with De Kooning, his work was featured in the U.S. pavilion at the Venice Bienale. The record of our conversation proves that he is not only a penetrating and candid conversationalist about art, but also a compassionate com-mentator on modern life.

BRANDON: Europeans are becoming increasingly aware of the impact that America makes on their way of life, including the field of art. In the past it's been a one-way street, as it were, but now for the first time American trends seem to exert influence on European painters. What do you think caused this reversal of artistic influence?

SHAHN: It's part of the general influence that is going on now in ways of living—in hot-dog stands and automobiles and in the landscapes that have been shockingly ruined in Italy by the American-style gas stations. And I suppose art comes along with the rest of the culture.

BRANDON: You don't think that it is the strength of the abstractionist movement here that focussed the art world's attention on America?

SHAHN: I don't think so. I think that within a short period of time we have had two strong abstract waves in our country—after the famed Armory Show of 1913—and then it seems to have gone into a kind of a limbo, but we're now reviving the names and reputations of people whom we've forgotten entirely. Then we have had a second wave—after the First World War. My own feeling is—I don't know if anybody will share it with me—that every artist wants sponsorship and patronage. If not in dollars, he wants it in adjectives. And he's going to turn in the direction of the adjectives, failing to get dollars. It takes a very strong individual, I think, to resist that kind of a wave. Paul Klee is a wonderful example of a person who resisted endless waves of isms that flowed over European art during his lifetime and he was in a sense a little bit like China absorbing the invaders rather than being influenced by them. We had in this country during the period of the WPA* —we had almost a national sponsorship—something that hadn't existed historically perhaps since the Egyptian period, you know. And most of the painters that I knew were fairly happy with such a sponsorship. Economically, we were all leveled. The effort to show each other up ceased to be so strong because the outlets and facilities for showing each other's ability against—one against the other—didn't exist. We had, maybe, ten galleries functioning in New York during those years, and we have 150 to 175 functioning now. Then the war came along and ended it all suddenly.

The artist craves patronage somewhere, and he looks around.

* Works Progress Administration—a governmental agency during the depression to deal with unemployment.

Who else is now going to be the patron? Will it be the Museum of Modern Art, the Whitney Museum? After the last war it ceased to be the ordinary man, so to say, as represented by the government. Many a painter I knew made an about-face with such speed that it was simply shocking.

One I remember particularly who was doing a beautiful thing—almost like Fra Angelico—I would call it "moral realism"—"social realism" of our particular time—and one day he suddenly began to do things like Mondriaan. He said to me: "Well, I've made up my mind and I'm going this way and nothing will stop me!" Now, what did he want? He wanted approval from certain sources. I think we all do. I do. Every one of us does. But sometimes we're not clear where we want that approval from. Granting that every painter paints primarily to satisfy himself, once he has finished his painting he does want approval somewhere.

BRANDON: But isn't it strange for the Europeans to want approval in this country?

SHAHN: Why not? Italians with means ignore their contemporary painters, except for a few collectors around Milan and Turin and so on. The contemporary painters know, or have heard, that in America there's an audience for them. And if painting is an international language, there we are.

BRANDON: What do you think are the predominant influences —I mean, indigenous influences—on art in the United States?

SHAHN: It's not indigenous, but I suppose the greatest influence today has been Picasso. A friend of mine once divided the whole thing into three broad categories: The Maze—as represented by Pollock; the Order—as represented by Mondriaan; and the Monster—as represented by Picasso—as of the Guernica period. It's oversimplification, of course, but I think you could almost divide our art today into those three broad categories.

BRANDON: Have you ever met Picasso?

SHAHN: No, I haven't. I have a little bit of a—I don't know—shyness before such prominent people, and a meeting was arranged and I confess I broke the engagement. He's, you know, a monument. I had the same feeling with Frank Lloyd Wright. It wasn't he that spoiled it for me, it was his students at the school in Taliesen. They referred to him as "The Master" you know—"The

Master" and I just couldn't take that. And they showed me where he sits on two chairs in a little theater higher than the rest of them . . . I can't feel anybody being a "Master"—

BRANDON: Where do you put yourself in?

SHAHN: I don't know where to put myself. I just leave that to others and then they argue the point. I've read so many of the reviews of my show in Venice during the '54 biennial that I am completely confused. If I had ever had any idea where to put myself, they certainly made it much more difficult for me. I've been called a surrealist; I've been called an expressionist; I've been almost called a cubist, a primitive, a social realist, an unsocial realist, etc., etc. So I don't know where to put myself.

BRANDON: It's been said that you belong to the great satirical tradition which reaches from Hogarth through Daumier and the early George Grosz.

SHAHN: Well, those are just flattering things. I admit that I was very much influenced by all those people, but I have been very much influenced by the Japanese, too, you know.

BRANDON: In what way?

SHAHN: Well, in their whole outlook on pattern, the flatness of design, and the kind of color I use. I once studied them very assiduously.

BRANDON: I was in Japan four years ago and I found that the Japanese are also very much influenced by American art.

SHAHN: Oh, completely so. I just had a visit from the editor of a Japanese art magazine—he brought me a lot of photographs—and it was incredible. You could take the reproductions from the magazines he showed me and put them over English titles and it would take an expert to identify their national origins.

BRANDON: Do you always paint with an intention—?

SHAHN: Of communicating—yes, I make no bones about that at all.

BRANDON: But there are some painters today who deny that intention, don't they?

SHAHN: Well, they also would communicate, but they have another gauge for measuring communication. In other words, the fewer the people they communicate with, they feel, the sounder is the quality of their work, the profounder is the quality of their work, whatever term you want to use. And there has grown out of that view a kind of philosophy that if the audience is small, then the very quality is inversely great, and vice versa. And that, to me, is as silly as the other point which says: If the audience is great, the work is great. And I think that holds for every field of work. You, yourself, must feel in certain areas of journalism, even though the audience is not world-wide, that the thing you do has a certain depth, a certain profundity that you are impressed with, regardless of the size of the audience.

BRANDON: Your painting shows an extraordinary discipline, and a repetition of themes and ideas. That discipline is missing with most contemporary American painters.

SHAHN: Well I don't know whether you mean to be flattering about this or you mean to be—disparaging . . .

BRANDON: Personally, it's flattering.

SHAHN: Well, I've heard the identical words used in a disparaging way. I throw my hands up in desperation and say: This is what I am and this is all I can do. I don't think it's a particular virtue as such, it is my nature and temperament to be that way, that's all. However, I don't hold it out as an absolute and I wish other people wouldn't hold out other directions as their absolutes. I've been accused, once in delivering a talk . . . "But, my goodness," some student said, "I thought artists were emotional and yours was an intellectual talk." Again, I threw up my hands and said: "I can't help it, I'm that way, you see."

BRANDON: If you compare Mondriaan, how he painted in his earlier period, and in his last period, there's an extraordinary difference. Picasso went through different stages, but with Mondriaan it seems to have come suddenly.

SHAHN: I wouldn't agree with you on that. I think one can trace the steps of Mondriaan painting. I remember seeing recently a study of trees, in which the direction—if one already knew the direction—was apparent, as with Joyce, *Ulysses* is apparent in his *Portrait of the Artist*—you see, in that sense. If you were to take them apart, not knowing that one was the author of the other, you would not think that were possible, but if you knew that he was the author of both, you can see that logic. And there are actual logical steps from one to the next. As I always felt that one should really read some of Mondriaan's own writing. He's a man disturbed by the social scene, the disorder of the social scene, and tried in *his* medium of expression to say that.

BRANDON: Well, he tries to impose rigidity . . .

SHAHN: All people that try to impose orders impose rigidity. There's no doubt about that.

BRANDON: Yes, but you are also seeking a certain order—

SHAHN: Not of that kind. Perhaps mine is the order of what the French call *"Le moment après vu"*—the unexpected thing that comes along. I think that my order is more of a critique of the disorder without actually holding forth an order.

BRANDON: What is life for a painter like in the United States?

SHAHN: Well, we have something happening in this country that doesn't exist anywhere in the world. We have our colleges and universities becoming sponsors and patrons of the arts. We have, I think, 1900 colleges and universities in the United States. I would say there are, on an average, two artists teaching in every one of them, some having as many as twenty teachers in their art departments. Now that offers security of a kind—economic security, certainly.

I have been terrified by it because it has been done without much thought—it just happened. It's become a kind of a super WPA without a pauper's oath. And one has yet to see whether that has been a worthy thing, either for the universities or for the artists. It has become so prevalent that when I was out at Ohio State a couple of years ago, they had a staff of some twenty-five people in their art department. They all referred, rather enviously, to one man as an "independent painter"—and it meant only that he was not teaching. I don't object to security, but I am skeptical about the peculiar removal from the outside world that the university always means. I get nightmares when I think that Goya might have gotten a Guggenheim and, being talented, perhaps they would have renewed his Guggenheim. Would we then have had from him what we got from Goya? I doubt it.

Security makes a great many also turn temporarily to so-called commercial art. The danger here is that they begin to make too much money too soon and then the flame of their own creativity begins to get weaker and weaker. At best, it's a very weak flame because the world and all the outside isn't putting any great pressure on the artist to paint, you know. And if, during the youthful and creative years that flame isn't nurtured, it will finally subside and there will be nothing left of it.

BRANDON: Art has come very late to the United States, hasn't it?

SHAHN: Naturally so. It hasn't been very long since we said that our geographic frontiers have been practically used up. We now have to begin to look to our social frontiers. So it is very natural that it has come late. There have been efforts by scholars to show that we have a tradition going back to colonial days, but that was so rare and so occasional, it wasn't very important.

BRANDON: Perhaps it's because art is a kind of nonmaterialistic enrichment, a taste for which has been slowly developing here—

SHAHN: Yes, yes, when I asked the headmaster of a very important prep school in our country fifteen or twenty years ago about teaching art to his students, he said: "We don't bother with that at all. Our graduates will go to universities, become executives, and their wives will take care of that sort of thing."

However, since the war something has happened, there's no doubt about it. As individuals often begin to question the validity of a material culture, so a country can sometimes begin to question it. Certainly today this self-questioning is all over the place, as you very well know.

BRANDON: Has art had much influence on shaping life in America? I mean, in other countries it had a certain cohesive force . . .

SHAHN: Oh yes, no doubt about it. Yes, there was a time when an artist was appointed an ambassador. It isn't very likely today. But whether it's had an influence? It began to have such an influence during the period I speak of, the so-called WPA period. It was the sheer volume, not the quality, that was slowly beginning to exert an influence and there are echoes of it left, little art centers all over the country. For some reason art seems to be an influence when people get a little older, when they've satisfied some of their material needs. You've probably read this book about Lord Duveen and how these older people felt that what they had struggled for so much and for so long had *not* given them the satisfaction that a work of art had done four centuries ago. And they preferred to associate themselves rather with this work of art than with the very plant which they had used all the energy of their youth and manhood to build.

BRANDON: Museums rather than factories help to preserve names for posterity . . . Do you think the artist in this country is still suspect?

SHAHN: Yes, I do. It took twenty years—carefully paying my bills on time—for me to receive acceptance in a little community like ours here, for instance.

BRANDON: You said once that there is a great difference between having a Van Gogh on the living room wall and having him, himself, in the living room.

SHAHN: When I said that I was thinking of a particular situation, of a terribly talented youngster of sixteen, amazingly advanced, an only child, whose parents wanted him to go on from his prep school to a university and then to a law school. He would have been the seventh generation to follow through this pattern. And he was fighting—politely—as he had been trained to fight in a situation like that—to go to an art school. His parents finally won out; they were collectors, but the thought of their own boy becoming a painter terrified them. And when it was all over and he was safely ensconced at Harvard, his mother said: "Had I two sons, I would have given one to art." Artists, I believe, fall into three categories here: the lowest is the painter; second comes the musician; if the boy had turned to writing, I don't think there would have been too many obstacles put in his way.

BRANDON: Why is there this difference in this respect between the musician and the painter?

SHAHN: Well, I think you, you English, by and large are responsible for it. For generations now you've written novels which we've read and devoured, in which the artist is turned into a character that may have existed, but I've never met one. I've never met any of the characters that exist in *The Moon and Sixpence*. And along comes your latest one, Joyce Cary with *The Horse's Mouth*, an absolutely incredible character. I cannot conceive a character just out of jail walking along the Embankment and thinking what colors he would use for a sunset. And we, in America, who became artists were very much influenced by those novels. But those who did not become artists who were, you know, out in real life, they were terrified of these characters. That's part of it.

BRANDON: Well, I'm sure that's partly true. But isn't it also because the painter is not considered a man who can make much money? Doesn't that play quite a part in this country in judging professions?

SHAHN: I think it does. The only difference is this: we don't have a tradition. A youngster in Italy wanting to paint . . . his father without ever having seen his work would know the names of Michelangelo and Raphael and so on and he might even have seen some of their works . . . so he'll be distressed but not to that degree. If money has not accrued, certainly glory has accrued to those names. And, in that sense, we are different from the European. But it isn't only money, it is the instability of the whole thing. A youngster in Harvard last year expressed the desire to become a painter but had reservations because he said you can't hang out a shingle as a painter; if you're a doctor, an architect, a landscape architect, an engineer, you can always hang out a shingle, but you can't say "Painter" on a shingle.

BRANDON: Do you think that abstractionism is abating or—

SHAHN: I don't think so at all—no. I have a silly notion, which I don't think anybody shares. As a democracy we have very genuinely tried to distribute the good things of a democracy to everybody. Now we feel we've exhausted the distribution of material things and we must distribute the things of the spirit. So we print paperbacks, produce hundreds of thousands of phonograph records—millions—now we come to distribute art.

But people don't feel that a reproduction is as good as an original painting. By God, we're going to teach them to make their own! We can't have enough artists to distribute original art with the largesse with which we distributed automobiles—so we'll teach people to do this kind of painting—that requires no particular training. Kids who come into an art school within six weeks can turn out a very creditable abstraction, a nonobjective painting. I think that's how we'll resolve this particular problem.

BRANDON: You mean to get around the need for draftsmanship?

SHAHN: Yes, yes. Teachers in art schools, particularly those who were trained in an earlier time, try to stress drawing and the kids just say: Well, what for? Nobody draws. We just won't go and look at the work of X, Y, and Z, just because X, Y, or Z is a competent draftsman. There's a rebellion against drawing and consequently the teacher is just barking up a tree with the idea of teaching draftsmanship. And then another thing that is happening here: despite all the attacks on us about conformity, and maybe because of it, each artist is desperately trying to be as individual as he can. Perhaps in his very rebellion against conformity he will just try to express that which is most individual in him. The fact that an exhibition of a group of such individual expressions begins to look quite anonymous is another matter. So there is a growing tendency toward abstract art.

And should the artist, himself, try to counter this tendency, his audience won't let him. The millions who have been given art appreciation courses over the last twenty years since the war will think this is the only art expression that exists and they will demand it.

BRANDON: Perhaps it has become a vested interest for too many people who bought abstractionist paintings at high prices.

SHAHN: Well, I don't ever want to accuse anyone of venality in those situations but it's possible. There was an amusing reaction to the German expressionist show which was held in New York some time ago. When I expressed my strong liking for some of the works in that show to some prominent collectors of other directions of painting, I was startled that they did not respond to my enthusiasm. There might be a fear, as you say, that this particular thing was a threat to their investment. But, by and large, I don't think there are many people who buy exclusively for investment—there may be some. Likewise I don't think there are many artists who enter art to exploit a particular fashion. I think they believe this or that direction is more closely allied to their personality or way of thinking.

BRANDON: Don't those painters who are not abstractionists somehow feel that they are suffering from an established monopoly? I know the anti-trust laws here do not yet apply to painters . . .

SHAHN: I think they do. Some five or six years ago a group organized itself and called itself "Reality." And they held meetings, they put out a little publication, and I went along with them for a

74

bit, but when they began to exclude people on partial loyalty to their belief, then I said: Well, this is the end. You would exclude X because he leans in a direction that you don't like, and I will follow by excluding Y who also leans too much in another direction, and, finally, it will be left for just the two of us. And then, I know what you think of me, and you probably know what I think of you—and then we'd have nothing, you see. So, I just can't go along with you—and I sort of pulled out on that basis. But they do sense being outside of things.

BRANDON: Of course, what may help now is a revival of the importance of the egghead . . .

SHAHN: This is the thing I fear now. You know, it's been so nice being part of the minority for such a long time. I consider myself an egghead, willy-nilly, and if the egghead should suddenly be put on a pedestal as was suggested on television last night—"We *must* change our attitude toward the egghead"—it would make me shiver. I think we've been insane on the subject of eggheads. Here you will find fathers using every influence in the world to get their kids into college and then ridiculing the teachers of their sons. That, to me, is one of the most ironic things. They are out raising funds for one university or another—the alma mater or something —and then in the next breath, they're tearing these very people apart. This is one of the fantastic contradictions we have here. In 1952 I gave a talk which the U. S. Information Service broadcast overseas; it was called "The Integration of Sculpture and Painting in Modern Architecture." They also assigned some young woman to turn it into a little booklet, and she began to pick illustrations for it. She brought in some of my things among others, and the man above her didn't quite say No, but he hinted that she bring something else and finally he said: Bring in some nonobjective work because that is absolutely noncontroversial.

And here is another interesting point: When Russia issued that edict about cosmopolitanism—whatever they called it, you know, about 1948—we immediately were euchred into a kind of position so that we had to say: If this is what you claim to be the direction of "social realism" as they called it, then we're going to go in the very opposite, as we have been opposite, as we have been going in every political situation, you see. And suddenly we found a magazine like *Life*, which supposedly understands the temper of our people, shifting from the regional school, of which they had been the great exponents, to suddenly extolling the work of a Jackson Pollock, even while they knew full well that their audience didn't care. It was an echo of the political situation.

BRANDON: Do you think painters will continue to avoid controversial problems?

SHAHN: That will depend entirely on our political and social situation.

BRANDON: But then you really imply that these people have not the kind of courage to comment on the world events—that, for instance, you have in your paintings.

SHAHN: I don't want to be boastful about that, but I feel myself in an isolated position today. There are very few people I feel I can go along with. I've been fortunate the last few years. Despite all this, I can get by economically, you know, but beyond that I feel an isolation, there's no doubt about it. But I'm both too stubborn and too old to do anything about it.

BRANDON: But you find, for instance, that people buy fewer of your paintings than they did previously?

SHAHN: I don't think so. You see, the artist is very fortunate in this sense. He needs only one maverick. The author has an editor who looks upon his work as an investment adviser would look upon an investment, you see. There are three thousand people who are going to spend $4.75 each and he has to protect these investors, as it were. But in the case of the artist, there is only one investor. And in that sense he's much more fortunate.

BRANDON: The other day I read that one of your colleagues criticized you for doing a cover for *Time* magazine of Freud—a portrait of Freud. I'm glad there are still some painters who dare to paint portraits.

SHAHN: Well, maybe this colleague can't paint a portrait, I don't know. I know the particular reference that you have in mind and it didn't disturb me one way or another. I would do a portrait if the individual who is to be portrayed is one to whom I'm sympathetic, you see. I've done two of these portraits—one of Malraux and one of Freud. I was asked to do a portrait of Teller by the same organization and I find Teller a very unsympathetic person and just refused to do it. I told them point-blank, I don't like this character. I know they're going to say some glowing things and there'd be an awful discrepancy between my portrait and what they're going to say. Oh, you have to harden yourself to criticism, you know, and you develop very early a kind of a carapace like a lobster, which is good as a protection but, perhaps, in the long run it also protects you against the nice things—it has a dual effect upon you—it acts as an armor against that as well as the other. This I know . . . when I am painting I'm so alone, you can't conceive anything like it.

BRANDON: But as you said, by painting a portrait, you can put a lot into it—your sympathies and antipathies. Nevertheless, painters today seem to be very reluctant to do portraits.

SHAHN: I don't know the reason for that. Most people seem to be content with a camera portrait. They're not awfully good; they're instantaneous impressions. Even the most insignificant portrait is an effort, if there's any competence on the part of the artist at all, an effort to bring together many facets of the individual he's portraying. During the several hours, or days, or week or two weeks during which the portrait painter is engaged in working, the subject will have been going through a thousand moods. When he's painting this side of the mouth, the man may be thinking of dinner; on the other hand, when he's painting this corner of the eye, the man will be thinking of the stock market. And those all get together and you get the essence of the individual, which you don't in the camera portrait.

BRANDON: Berenson once wrote that the great painters of the past taught us to see nature—that is, what is outside ourselves—as art, and that the artists, the great creative masters, from them to the humblest artists in the sumptuary arts, have played, perhaps, the most decisive part in civilizing and humanizing that ferocious beast, primitive man. And are we now passing, he asks, through some abyss of despair about human nature and its destiny—without having the exciting fear of hell and the hope of heaven—of the early medieval man? Instead, he says, of communicating pleasure in everyday things and hope of the better, the nonrepresentational artist of today ignores shape and substance and fails to make us long for the realms not only of actuality but of aspiration.

SHAHN: Well, you know, I feel a little bit about that quotation as the folk of ancient Rome did when a new Pope came into power. The Jewish residents of the ghetto had to go through a ritual of presenting a brand new scroll of the Torah to him. And the Pope said: "I agree in substance with what you say, but not with your interpretation." In substance I agree with him, but I must confess there are so many factors that enter into it that would make us differ. To begin with, if I ever reach the age of ninety, I would only look for joy in painting, naturally. Also, there is a time when a human being, like an old radio-receiving set, ceases to receive. You cannot apply his values, which were formed more than a half century ago, to what goes on today. And it would be very hard to agree or disagree with him on that. I agree to this point: there is a dehumanization—the artist disclaims any responsibility on the theory, that has always been held, that he merely mirrors his society. That would be very well, but I expect more of the artist than a mere mechanical mirroring of his society. In other words, if the brutality and disjointedness and fragmentation of society that is going on today can be interpreted in the paintings that are being made today, that would be very well, but I think there was probably more violence in a Giotto's time, or a Fra Angelico's time, and if they merely mirrored that kind of society, I don't think that would have been enough. I think the role of the artist is to transcend, you see. He must not only mirror his time, he must hold something beyond that. And in that sense, I accept that interpretation of Berenson's. But I think his comparisons are not based so much on time as on the actual outer aspects of the painting. And I think—I flatter myself in thinking—I can look beyond the immediate exterior of painting. And as I've heard people often say: Oh, this painting is much too strong for me, I just couldn't live with that. Well, they may as well throw out most of their books that are of any value, because you just literally can't live with Dostoevski's characters, but still we are content to keep them on our shelf. But if you begin to look at a painting purely as decoration, then you really can't live with it. Neither does Dostoevski fit into a musical comedy scheme. And by the logic and values that Berenson uses, he cannot accept contemporary work today; his values are set, you know, as well as his means of measurement.

BRANDON: But with a book you have the advantage that you can put it back on the shelf, and you don't have to read it in order to look at it.

SHAHN: I am aware of that . . . for instance, a book that disturbed me very much was Céline's *Voyage au bout de la nuit.* It moved me. And whenever I see it, I'm aware of its content, you know. And still I'm content to keep it because I think it's an impressive book, it was an important thing to have said when it was said. And I just do not look upon pictures as decoration. They might, incidentally, serve that purpose, but that's very incidental.

BRANDON: Isn't it true, though, that artists today go to the other extreme of ignoring almost everything around them and being too much concerned with themselves?

SHAHN: They think they do, but I don't think they really do. I think that every artist, no matter what direction his work takes, is saying or stating his beliefs. If the world around him is too much for him, he can withdraw within himself, but this is a statement of what he believes. And it is, in a sense, the content of his work. Even the lack of content is a content. He makes that as his statement.

BRANDON: But isn't there the danger that the artist isolates himself?

SHAHN: There's every danger in the world. I have begun to believe that just as science has begun to speak to a select few, who have had to have a long training to understand, so, I'm afraid, the same thing is beginning to happen in the arts. It's certainly happening in some of our poetry. Ezra Pound once said somewhere— I hope I'm not misquoting him—"I have nightmares when I think of what would happen if the classics were made available to the masses." Now this kind of a philosophy has grown up in the arts to such a degree that it has become a measure of value. If the audience is smaller, the work is better. If the audience is larger, the work is worse. That is as ridiculous as the other gauge which says that a large audience means necessarily that a work is good. Radio and television evaluate their programs by high audience ratings. One is as ridiculous as the other. What Mark Twain said is something that concerns every artist. And that is that at one time or another he must ask himself: What shall I paint, for whom shall I paint? As he asked himself: For whom do I write? And I, personally, paint—well—I paint for you. If I can sit here and talk with you, I feel I can paint for you, and I feel pretty sure that you'll understand what I'm trying to say. I don't necessarily paint for the museum director; the museum director is a person whose life is filled with pictures, and whose response sometimes becomes a little jaded. He needs something awfully stimulating, you know, for the taste buds to react. Well, I made up my mind long ago that it isn't for him that I paint. But if he likes it, I feel delighted.

BRANDON: You feel that you have your own audience—

SHAHN: Yes. It's a limited audience. I'd like it to be bigger, everybody likes to have a big audience, but I do not make a single effort to create a larger audience.

BRANDON: When you start painting, what moves you? Is it the idea, the form?

SHAHN: It's quite inseparable. Recently I talked to someone on that very subject. It was just an incidental conversation, and I said: "I am going to do my next painting in yellows." I have a vague idea of subjects and form, but yellow is a form—it's one of the forms—because the last one had gone quite blue and I wanted to just go off on another extreme. So in this case you might say it was form that started me. On the other hand, and more often, it will be what I call the content of the thing, the idea, you see. And I must confess to you that I am not consistent in that. I was once asked how I judge other people's work and I spoke of design and color and texture and *then* content. And when they asked me: Is that the way you work? I said: "No, I work just the opposite." But not always. I'm not consistent—I just want to put it that way. So, this picture that I called "Epoch" in which there is a little creature balancing himself precariously on some acrobatic cyclists, each of whom have in their hand a little sign of some kind—one which says "No" and one which says "Yes." They, themselves, are in a very precarious position but they're professionals, they'll come through. But the character that is balancing himself on them is really in a dangerous position. I set the whole scene, as it was, in a circus-like or country-fair-like atmosphere. It does have a kind of

a depressing look—an abandoned kind of a look, if you wish—for I
was disturbed by the world situation, by our own national situation
—that was at the beginning of the high point of this endless suspicion of one toward the other for one's own security, for the
national security—one's loyalty, and so on . . . those words were
so much used that they ceased to have any meaning. There was I
balancing myself between these "Yeses" and these "Noes"—and
it wasn't only I, it was all of my friends, it was everyone I knew or
cared to talk to who were in this same precarious position. I don't
think I feel any more secure now except that I am getting used
to precariousness. The two characters—the professional cyclists—
who are carrying us, as it were, through this time, I think are rather
sinister, they're almost inhuman. The character that represents me,
or represents you, isn't much more human, except that in his
fright he does look human; his clothes are rumpled, his expression,
his pallor is very apparent.

In this next one here, which I call "The Blind Botanist," I'm
afraid it's a theme that has gone through my painting in one form
or another for a number of years now. About fifteen years ago I
painted a picture called "The Red Staircase." It showed a crip-
pled man walking up an endless stair, and then when he came to
the top of that stair he went down again. And the whole thing
was in a ruin of rubble and burned-out buildings. To me this is
both the hope of man and the fate of man, you know. It's obvious
almost, that he seems to recover from the most frightful wars, the
most frightful plagues, and goes right on again when he knows
full well that he's going into another one; but that's that eternal
hope in the human being.

In this one, that I call "Goyescas"—and is the most recent
painting—I painted a creature that may be interpreted as military
or militantly religious, or conservative because of the old-fashioned
hat he's wearing of a century ago, the admiral's hat. His costume
is noncommittal, it could be of any country, of any religion.
Curiously enough, he has four hands, a kind of symbolism I don't
often engage in. His hands are clasped in an agony of distress over
a group of heads that might be dead or dying, in great, overwhelming pity for them—and then another set of hands that rise
out of those hands, which seem not to care at all what the other

set of hands are doing, engaged in playing this child's game of cat's cradle, a game that is as far removed from reality as one can imagine.

Or this painting, which I call "Cybernetics"—a word that used to be unfamiliar; it's part of our vocabulary now. It is a word which, I think, Professor Norbert Wiener invented. It means, as I understand it, the whole modern system of electronic communication, which, in turn, can be used for automation, which, in turn, can be used for making fantastically rapid calculations. It seems to me there is a tendency, certainly in our country, to lay a great deal of faith in that machine. Every once in a while the papers will carry a story that it has begun to think. When they are a little more sober about it, they will deny that they ever said such a thing, that it cannot think beyond the thoughts of the person who put thoughts into its mind. In other words, when "information," as they call it, is not fed into it, it is doing absolutely nothing, it's a piece of static machinery. When "information" is put into it in the form of punched cards, and the surge of electric power sent through it, then it will come to certain conclusions, mostly numerical ones, hardly more than that. Efforts have been made to transmute this machine into a translating machine by feeding symbols of one language which will give you an equivalent of another language. However, the thing that distresses me about it, and the reason I painted it the way I did, was that I am so completely skeptical of the faith that is put into this—that this will solve every problem, including all the diseases of mankind. My boy, a couple of years ago, worked in a laboratory on cancer research. He worked on that sort of machine, merely feeding statistics into it. And he said: "Any day I expect something to develop on the side of that machine, I've been feeding so many cancerous statistics into it." In my painting it is surrounded by a group of seven figures. I tried to get about every expression into the thing: of hope, of fear, of skepticism, of agnosticism, maybe, on one face—but, in general, the machine is looked upon with awe by everyone of the onlookers. And to me it has almost a religious quality; it is comparable to a group of patrons looking at a religious image that El Greco might have painted on order. In discussing this painting with a friend first, he wanted to know whether I would have the machine dominate man, or man dominate the machine? I said: Do you mind if I'm neutral on this thing? There's a danger in both of your suggestions—that man can dominate the machine, I hope, or this machine can dominate the man, I fear. But let me be neutral about it.

BRANDON: What really inspires you to paint?

SHAHN: The life that goes on here. I once told a student there were just two things to paint: the things you are very strongly for and the things you are very strongly against. And I feel pretty strongly about a lot of things. I keep notes constantly, both drawn notes and verbal notes, and I mull through them fairly often; and something that is just a very slip of an idea suddenly—and I don't know why—becomes of great significance and it can become a painting. But it's generally based on what goes on around me: what goes on politically, what goes on socially, what goes on in the seasons, what goes on emotionally, etc.

BRANDON: Now you, yourself, have not gone in for abstractionism, except in a limited sense.

SHAHN: Well, in a sense, a general sense, any painting—a Joshua Reynolds, if you look at it very closely, just a tiny fragment—would be an abstraction. Brushes, stroke brushing and so on, are abstract forms, if you wish. It all becomes a matter of degree. I use abstraction as a tool, as I use realism as a tool. They're all part of a much larger thing, and anyone who holds realism as the very essence of painting is to me as wrong, perhaps, as someone who holds the other direction—abstraction—as the only way of expressing oneself. Painting is made up of too many factors; it's made up of one's thinking; it's made up of color; it's made up of realism; it's made up of abstraction; it's made up of all these things, and a great painting, I think, is one in which all of those things are in a delicate balance so that none jumps at you out of all the rest asking for your attention.

Recently the dean of the art department of one of the universities came to me with a problem that illustrates this confusion about form and content. A young man was applying for his Master's—you know, we give Doctorate's in Art here—and he was applying for his Master's, and during the interrogatory, he was asked to comment upon the philosophic influences of certain predecessors of Michelangelo on his work on the Sistine Chapel. And this young man, a nonobjective painter, said: "I haven't the slightest interest in the idea of the content of work—I'm only interested in line, color, and form." He said that with such an arrogance that it offended the professors and they didn't know whether to give him his degree or not.

Well, the dean told me this problem, and I said very simply: Let's put it the other way. Suppose you had asked him to discuss the line, color, and form of the Sistine Chapel, and he had said: "I haven't the slightest interest in line, color, and form—I'm only interested in content." Would you have given him his degree? And he said: Oh no, no. I said: This is just the obverse of this medal, you know. This is this darned fragmentation that is going on in our society and you're getting a reflection of it in your art department.

The Critic in Isolation:

a conversation with

EDMUND WILSON

My arrival at Edmund Wilson's Talcottville home upset his serene seclusion: he questioned me so eagerly about what was going on in Washington and the world at large that inadvertently I upset his inner calm and set his mind going on current problems which interest him intensely, but which, in some sort of escapist mood, he tries to avoid. And so it took him almost an entire day until he was able to concentrate again on what I had come to talk to him about—literature.

Most of the year Mr. Wilson lives on Cape Cod in Massachusetts. But when the holidaymakers invade it in the summer, he flees to his ancestral home at Talcottville. It stands isolated and remote outside the village on a not too heavily traveled road and the view from the old-fashioned porch is over wide fields, with woodlands in the background. The house is simple, almost austere; but it exudes the warmth and earthiness of early America.

Mr. Wilson has not only a strong jaw, rather reminiscent of Sir Winston Churchill's, but also something of Sir Winston's strong independent sense of authority in his own field. His statements always carry conviction, yet they never sound pontifical. It is impossible to pin him down on such broad subjects as "American culture," or "schools of literature"; he does not like to generalise in the French manner. He insists on treating every writer, every book individually and separately. Justice Felix Frankfurter, the highly erudite member of the United States Supreme Court, who has known Wilson for a lifetime, put it to me this way:

"Bunny Wilson approaches every book critique with the judicious-
ness of a judge. It seems to me that before he writes about a
man he studies his whole corpus. Theodore Roosevelt, for instance,
was to him something of a Kiplingesque swashbuckler. But after
he got through reading his collection of letters, he gave the
cultural range of the man full recognition. This bespeaks the
kind of self-discipline a judge should be capable of. For a judge
should divest himself of personal prejudice and idiosyncrasies,
he should be able to show a deep sense of responsibility, detached
from his own ego."

Our two-day conversation went on from morning till late
evening and during mealtimes. It was impossible to stop, and it
always seemed a pity to interrupt a train of thought. Mr. Wilson,
who was sixty-three when our conversation took place, has an
unusual gift for languages. He is one of the very few literary
critics who can read French, Italian, Russian books in the original,
and also in German and Hebrew though with the occasional aid
of a dictionary. It is strange therefore that a man with his
broad international learning remains politically an unrepentant
"old-fashioned isolationist." He is a man hankering for the past.
He was a penetrating social critic in the thirties, but today he
is too disgusted with the present to write about it.

In spite of his profound distaste for modern gadgets he agreed
to my tape-recording these explorations of the mind of one of
the most distinguished American men of letters.

BRANDON: Stewart Hampshire in his review of your book *The*
American Earthquake in the *Sunday Times* said that in your
attitude to Europe you alternate between moods of chauvinistic
contempt and moods of reverence.

WILSON: That's quite true—a good point on his part. And he
also says it's rather the same attitude as that of the old Russian
intellectuals, and that's perfectly true. I think that there's always
been a good deal in common between the Russians and us. In
reading Turgenev lately, I found that he would write to his
Russian friends how awful the Europeans were, but that when

he was back at home he would brood about how awful Russia was.

BRANDON: What is the basis of your disillusionment with Europe?

WILSON: It's the same thing as with the Russians. It's the idea of a new country. You find it in all of our literature from the very beginning, especially in something like Walt Whitman. We felt that they'd had it in Europe; that they were in a decline. The time had come for us to pick up, show the world something better, or something new.

BRANDON: But what assurance of new nourishment do you have from here?

WILSON: It's been just that any kind of new start has always meant new hope.

BRANDON: But do you see any possibilities?

WILSON: Well, I think we've got into a new phase in this country now vis-à-vis Europe. One thing that is important is that the English Revolution did not occur in the seventeenth century; it occurred over here, in the eighteenth century. So you have the peculiar situation of a national revolution occurring geographically in another part of the world. The trouble was in France that when the Revolution came, they had the whole thing on the premises, they had the old order still there along with the new, and ever since the whole thing has been scrambled. Whereas here, a definite break occurred; the seventeenth century revolution really left "The Establishment" more or less intact. But over here you had something different. And we always had this impetus from having made a new start. But I think we are in a further stage now—the whole world is getting to be more alike in certain ways. We're all having to deal now with more or less the same kind of society—so that national literatures and all that—and talking about things in those terms—is becoming less important. Obviously, Europe and America are merging more all the time, and even in our peculiar relation to the Soviet Union we're getting more and more alike all the time. There are moments when I think the great menace is the time when we'll discover that we understand each other perfectly. But I've been cultivating Russia myself as much as anybody. I went to Russia in '35 and learned

Russian in middle age; my boy is learning it much more quickly.
He's had a year of Russian at Harvard and is going on with it
in summer school. I mean in America now it is not merely a
question of our relation to Europe, which in my youth was the
important thing, it's also our relations with Russia and Japan
and other parts of the world.

BRANDON: You're talking about political relations now—

WILSON: No, no—cultural, too! Russian literature both old and
new has had a great deal of influence here.

BRANDON: Do you feel that there's anything like a revival of
pre-revolutionary Russian literature here?

WILSON: I think it's still tremendously important everywhere.
I mean, everybody reads Tolstoy; everybody reads Dostoevsky;
and everybody reads Chekhov in the Katherine Mansfield period.
Isaiah Berlin has been writing about the nineteenth century
Russian intellectuals and so on.

BRANDON: Apropos this increasing similiarity all over the world,
it seems to me that you and Malraux have quite a lot in common;
you both have a world point of view, a universal interest.

WILSON: I think that's true, and I tremendously admire
Malraux. I think, in fact, that he's the greatest living European
writer, if not the greatest Western writer.

BRANDON: You're both attracted by the literature of ideas, isn't
that it?

WILSON: No, I don't think that's true. I don't think that either
Malraux or I go at things from that point of view. I don't go at
things from an ideological point of view at all. The ideas seem
less important to me than the concrete books of an author or
the way some given group of people lives. And I know from
talking to Malraux that although he's very clever at all sorts of
formulations, as all the French are, his approach to politics is
far less ideological than practical. He's quite different from Sartre
in this respect, because Sartre really is an eighteenth-century
mind. The curious thing is that he's transposed Marxism back
into eighteenth century terms, the kind of thing that Marx
thought he was getting away from. And his approach to politics
seems to me completely unrealistic, that is, it's all a theoretical
approach. His novels are very good examples of a kind of novel

that is characteristic of this period. They're really a sort of super-journalism. They're very interesting and readable because they deal with things that are happening at the time, or have just happened. It's a kind of fiction that is also produced by Moravia, the Italian writer; Leonov, the Russian writer; and John Steinbeck in America. Of course, they're all very different, but there's something of this interest of immediacy, they're writing about the same world that you're living in and events that are happening around you.

But to get back to Malraux, his books about art are extremely original works. His conception of "the imaginary museum," in which you have pictures from all sorts of civilizations and periods put together so that you can study them side by side, has really revolutionized books on art, and Malraux's text,* I think, is as important as any of his fiction. It's both a work on the history of art and a sort of philosophic poem. These books are no more merely books about art than *War and Peace* is merely a novel about the Napoleonic wars, or Gibbon a mere history of the fall of Rome, or *Das Kapital* merely a work on economics. Like these others, it's really a discussion of the destiny of man on the earth. Malraux seems to me to be one of the few living Frenchmen who have the international point of view that the great French writers of the past had. I was reading something of Renan just after I was reading these books of Malraux, and I realized how the French point of view had shrunk between Renan's time and Malraux's. One of the curious features of Malraux, though, is that—unlike Renan and the nineteenth-century writers—he doesn't seem to write like a Frenchman any more, in spite of the fact that he's full of a kind of generalization that's French. His way of writing, as my wife says, sounds more German than French. He's a great admirer of Nietzsche, but Nietzsche is not a typical German writer, and I don't know how he's come to write in the way he does. His sentences are sometimes so balled up that you have to read them twice to find out which way they are flowing, if you can call it flowing. This style has been growing on him—it appears to some extent in the last of his novels, too. But I feel about him that he's head and shoulders above any

* *The Voices of Silence*

other French writer I've read. Sartre, by the way, is the one who sees everything in terms of ideas; whereas for Malraux politics is a way of getting something in particular done.

BRANDON: When you write about literature, do politics influence your selection?

WILSON: No. There are certain kinds of writers that are more congenial to me than others. There are writers that I think are very gifted that I haven't any special interest in reading. For example, D. H. Lawrence. I think he was an extraordinary writer, and yet I have very little appetite to read him. Thomas Wolfe, of whom some people in this country have a tremendously high opinion, is completely unreadable to me, but I've read enough of him to know that he did have a good deal of talent. But he's not for me.

BRANDON: How would you define your taste?

WILSON: Well, I suppose that, in general, I don't like loose or romantic writing. That is partly what puts me off in the cases of Lawrence and Wolfe.

BRANDON: What do you think of the standards of literary criticism today?

WILSON: I don't think about those things *at all!* Literary criticism is a department of literature for me, and when I read literary critics I read them as literature; the others I can't read at all. I never think of myself, for instance, as a literary critic; I think of myself simply as a writer and a journalist. Usually I'm tagged as a literary critic, but actually I've written more books which are not literary criticism than books that are. I write about things that interest me—just now I'm writing about the New York State Indians. I never think about schools of literary criticism. I'm likely to write literary criticism when I want to make a little money, because it's easier to do than other things. All you have to do is sit down and read some books—you may already have read them. I never think about the kind of problems that are discussed in the literary quarterlies. The great thing with me has been the fact that I read Taine's *History of English Literature* at a very early age, at the same time that I was reading the English writers he deals with; that made a great impression on me. Then afterward I read Michelet and Renan and other

French writers, and I have been influenced by them in this field probably more deeply than by anybody else. I'm as much interested in history as I am in literature. I'm writing a book now about the Civil War which is as much historical as literary. All the people that I deal with are articulate and write, but I don't confine myself to belles-lettres. I deal with speeches and diaries and military memoirs, and official and personal correspondence. This is all much more in the nineteenth-century French tradition than in any of the fashionable current modes.

BRANDON: Do you think that the stranglehold on world-wide interest that European writers held in the nineteenth century and earlier has been broken by American writers in this century?

WILSON: I suppose it has to some extent. Since I live in this country and since I've always been occupied with our own writing, it's rather hard for me to tell. I can see evidences of it coming from England and France and Germany. Thomas Wolfe is a great German writer, and actually he *is* a German writer. His family, apparently, were partly German, and it's all very much in the tradition of German romanticism, I think. At any rate, in the bookstores in Germany now, Thomas Wolfe is all over the place. When I was in Munich they did a play of his which was rather interesting but which has never been done in this country. And, of course, Faulkner has rightly made an impression everywhere. I think that he's probably our greatest writer now.

BRANDON: If you compare the standards of American literature to European today, do you think the creativeness in this country is today greater or—

WILSON: I think that in Europe the French have been holding up marvelously. Malraux, as I said before, is the greatest European writer, and I think that there's been more vitality in French literature than anywhere else. Their wonderful literary tradition is stronger than that of any other country. But it's rather hard for me to tell about this country, because I grew up in a period that was probably one of our best literary periods.

I think we've had two great literary periods in this country. One was in the fifties of the last century, when you had Hawthorne, Emerson, Thoreau, Melville, Walt Whitman. These writers, as well as lesser writers like Oliver Wendell Holmes—I've just been reading an essay on him, a very good essay, by Virginia Woolf—lesser writers like Holmes and Longfellow were all pretty well known in England. Whitman was even something of a sensation.

And then there was a lapse. The period after the Civil War was a bad period for literature for various reasons. It was the time when the American writers and painters and other artists emigrated to France and England. It was the period of Whistler and Henry James. But after that a whole new cultural era began for the United States—definitely, I should say, with Theodore Roosevelt's administration. It got under way slowly and really came to a boil at the time when I was in college, 1912 to 1916. So that the period of the twenties, which was awful in some ways, was a good period for literature and art in America.

Then we began to reach Europe again in a different way. Eliot still had the mentality of the Henry James period—he studied in France and Germany and finally settled in England. You can see the whole thing very clearly in the relationship between Eliot and Van Wyck Brooks. They went to Harvard together, and at that time it was quite natural for somebody in Eliot's position to go abroad and live there. In fact, for many people it was the only thing to do. But this was just at the moment when a new literary movement was beginning in America, and Brooks became a part of it. This incident is important, I think. Brooks and Eliot have always been at odds with one another, and yet they're rather alike in some ways. Eliot went to England; Brooks, who was his contemporary at Harvard, also went to England, but he tells me that when he went to England he thought of nothing but the United States and that he wrote there his first book on American culture, a book called *The Wine of the Puritans*, which was published in 1909. And then he came back and devoted the rest of his life to American literature. His first books and those that he wrote in the twenties were in their time revolutionary and made a tremendous impression.

BRANDON: Revolutionary because of what?

WILSON: Because his books were a very severe criticism of American literature and culture generally. He pointed out all the deficiencies of our classical nineteenth-century writers, and this was so unconventional at the time that Scribner's wouldn't even publish a book of his called *America's Coming-of-Age.* W. C. Brownell, who was one of the most highly esteemed American critics, was editor at Scribner's then, and he told Brooks that, although he agreed with many of the things he said, the time had not come when they could be said in public. Later, Van Wyck Brooks set himself the immense task—which he's now finished— of doing a history, five volumes, of American literature, which is more or less based on the same kind of tradition that I have been talking about in connection with myself. This work seems to me quite unlike anything produced in England; it's more like French literary history. Actually, so far as I know, nobody before Brooks had ever read American literature from beginning to end, and there's a terrific lot of it—even leaving out theology and politics, as he does. He has devoted his whole life to the subject, and his labors have been prodigious. In a sense they have handicapped him somewhat as a critic, since he hasn't had time enough to read the literature of the rest of the world. Eliot went to Europe and read everything that Matthew Arnold had read—as well as quite a lot of things written since Matthew Arnold's time— whereas Brooks came back to the United States and immersed himself in American literature. In this he is very typical of the whole literary movement in the twenties.

We were preoccupied with American matters, and the whole situation was, again, more like the early part of the nineteenth century before the Civil War, which had certain things in common with the early phases of the Soviet Union.

At the time I was in Russia in '35, they were going through a relatively liberal phase—they were talking about how in a cultural way they had to learn from the West and learn from the bourgeois world. They were making the new humanity in the Soviet Union, but they had to know about the best that had been done in the West and the best that had been done by the bourgeoisie and the feudal world, and use it for their own purposes. That was almost exactly our point of view in the early nineteenth century; the Americans who went abroad at that time, and who studied European literature and other things, were doing it with the intention of bringing back the best that Europe had produced and using it for making the new humanity over here.

Well, then, in the twenties this idea somewhat revived, and although a great many Americans still went abroad—Hemingway went to live in Paris and a number of other people did—still, we were all preoccupied with American literature; we were trying to make something of America, to make an American culture. This was what everybody talked about. I go back over my own articles written in the twenties and thirties and I realize that this was what we were always doing. We studied German Expressionism and then tried to adapt this to American life and produce American plays that exploited these devices. Some of O'Neill is based on that, you know—a play like *The Great God Brown.* And Dos Passos went to Russia and met the Russian writers; he'd read Jules Romains; and it was evidently partly from them that he got the idea of writing novels and plays that would deal with groups and not individuals. He tried to adapt that to American life.

The thing that's upsetting now, in politics and literature both, is that from the moment we lose the idea that we are concentrating on this country—and that idea seems completely to have gone by the board—we don't know where we are any more. I've felt that myself very much, beginning with the last war.

BRANDON: You were really talking about an imitative culture. Do you think there is now something like an American culture?

WILSON: In the early nineteenth century—and in the twenties of this century, in the thirties, too—the thing we were always debating about was: How was this or that to be Americanized? We wanted to be not merely imitative, we wanted to make an American culture. And what we produced were writers and works of very diverse kinds.

Nowadays, you read quantities of things about the American tradition and what it consists of, and what the apparently diverse writers have in common, and actually I think a great deal of it doesn't make very much sense. I don't really know what American culture is. Foreigners say they see certain things that the various writers have in common which I don't always see, but maybe that's just because I'm here.

One of the things that seem to me strangest is that everybody from England always thinks that we're terribly lonely in America.

V. S. Pritchett, for example, says that I strike a note of loneliness, but I'm not conscious of being lonely at all. But since we don't have any cultural capital—like London or Paris—we're scattered around all over. I mean, there aren't any Existentialist cafés, there's nothing like the literary groups in London. But that doesn't mean that American writers are lonely. Foreigners perhaps are lonely when they come to America. But we are not. In England, as Auden said, it is all like family life. He wanted to leave England to get away from it. Hemingway, Dos Passos, Faulkner, and others all have their country places. I live up here. A good many American writers aim to live in this way, though a good many, of course, teach in colleges, and some lead an international life like Thornton Wilder. There is a definite literary world in England, but not here. American writers have their families, they occasionally see each other and correspond. It may be that Europeans think of American writers as solitary on account of Thoreau and Hawthorne. But it is only geographically that most American writers are solitary. The point is, I think, that Europeans are not used to the spaces and distances here. They can't imagine that we are used to them. New York and Chicago, however, were once intellectual centers more than they are now. If we have any such centers now they are around universities such as Harvard and Columbia.

BRANDON: But do you think that out of the European influence American writers were able to develop something that could really be called "American culture"?

WILSON: I don't know, I'm sure. I read quantities of articles about it—in English and American and French periodicals—and I don't really know.

BRANDON: It's been said that this vigor of the American personality in writing is something characteristic and, some say—

WILSON: I really know very little about contemporary writing. I did read one book of Kerouac's: *The Subterraneans.* He has traces of talent, I think, but it seems rather feeble and decadent. I think that Salinger is very good—he's one of the few I've read. The writing of my own generation seems to have reached Europe recently, and they have the illusion that all this is new—actually the writers they like are mostly between sixty and seventy.

Thomas Wolfe has just hit Germany, but Wolfe has been dead for years, and other writers have hit the French rather belatedly.

BRANDON: How does the "lost generation" of the time of the Eliots and Gertrude Steins compare to our generation? I mean, they have to meet a similar intellectual vacuum.

WILSON: I don't think there was an intellectual vacuum in Gertrude Stein's time. I was explaining that that was a period of intellectual fermentation. The Americans at that time had been through upsetting experiences in war, but also stimulating ones; I don't think they were a lost generation at all.

BRANDON: Today's lost generation in England we call the angry young men—

WILSON: I think that our "beat" generation here more or less corresponds to them. These antisocial writers are typical of the world in its present state. The best of them is Jean Genet, the French writer, who carries the antisocial attitude further than any of the rest and also has more ability. I think that after Malraux he's probably the most important French novelist.

BRANDON: What do you think generated this "antisocial" reaction in our period?

WILSON: I think there's been a general dissatisfaction with the kind of world we live in. In the thirties, there was a tendency for the various kinds of intellectuals to react against it by way of Marxism, and, of course, the great hope of the Marxists was the Soviet Union. But the Soviet Union turned sour on them—turned out to be a great, big, old, terrific, Russian despotism. So there was nothing for them to believe in at all, and now they don't know what to do with the present world.

I was born in the nineteenth century, and, like most people born in the nineteenth century, I still have—entirely instinctively—the belief in human progress, the conviction that the world won't fall apart, the faith in the value of reform. But it is obvious that the people born later are now quite remote from this.

Many young people who, in my time, would have gone in for the humanities in college, now go in for physics and don't have any political ideas at all, or they go in for psychiatry or something of the kind.

Oppenheimer is a very interesting case of this. His career has been of a kind that wouldn't have been possible in my generation. He went in for mathematics and physics, and he lived, as he says, in a completely abstract intellectual world. Then he got interested in communism, but it was also something completely abstract for him; then when he had to abandon that, he went back to his abstract world of physics and worked at these confounded bombs. From the point of view of anybody of my generation, this career makes no sense at all, yet it's typical of Oppenheimer's age group.

BRANDON: You mean, it doesn't mean a progressive developing of an idea, of a mind—

WILSON: It has no connection with human society at all, it seems to me.

BRANDON: But isn't it partly the welfare state—after all, the United States is also a welfare state—that makes it so much more difficult to find new goals to reach for, to fight for? Youth wants above all security and it is getting it increasingly. What is left for radical youth to—

WILSON: Yes, of course, but I haven't any solution to propose. I think in Britain you had the welfare state after the war. We had something that could be called a welfare state in the early days of the Roosevelt administration. But then the whole thing turned into a big war-making exploit on our part, and that's what it still is, it's never gotten away from that. I'm very unsympathetic with America's present role in the world and its effects on our life at home, and I think that there's a good deal of such dissatisfaction. In the case of the beat generation, it is not surprising that they should be completely antisocial—they have gone in for Zen Buddhism and things like that, which divorce them from social reality.

BRANDON: Perhaps mass education here is contributing to this.

WILSON: It's bound to, of course. The whole idea of equality is something that doesn't work beyond a certain point. The Declaration of Independence says that "all men are created equal," but it goes on to specify the equal right to "life, liberty, and the pursuit of happiness." This is a very sound formulation, because it *is* true that everybody ought to have a chance to live, and to make the best use he can of such abilities as he possesses, to enjoy himself to the best of his capacity. And

I think that, beyond that, the ideal of equality is rather a misleading one.

With socialism—and all the socialists have been utopian, including Marx and Engels—the whole idea was that wage slavery ought to be got rid of. The abuses they objected to were real. Once these rudimentary rights have been guaranteed, you will not be able to get people excited about the ideal of equality. The equality that people fight for is really the chance to excel. If they're debarred from certain kinds of professions or certain degrees of distinction, they first want to get these barriers removed. And this brings us back to mass education. It makes it more difficult for the able to excel, because they're held back by the less able. Since different people are variously gifted, I'm in favor of unequal schools for students of unequal abilities. But assignment to a higher or lower school—or department of a school—should, of course, depend solely on ability, not upon race or color.

The appearance of this phrase The Establishment in England is very significant and interesting. I don't think that in this country we could talk about anything equivalent. I'm not sure that they could in any other country. It's as if institutions in England were turning out to have a strength that is even independent of the old hierarchy of class.

BRANDON: It's almost another way of saying "The Traditions."

WILSON: Well, it's not merely "The Traditions" because it's people who are trained in a certain way and who fall into certain relationships with one another. I don't see that we have any Establishment here.

BRANDON: One reason, perhaps, why stability here is lacking.

WILSON: Exactly, yes. I agree. There are considerable advantages, I can see, in having a durable Establishment. By the way, in spite of the fact that the angry young men are trying to knock it around, it seems to me that they can't get out of it; I mean, every time John Osborne tells you that his mother kept a pub, he tells you that his grandfather went to Eton! Or take John Wain and Kingsley Amis. They went to Oxford . . .

BRANDON: What do you think should be the role of the drama critic?

WILSON: I believe that the kind of criticism which formulates a recipe for the right kind of works, for masterpieces, is always sure to be quite useless. Our American critics like Paul Elmer More and Irving Babbitt who called themselves humanists, are an example of it, and the Russians who talked about social realism are another example of it. The critic compares the actual works that come to his attention with ideal works that don't exist, except in his own mind, and this is a perfectly useless kind of criticism. Aristotle didn't formulate his rules for tragedy until years after the great Greek tragedies had been written, and you can't—the critic can't provide a formula and expect the artist to fulfill it.

BRANDON: How do you feel about English literature since the war—postwar English achievements?

WILSON: I don't want to criticize the English in such a way as to imply a superiority on our part in America, because I don't think that what we're producing is terribly interesting or distinguished now. I think that something has happened in England that's very curious.

For one thing, in the last century the complaint of writers who had been influenced by the French was always that English novels were in general lacking in form. The writers who were interested in form—Henry James and George Moore and Conrad—all admired the French novelists and Turgenev and were trying to do something which was closer to their works than to that of the traditional English novelists. But none of these writers was English. Whereas now you have in England, it seems to me, a highly developed sense of form and style, but you don't have any such substantial novels as you had in the nineteenth century. The whole thing seems to me to have dwindled. You have a lot of people who are quite good, who write rather small-scale novels. They're sent over, as my wife says, like a lot of little cakes that we eat.

Actually, I read more contemporary English fiction than I do American fiction, because the American stuff is likely to be badly written and extremely formless. But the English stuff is mostly on a much smaller scale than Dickens and Thackeray, George Eliot and Meredith and Hardy—or Bennett and Wells, for that matter. Of course, Bennett was enormously influenced by French fiction; he says that *The Old Wives' Tale* was inspired by Maupassant's *Une Vie*, but it's so different that nobody would ever have guessed it, and it has all the solidity and scope of the traditional English novel. That is something that seems to have disappeared. Angus Wilson actually admires the nineteenth-century English novelists, and he greatly admires Zola, about whom he's written an excellent little book. But his own novels, in spite of their complexity, remarkable though they are, fall short of the old dimensions.

Another curious thing about English writing is the present standardization of the language of prose. This language has lost its richness. Think of the inventiveness of English prose. Virginia Woolf is the last great example of it.

But this richness survives in the poets. Auden and Day Lewis and Louis MacNeice have a large and varied vocabulary and a wonderful command of language. By the way, do you think that there is any chance of John Betjeman's being the next Poet Laureate? I think he is one of the very best poets in English, and I should like to see him Poet Laureate—I should like to see him make the Royal Family look suburban.

BRANDON: You said earlier in our conversation that French literature is so much more vital than English literature today.

WILSON: Yes. In the first place, the French literary tradition is still so important, it's so old and well developed, and it's taken so seriously that it's very hard to discourage. But another thing is simply that the French were not involved in the war to the extent that the English and the Germans were—German literature seems to have been nonexistent by the time the war was over, except for Junger and Brecht. Also in France fewer people were killed. Even under the occupation, the writers were able to write. And at the end of the war you had Malraux, Sartre, Genet, and a lot of other people. Céline had gone into exile, but he's now back. Léger went on writing in the United States. A great many English writers were killed in the war. And I sometimes feel there's a tendency to boycott writers who left England before the war. It seems to me that Auden and Whitehead have been certainly the greatest Englishmen in the literary world between the wars.

I exclude Yeats and Joyce and Shaw as Irishmen. But Auden and Whitehead are very, very English. Both of them, as I was saying about Malraux, have an international point of view without ceasing to be very English. They both came to live in America, and I get the impression, especially in connection with Auden, that their pictures have been turned to the wall in England.

The same kind of thing was true of Whitehead, because it seemed to have become fashionable to say about Whitehead in England that he'd been admirable as a mathematician and symbolic logician, but that he was no good as a philosopher. Bertrand Russell more or less says that about him, although I don't think for that reason. Russell, after all, lived over here a long time himself.

BRANDON: You feel that Americans have treated their own expatriate writers better?

WILSON: Yes. Our admiration for Eliot has known no bounds. I don't think that Ezra Pound was treated well, being kept in that asylum for years, but he's always had a great deal of influence and has been very much respected. But what really discourages me about literary life today is how ineffective the influence of writers on people's minds is. I am not thinking about myself but those writers who are enormously read. But what is one Bertrand Russell —even with Priestley and Taylor and the rest of them behind him —against the drive toward annihilation, against all the people who insist on keeping the bomb?

Sex, Theater, and the Intellectual

---

a conversation with

MARILYN MONROE
AND ARTHUR MILLER

When Arthur Miller suggested that my best chance of finding him and his wife together was to come to Hollywood immediately, I took the next plane and flew out to Los Angeles. I did not find the famous pair in a luxurious twenty-bedroom villa, or beside a heart-shaped, heated swimming pool, nor were the faucets in their bathroom made of gold. They occupied a first-floor apartment in one of the bungalows hidden behind palm trees in the garden of the Beverly Hills Hotel. The spacious living room with its oversize, cold fireplace was comfortable, and the furniture had a lived-with look, but it nevertheless felt impersonal. This was clearly a temporary camping ground for the Millers. The double bedroom and the kitchenette which made up the rest of the apartment did not alter this impression. The Millers prefer to live in New York or in their country house in Connecticut. That is where Arthur Miller does all his writing. The few personal effects in the living room were a phonograph and a few books on the chimneypiece: De Tocqueville's Democracy in America, Strunk and White's The Elements of Style, D. H. Lawrence's Sons and Lovers, Moss Hart's Act One.

Arthur Miller was very much as I expected him to be, except for his startling height. Marilyn Monroe was utterly different. Arthur Miller was as informal as his open polo shirt, and as powerfully intellectual as his high forehead, his penetrating eyes and his sharp chin make one suspect. His nonchalance, however, is deceptive. Underneath there is a fierce intensity and a nervous *restlessness. Only in serious debate do they come to the surface, and then very suddenly, and his dark-brown eyes begin to flash with passion. When he looks at his wife however, they seem serene and content. He is easy to get to know and it does not take long before one is in intimate conversation with him. But he is not the type of American who calls a stranger by his first name.*

Marilyn Monroe made her entrance into the sitting room after dinner in a startling ankle-length, off-shoulder negligée, in scarlet velvet. Her light blond hair was pinned up and she had a minimum of make-up. Despite her dramatic get-up, hers was not a diva's masterful entrance. Nor was the room suddenly electric with sex. This was just a beguilingly pretty girl who looked at me rather shyly and coquettishly as she stretched out her small soft hand: not a seductive, man-consuming vamp but a little kitten one felt like stroking. Her voice was girlish, high-pitched with an occasional uncertain tremolo.

We settled around the empty fireplace, Arthur Miller lounging comfortably at the end of the long sofa while Marilyn Monroe stretched out over the rest of it with her head, slightly tilted, against his shoulder. She eyed the tape recorder uneasily and her voice faltered once or twice when I first brought her into the conversation. Miller immediately reached out for her hand, affectionately and protectively, and she quickly grew calm.

As the evening progressed, I realized that his intellect and masculinity give her a sense of security and pride. The conquest of a famous beauty, and the intellectual protection he can offer her, give him likewise security, pride, and contentment. The tragedy of her past is also something of which he is very conscious.

Marilyn Monroe was an orphan, an unwanted child. She grew up without affection and at times she was near suicide. When she talks about herself the awareness of her bitter past is never quite absent. Yet as her reserve dissolved and her shyness in competing in conversation with her husband waned, both her common sense and happy outlook on life, and her ability to transfer it to others, came to the fore most disarmingly. Occasionally her girlish irresponsibility caused her husband to raise an almost unnoticeable eyebrow.

Arthur Miller's outlook is not influenced so much by a personal sense of tragedy, though he too had his dose of it, as by the collective effect of such tragic events as the 1929 depression and McCarthyism. It was their shock to the American nation that caused in him deep emotional upheavals. His family suffered from the depression and that left indelible memories, but it was he himself who was caught in the maelstrom of McCarthyism.

Called before the House Committee on Un-American Activities he testified that he had never been a Communist. But he freely admitted that he had been present at several so-called "Communist front" group meetings and was then asked to name some of those he had seen there. He declined. "My conscience will not permit me to use the name of another person to bring trouble to him," he explained to the Committee. Though pleading the First rather than the Fifth Amendment of the Constitution he was convicted of contempt of Congress. His able and militant attorney Joseph L. Rauh, Jr., did not give up, and finally in 1957 the contempt conviction was unanimously reversed by the Court of Appeals and he was acquitted.

Miller is a man of burning beliefs, impulsive compassion, and vehement bitterness. These are all potent ingredients for the making of a dramatist. He wrote his first play at nineteen and at thirty-three his Death of a Salesman *won the Pulitzer prize. Miller reads avidly and sees that his wife does too. He seems to be trying to educate her. He is an intellectual, but not quite in the European meaning of the word. His passions are too strong for that. He is fiercely interested in ideas, but he also resents them. He is a thinker but he also reacts viscerally. He shies away from extreme European intellectualism while being appalled by American anti-intellectualism. But these qualities energize his creative power and enable him to reach audiences everywhere.*

The morning after our first session, which lasted until late at night, Marilyn Monroe invited me to the studio. Miller drove me out there, and while his wife went through the long processes of dressing and making-up he showed me the fascinating outdoor sets on the studio grounds. In half an hour you can travel there from a square in Montmartre to a Persian palace, from a German castle to the Wild West. When we got back

Marilyn was in her full make-up and in the costume of an acrobat, skin-tight from top to toe. Yet there was still the air of girlish innocence about her. Again it was not her adolescent sensuality but her puckish sense of fun that intoxicated everybody. That is her real gift—her ability to turn boredom into bliss, misery into joy. A lighthearted atmosphere pervaded the studio; not even the hard-boiled stage hands could resist it. She dominated everybody and everything. She was in her element. Arthur Miller meanwhile stood with Mrs. Strasberg, her drama coach, and me in the darkness behind the klieg lights. He seemed withdrawn, even a little shy and uneasy. This was Marilyn's show.

I asked Mrs. Strasberg how soon she thought her star pupil might venture on the legitimate stage. "She can do anything if she puts her mind to it," Mrs. Strasberg answered, "and further more my husband Lee" [who runs the Actors' Studio in New York] "says that acting is 'being private in public' and that is basically what Marilyn does . . . but she still will have to work hard before doing it."

We were now watching Marilyn before the cameras. They took only test shots for the make-up and she seemed to enjoy it. It was as if she were basking in the sun. Suddenly during a relaxed moment I caught her eye. She rushed forward, grabbed me by the hand and dragged me in front of the cameras. In a mood of coltish playfulness and sparkling delight she made the cameramen take pictures of us. And before I could protest she began to parody the opening of a love scene. The lids over her big gray eyes became heavy and looked their most seductive. Her body came heaving forward and her mouth beckoned challengingly. In my surprise and embarrassment I fluffed the scene.

BRANDON: Last summer I was traveling on a rickety bus from Athens to Delphi and above the driver hung the image of a saint—and next to it dangled a picture of you, Mrs. Miller. The god and a goddess, I said to myself. It is fascinating that what you represent in terms of taste, beauty, has become an international symbol, even in Greece, the home of Aphrodite!

MILLER: I don't regard her as a symbol. I know she certainly doesn't regard herself that way. She is the most direct human being I ever knew. I don't know what explains it, if anything does, excepting that she's had a life as an orphan that left her unprotected from danger and from others around her in a way that people who have lived in secure families never know. From way back she's had to estimate her situation in life on the basis of the sternest realities, and not to allow the ordinary obfuscations of sentiment, of family sentiment, to mislead her. The net result of it is that she responds to the most elemental part of the human being near her—that is, his propensity for hurting or helping, and he is immediately stimulated by the fact that he is really being looked at.

BRANDON: You don't think it's also a reaction to the most elemental parts of her—

MILLER: Of course. Her beauty, in fact, makes all the rest even more surprising. People do not expect such strong reactions in her; each scene in life has its own immediate and powerful importance to her. Her wit is based on frankness, and quite often people laugh in order to separate themselves from its unhypocritical implications. She is enormously active within herself, because her beauty alone will never account for the impression that she makes even in the smallest role.

She's one of the few stars who never had her own cameraman, her own lighting man, and all the rest of the techniques that go to packaging the jewel for the public. They've depended upon her to, so to speak, light herself from within, which is just what happens. She has what they used to call incandescence.

BRANDON: You've become a symbol for feminine sex in America, but such symbols don't exist in England or in other countries. In France, I think Brigitte Bardot was simply created for export to America. Why is it that you have become, as others have before you, a symbol of sex?

MILLER: I think she's just a genius . . .

MONROE: He's crazy.

MILLER: There may be a difference in the seeming obsessiveness with sex in various countries, that is, how much in stride it seems to be taken, and how much it seems to be isolated from the rest of existence and made very much of. And possibly we do more of that than other countries do, although I'm not so sure that that's any longer true.

BRANDON: The Swedish approach is a naturalistic one—yours relies more on femininity, charm, and sense of humor.

MILLER: She has made sex a part of existence—

MONROE: Well, I hope so—since it's so. In Swedish films sexuality seems more natural. I think their code is quite different from ours, and also perhaps more natural. It reflects their attitude and ours reflects ours.

BRANDON: When you say code, you mean social code or film code . . .

MONROE: Social code, which the film code reflects. This is still a puritanical country. I think we got that from England originally, didn't we?

BRANDON: Do you feel hamstrung by American puritanism?

MONROE: I don't pay any attention to it. I'm not aware of it.

BRANDON: The curious thing is that while the code here doesn't permit you to do the kind of pictures, say, Brigitte Bardot does, they are permitted to be shown here.

MONROE: Yes. I'm not permitted to go without clothes—no one is in this country, you know. They'll arrest you or they'll do something. They surely would not show the movie. Yet they like it in foreign movies and they accept it.

MILLER: That's part of the puritanism, too.

MONROE: And partly, I think, the eroticism of one nation differs in the imagination of another. One nation imagines more sexuality in a strange nation than in itself.

BRANDON: Sex preoccupies films and the theater as never before. Don't you think so?

MILLER: Maybe it's simply an expression of the confusion of life which makes it so difficult to say anything about it. You can always say something about sex! I think that's one crude reason for it. It evidently also draws people to the theater, and the theater, to a certain degree, is a merchandising operation. I believe now that the obsessiveness with sexuality is a convention. A lot of plays are driven to that because it's a kind of shorthand through which we can appear to enter into the lives of the people we're seeing. We feel we are entering into their lives through their sexual complexes. For many people it is the only thing left that is real any more.

BRANDON: Do you think that the obsessiveness with sex in the United States has something to do with the fact that this is a women's world, as Thurber says?

MILLER: There's a theory about the pioneer society, where a woman necessarily—dictated by the economic and social circumstances—took over an enormously greater importance in the scheme of things than she would have in a settled society. The nature of the work was such that she had decisions to make that she wouldn't, let us say, in the European society of the same time. I don't know whether nowadays it's the effect of industrialism, where men have to be away from home all day long and necessarily leave the decisions of life to the woman because she's there and on the spot. And whether that will happen all over the world in due time . . . I don't know enough about the other societies.

BRANDON: Some people say it has something to do with the idea that women are really brought up in this country to think it's they who permit and forbid sexual relations with men.

MONROE: I think there's a different outlook now. The other was kind of left over, excuse me for saying, from the Victorian age.

BRANDON: Perhaps it seems so to you—you are in a privileged position. You are a symbol.

MONROE: I haven't always been the symbol, though . . . I have a good memory. What do you mean by "forbidding" sexual relations?

BRANDON: That it's the woman who says Yes or No—that it isn't she who succumbs, that she determines it—consciously.

MONROE: Isn't it that way in nature?

BRANDON: That she determines it?

MONROE: She has a lot to do with it.

MILLER: I think it's a question of emphasis here that Mr. Brandon is talking about. In other words, if the decisive factor in it is the woman, the male aggression is dissipated. Then it's not what it is in nature.

MONROE: If that's so, I should think it would arouse it.

BRANDON: It makes me wonder whether this confusion about

sex is not one of the main explanations for the prosperity of psychoanalysts in this country. Are you interested in Freud?

MONROE: Very much. I think he's a great help to society. He's discovered a science that mankind benefits from. It can make it live happier, more fruitful lives. Mankind deserves to be happy, I think. What makes the psychoanalyst important is that one can't always be objective about oneself. You might sometimes keep going in a circle, in the same circle if, under certain circumstances, one tries to rely on oneself to deal with one's own problems.

MILLER: The theater, certainly in this postwar period, the serious theater has become more and more bizarre in terms of preoccupation with odd sexuality, on the one hand, and very sentimental on the other. Maybe it's because you can write passionately about sex and not have to jar the audience with disturbing questions. But it has one great virtue: I think we use on our stage—more than other countries do, possibly—any kind of person. Until very recently the British theater would not take seriously a play unless it had elegant personages in one form or another on the stage. I know when I was there with *View from the Bridge*, it was hard to find people who would play, or could play, working-class people . . . There were plenty of actors who had come from lower middle-class families, but they had trained themselves out of being that kind of person any more.

Ours is a democratic theater at least in that respect, and I think that's part of its strength all over the world. The range of personality in our theater is, I think, greater. It reflects better the general population of this country than English drama.

BRANDON: What social consequences do you deduce from this?

MILLER: I think we're in a stage of society—this is my own prejudice—that the rest of the world is arriving at. I think we may have gotten there a few hours earlier in cultural matters, and industrial, too. The largest crowd—to forget sex for the moment! —that I ever saw in Paris was about 1947 or '48 in front of a store that was displaying a clothes-washing machine. And everybody says the Americans are crazy about machinery. Well, these people were really absorbed in this thing, and it wasn't just because it was a tricky mechanism—it washed clothes and it was a time-saving thing—the same reasons, I think, that we are mad

109

about them. I have a feeling, that for good or ill, culture is more international than anybody wants to admit.

In a way, it's terrible, because differences are always interesting. The Coca-Cola sign goes all around the world now and you kind of wish it didn't. The most easily assimilable part of the culture, that is, part of the culture which is designed for the least cultivated, vegetative part of the American people—is the one that seems to be transported to Europe. I know I've been in countries in Europe where they expressed astonishment that we had symphony orchestras, that we sell so many symphony records, that there were serious writers in this country . . . it was necessary to remind them of some of the big American names, and then it came back to them and they had to make a connection between those names and what I was talking about. What they do know are the comic books and comic strips and the movies and the rest of it—that's the appalling thing. People who adopt an exported culture are always made its slaves—they can never contribute to it but must merely try to keep up with it, and its charm can never be transplanted. Also the advertisements in Europe are aping our own. They've lost all the . . . what I used to think was the European dignity in advertising, but now they're indistinguishable from American advertising excepting that they're self-conscious. Basically I have the feeling we're where you're getting.

BRANDON: Well, how would you define this state of the international culture?

MILLER: A thing gradually gets to be judged solely for its mass appeal, its ability to be merchandised. That goes for a novel, it goes for a poem, it goes for a movie. The older idea that a thing had an intrinsic value, which gave it the right to exist even though it could not gain a tremendous mass audience, is going by the boards. An analogous situation is your B.B.C. in England. You support it because it has value, you think, which can't be translated into money. And now you've got commercial television—standing alongside of it—which is a beautiful American invention, and it's eating up the audience. And in my opinion, you will soon have to make a decision based upon some old cultural values, and it will have nothing to do with economics. They're going to tell you that democratic ideology says that this is what the people want, and therefore they have a right to get it, even from their own government. And who are you to tell them what they should listen to? And if this country's experience is any guide, it's going to be very difficult to withstand that argument, because for one thing it lends an ethical justification to naked avarice. I don't mean that it's altogether bad that this should be, but just relying on the so-called majority vote is a way of divesting yourself of responsibility too. If popularity is the single determining thing that establishes value, it will be harder and harder to do anything but repeat the tried and untrue. A genuinely new idea must meet great resistance. That is its definition. The art of selling is the art of evading resistance.

BRANDON: What stimulates you into writing?

MILLER: I wish I knew. If I knew, I could probably control the inception of it better. I'm at the mercy of it; I don't really know. I cannot write anything that I understand too well. If I know what something means to me, if I have already come to the end of it as an experience, I can't write it because it seems like a twice-told tale. I have to discover it for the first time as I'm writing, I have to astonish myself, and that's of course a very costly way of going about things, because you can go up a dead end and discover that it's beyond your capacity to discover some organism underneath your feeling, and you're left simply with a formless feeling which is not itself art. It's inexpressible and one must leave it until it is hardened and becomes something that has form and has some possibility of being communicated. It might take a year or two or three or four to emerge.

BRANDON: So you really don't know how your play is going to end when you start it?

MILLER: I don't. I have a rough notion . . . for instance, if a play has a hero in it who will die, I know that. And I must know the core of irony involved. But little else in terms of the progression of the story. The shape and, so to speak, the tempo of the development, is created within the play itself.

BRANDON: When you, for instance, wrote your new film script, *The Misfits*, did you write it with your wife in mind—for a part in it?

MILLER: I was of two minds about that, because I happen to believe that she can do anything on the screen.

BRANDON: Does the stage hold any attraction for you, Mrs. Miller?

MONROE: Very much.

BRANDON: Why? What is the difference?

MONROE: Since attending the Actor's Studio, and I worked on a small stage, I found that in doing a scene, just one scene, it was more continuous. There was something to begin with and it grew and developed, and there was some place where you're going and some place where you've been—everything is sort of connected in a play. Movie scenes, you know, are cut, and often shot out of sequence. So, there's a lack of satisfaction. The theater makes more sense—for the actor, I mean.

BRANDON: Have you ordered a play?

MONROE: No, I've nothing in view at all.

BRANDON: I thought you could have one on the house.

MONROE: I don't think I'm ready yet for a play.

MILLER: It's impossible for me to write for a person, in as much as my vision is concentrated on something quite different, on some evolving paradox. The question of an actress, an actor, is the furthest thing from my mind at that time. Only as I was getting toward the end of *The Misfits* did I become thankfully aware that this would be wonderful for Marilyn.

BRANDON: "Paradox" in the French sense?

MILLER: A paradox in the sense that—or perhaps a better word is a dialectical situation—where Force A has moved Force B, which in turn has transformed Force A into C, which in turn has created D, etc. A play is made by sensing how the forces in life simulate ignorance—you set free the concealed irony, the deadly joke.

BRANDON: So it's really a rather tortuous birth, isn't it?

MILLER. The conception is. I'm a very fluent writer; I can write very quickly. The actual writing of a play—in this case a movie script—is a matter at most of eight weeks, and sometimes shorter, but that's simply the last stage of the process. By that time I have found the walls of life and I can feel them, and I can fill that room now and I can proceed. It's when there is no inner evolution that I am lost.

BRANDON: Do you think that drama is really an indigenous American expression of art?

MILLER: It depends on the level on which you're thinking of American life. Any people has a conventional idea of what they're like. Americans fancy themselves, for instance, to be open-handed, on the side of justice, a little bit careless about what they buy, wasteful, but essentially good guys, optimistic. Well, a lot of that is true, of course. That's on one level of awareness. But under that level of awareness there is another one, which gets expressed in very few movies and very few plays, but in more plays in proportion than in the movies. The level which confronts our bewilderment, our lonely naïvete, our hunger for purpose.

BRANDON: Do you see anything as "indigenous," for instance, in the theater as is the Westerner in films?

MILLER: Literally speaking, the Westerner as he appears in Westerns is the least indigenous person in the United States today. The number of people involved, let's say, in cattle raising, in being cowboys, is very small. The number of people in the West, however, who are involved in trade and industry is much greater. What the Westerner in the Western is, of course, is a folk hero, but he doesn't typify anything any more except escape and a memory of what people like to believe the past was like. The analogy that comes to mind is the feudal analogy, where there are no longer any knights, and yet people continue to speak of the character of, say, Jeanne d'Arc, King Arthur, or whatever it might have been. It's not been typical of England or France for hundreds and hundreds of years, yet the image evokes a sense of place and identity and a hoped-for personality. I think the salesman is much more typical of American life, both in viewpoint and numbers. God knows, for every cowboy there are one million salesmen.

BRANDON: To switch for a moment to a more modern feudal character. Do you think that McCarthyism is now dead in this country?

MILLER: As such it is. Two things happened: one was that the Army defeated him, not, I'm sad to say, liberals or the Left, not the people who knew what he was about. It was another con-

113

servative authority that knocked him down. I don't think one can push an attack on the integrity of the United States government itself to the lengths that he did and get away with it. However, the legacy of McCarthy is still with us. But it doesn't have the mass backing that it automatically could call up at any juncture a few years ago.

BRANDON: You mean he was defeated for the wrong reasons.

MILLER: Yes, he was defeated for the wrong reasons. He gained the antagonism of people who essentially didn't disagree with him very much—not all of them, but a good many of them. My own opinion is that he may have been demented toward the end; he misjudged his position and his power.

BRANDON: Well, do you mean to imply, then, that you think it could recur?

MILLER: If an international crisis sufficiently intense gripped us, I think something like it could happen again, yes. As you know, there were polls taken from time to time at various universities in this country in which the students and others were asked whether they approved of certain propositions; they were not told that these propositions were actually the Bill of Rights. The large majority did not approve of them. They thought they were too extreme and radical. I see nothing to indicate that that has changed. In other words, the educational system has not made any severe shift of any sort that I know about.

BRANDON: Still, he stands basically in most American eyes exposed as a bad influence.

MILLER: *He* does, but what he did doesn't. Guilt-by-association, for instance—I would say quite as many people believe that as believed it before. I don't think they'd recognize it as McCarthyism if it were presented in another form. When you don't defeat somebody on the basis of principle, he is only personally defeated, but that's all. His ghost goes marching on so long as the lesson has not been learned in terms of the principles that he was violating. And the defeat was not on that basis; it was never on that basis for the majority.

BRANDON: Not long ago I discussed with Peter Ustinov a complaint of yours that American playwrights write important social plays, but that they fail to grasp the total social problem. Peter felt that there was a lack of sensitivity involved in what you said, that you could say the same thing about Chekhov; that he was only dealing with a cross-section of weary landlords on the point of bankruptcy, but as soon as the revolution broke out these things were accepted as very valid criticism. It is part of their tendency, he said, to consider that perhaps Maupassant would have been more important had he written novels instead of short stories. After all, Peter said, a writer is here to stimulate and start trends of thought in the reader, he's there to ask questions, and that it was Shakespeare's greatness that he never answered any questions, he said "To be or not to be"—but didn't give any solutions.

MILLER: Ustinov is wrong about Chekhov and he is wrong about me. I have never been able to understand why one is insensitive because one looks beyond the individual to society for certain causations and certain hopes. It seems quite the reverse to me. I never had the illusion that Chekhov was only writing about some weary landlords. Bolsheviks, indeed, accused him of this, and defensive conservatives hoped it was true, but if it were he would be known now merely as a genre painter, a curio. It is an almost international mistake, even now, to see him as a writer satisfied to reveal life's absurdities, even as a celebrant of futility. Ustinov seems rather to laud Chekhov's inability to give answers quite as though Chekhov was not always searching for them, and was not, in fact, tortured by his inability to settle on solutions, accusing himself of deceiving his public because he could not tell them what they must do. The plays are great, for one thing, not because they do not give answers but because they strive so mightily to discover them, and in the process draw into view a world that is historical. It is not right to confuse the man's modesty with his accomplishment. *The Cherry Orchard* comes to mind, where you are shown the very history of his time; when the real estate developer destroys with his ax the lovely but unproductive basis of the characters' lives, Chekhov was not merely describing a picturesque piquancy, but the crude thrust of materialism taking command of an age. If this was subjectively apprehended, so much the better for his stature as artist. These characters are not ineffectual in a vacuum; they are ineffectual in contrast to this new force. And Chekhov is not content to weep over them either.

His plays are full of speeches about having to go to work and some-how to become part of productive society and building a better world. He was seeking some reconciliation for these much-loved people and the force displacing them. A playwright provides an-swers by the questions he chooses to ask, by the exact conflicts in which he places his people. Ustinov's implication is that the man was content to discover absurdity, but Chekhov was not cruel, and a genuine absurdity in life is a cruel cross to be nailed on; it was precisely his much celebrated compassion which drove him to seek to resolve absurdity and to discover thereby a meaning for life. I think he was a much more serious writer than Ustinov's kind of characterization would permit him to be. Listening to such a view-point makes it difficult to imagine the Chekhov who risked his health crossing Russia to examine and expose the conditions of life in the Sakhalin prisons. This, to me, was an esthetic act, an expression of his artistic sensibility. If he rebelled at Tolstoy's and Dostoevski's answers to mankind it was not because they had an-swered, but because their answers were overbearing and tyrannical to him.

You know, fine characterizations exist in many minor works. I think Ustinov has come close to saying what I would agree with—that is, if Maupassant had written novels he would have been a greater writer. Of course. If Chekhov had not written his plays he would have been a lesser writer. I am not denigrating smallness, I am simply trying to distinguish it. A fine writer, but a lesser one. It isn't merely a question of being a good psychologist or a good dramatist in terms of keeping interest alive and characterizing people. It's a question of how much of the world is allowed into your work that gives it its size. Chekhov certainly sought answers, and he gave as many as he knew. His distinction is not that he gave no answers or that giving answers was unesthetic, but that he halted before the Unknown. And that is quite another thing than is implied in Ustinov's point of view which, I think, is a con-descension. Chekhov wrote: "A conscious life without a definite philosophy is no life, rather a burden and nightmare." A writer who has not spent his life trying to find and articulate "answers" could not have written this. Nor is there any contradiction between this and his boredom with those who "know," that is, with purveyors of systems to solve everything with a single blow.

I am as bored as any man with works of fiction which schematize life to fit a preconceived philosophy. But it is simply blindness not to see that art is above all a need to interpret the chaos of existence. If a writer even sets forth actions "for their own sake," declaiming against any "ideology"—like Ionesco—he is indulging in an ideology nevertheless. The belief in disorder as an ultimate fact of life—this is as much an ideology as the belief of some inner human meaning of life.

I am not calling for more ideology, as Ustinov implies. I am simply asking for a theater in which an adult who wants to live can find plays that will heighten his awareness of what living in our time involves; a theater which presses its sensitivity into as many areas of causation as possible. I am tired of a theater of sensation, that's all. I am tired of seeing man as merely a bundle of nerves. That way lies pathology, and we have pretty well arrived.

I think Ustinov's viewpoint, if I understand it right from what you have said, is expressing not so much an artistic protest against the invasion of unesthetic qualities into art, but is rather a reflection of our mutual alienation from society: he sees art as something apart, something totally individual; Chekhov, to this viewpoint, for instance, is purely a sensitive portraitist, a man of pity, compassion, and so on. I say he is that, but pity gave him conscience, which is pity extended beyond individuals to all men. This is not necessarily a condition of great art—Goethe had none of it. But Chekhov did and I, for one, find it a beautiful quality in his work and in no way an impediment.

BRANDON: The last thing one can say of you, Mrs. Miller, is that you are alienated from society. Have you felt more American in some films than in others?

MONROE: Let's see . . . yes in *Asphalt Jungle* . . . *Some Like It Hot* . . . In a way I felt typically American in *The Prince and the Showgirl*. For instance, in the script I was supposed to say, "I'll just nip down and say good night to Mickey." So I explained to Sir Laurence Olivier that that would be impossible for me to say, being an American, unless, of course, I'm putting on British airs and then I would have fun doing it. He said, "Oh, no, no, you say this!" I said, "Straight"? "Absolutely!" And I said, "Well, I couldn't say 'nip down' because here 'nip' is—you take a bite of something or you take a drink, a 'nip', a little nip—and I can't say 'nip down'—they'll never forgive me back home."

BRANDON: You felt really American in contrast—

MONROE: Yes, and I've met Americans who've come back from England almost with a British accent. So I felt—well, I'll be the only American on the set, I must watch it.

MILLER: All the other characters, you see, were of a class unknown here. And they were all floating around on these bubbles of high-class manners and elegant conversations . . .

BRANDON: When you played "against" Olivier, it must have been quite a contrast to what you've been playing with or against here.

MONROE: Yes. Oh, I wanted him and only him.

BRANDON: Why?

MONROE: Because I would go to see Sir Laurence and myself in a movie. That's what I told the agents, too. I said: I wouldn't see it otherwise.

BRANDON: Did you yearn to play next to an actor of the classical school?

MONROE: No, I'm not looking for classic training at this time. I thought—chemically—it was good, it was a little incongruous and interesting and lifelike.

BRANDON: A sort of Lady-Chatterley's-Lover-in-reverse approach?

MONROE: I hadn't thought of that.

BRANDON: Well, I could imagine that you would have liked to play with an actor of the grand school, so to say, and see what it's like, but that didn't seem to be in your instinctive—

MONROE: No, I never like to play a part or with anybody to see what it's like; in life you find out almost what everything is like. And working is a different kind of matter.

Don't misunderstand me, I think the classical theater in England is marvelous for the training of the actor, but to be able to be contemporary is also important. It's good for an actor to have *that* training too, which my husband said he found lacking in England. He wasn't looking for Americans to play—or to be like Americans —he was looking for the common, everyday man, but the actors were in another class, no matter what class they came from, and that affected their acting.

But it was a wonderful experience to work with Olivier. And I learned a lot, in a way, from observation.

BRANDON: What sort of things?

MONROE: I don't know—they're all inside of me—and I'm sorry I can't express them, but one does grow.

BRANDON: Do you find British actors more stylized than American?

MONROE: My favorite actor is Marlon Brando. I think he could do any style. But I don't think that he's going along that path right now.

BRANDON: Is that the reaction of the actress in you or the female?

MONROE: I think both. Mostly, though, I think as actress.

BRANDON: Some critics think that the angry young men were influenced by America.

MILLER: I think that there is an American note in their writing. I don't mean that a play like *Look Back in Anger* could not have been done without the American influence, but there's a certain straightforward, even brash, thrust to these works which in tone is very American, and which to my mind does not typify English letters, which is much more oblique and remote—as the tradition seems to be, at least, for the last two decades. I found myself very much at home with the writing. I felt it was from our point of view a re-discovery of something that had become almost commonplace in this country since even Mark Twain. I mean, his attitudes were always that of the plain fellow overturning the well-mannered fellow and kicking through the conventional class lines in all directions. It was the triumph of the home-town boy against King Arthur's Court, so to speak.

The American play is preeminently active, relatively unreflective as such. It deals with nothing it cannot act out. It rarely comments on itself; like the people, it always pretends it does not know what it is doing. It must *be* something rather than be *about* something. But when a play does both at once it is most highly prized. It is a hard school to go to, but in my opinion the best one at the present time.

I don't know that the writers such as John Wain, Kingsley Amis, and John Osborne are even conscious of it and there's no reason they should be, but there is an echo of all that in their work.

BRANDON: With your ear being unused to religious drama, how does Graham Greene sound to you?

MILLER: I must confess that as a dramatist I find his work faintly formularized. His philosophic dilemma is real, but it seems to end in a bald assertion. The necessity which he seems to feel for conversion scenes reminds me of a kind of play that, on the surface, has nothing to do with this but actually does; it is the conversion play of the Left in the thirties. He's caught between two stools. On the one hand, he has to keep his works on a lay level, because that's his style as well as the level on which life is lived in this age; on the other hand, he has to broach a spiritual solution, which has no embodiment in the course of the play. God escapes realism. It is hard to turn intimations into proofs. So I find them to be good plays until they have approached the point where what is most important to him enters into them—the leap to another form of consciousness. I'm thinking now of *The Potting Shed*, for instance. That play requires you to believe in another world in advance. He's dealing in normal psychology, but I don't believe you can account for a spiritual conviction through normal psychology. I don't see how that leap is possible within his realistic form. To make it you would have to create an inspired world from the beginning; I could believe in that. I don't think I could explain it, but I could believe in it. But you can't thrust an inspired conclusion upon the kind of psychology within which he's operating, which is quite normal psychology. I admire the quality of his conviction, even of his dilemma, but he has forced it into a geometry at the end. A number of other people don't feel this way at all; they feel the thing perfectly motivated, but it may simply be that I have to look at his experience from the standpoint of the daylight world because Greene is presenting his vision as, so to speak, a daylight vision.

BRANDON: The American theater has no religious content; do you have an explanation for this?

MILLER: I don't know, excepting that there's one possible clue in this schizophrenia of the American mind in that respect. I'm told that ninety per cent of the American people go to church, or are members of churches; we're probably the most church-going nation in history. But there is a sharp line drawn between going to church and thinking that way, consciously seeking ultimate meanings. In daily life there is no more materialistic, or efficient, population anywhere in terms of our economic life. There's no attempt to mitigate or justify that fact; it's a thoroughly practical approach to economic life. However, on Sunday it's quite the other way. For a few hours we act with no thought of profit and are therefore good. Life is lived, so to speak, without reference to a religious ideology, excepting the weekly nodding toward the sky.

Now I suppose our theater would naturally reflect that as being the way life is. The American, anyway, has no patience with any theorization toward anything. He wouldn't necessarily see that there's any contradiction in what I just said—religion belongs on Sunday and the rest of the week one does something else. There's nothing wrong with that. I think the big change for our theater came when it was no longer possible to contain the increasingly absurd contradictions of existence within the formula of the play which presented a more or less evil influence, and a more or less good influence, and batted it out between them. The evil influences had become so pervasive and so ill-defined that we were left with, I think, a hero whose enemies were invisible; the victim *as* victim came to the fore.

Man has become such an apparatus of accommodation that we are unsure of his definition. The story of almost every important American play is how the main character got his corners knocked off. Our main tradition, from O'Neill to the present, revolves around the question of integrity. Not moral integrity alone, but the integrity of the personality. The difficulty is to locate the forces of disintegration. I have to believe they exist and can be unveiled. It is not enough to have the clues. For one thing, it gets boring; it becomes necessary to talk back, at least.

I wrote *The Crucible* in this frame of mind. It happened that it was written at the time of McCarthyism so that a kind of personification of disintegration existed among us again. But it was an attempt to create the old ethical and dramaturgic order again, to say that one couldn't passively sit back and watch his world being destroyed under him, even if he did share the general guilt. In effect, I was calling for an act of will. I was trying to say that injustice has features, that the amorphousness of our world is so in part because we have feared through guilt to unmask its ethical outlines.

The play of the forties, which began as an attempt to analyze the self in the world, is ending as a device to exclude the world. Economics, politics, these are widely regarded as mere gaucherie. Thus self-pity and sentimentality rush in, and sexual sensationalism. It is an anti-dramatic drama, and it reflects the viewpoint of a great many people who seem to feel that's the way life is today. The characters are tyrannized, but it is taken for granted that the tyrant is undefinable, perhaps not even there. To me it's a challenge to find a more defined structure which is creating these effects among us.

BRANDON: American drama is really still very young. How do you see its evolution?

MILLER: For all intents and purposes, we had a very slight indigenous American drama until the First World War. By that, I mean a direct reflection of American manners, American life, barely existed on the stage. Life was life and the theater was the theater. The plays were melodramas, for the most part, with a very few exceptions. It's after the First World War that real attempts were made to create a modern drama in this country in the sense of a drama that reflects the life of the people at the moment. And I think O'Neill has to be set aside from the main stream because his goal was not so much a journalistic reportage of what was going on, which is, I think, true of most of the other writers—

BRANDON: Which ones are you thinking of?

MILLER: Well, you take plays like *What Price Glory* and *The Front Page*, which were great influences, I think, and *Street Scene*. For the first time, for instance, profanity was used in the way that it's used commonly in the United States. The old hokum of sentimental idealism was destroyed. The war—for the first time I know about on our stage—was viewed in the modern manner, that is, without the usual ballyhoo of past plays, which made a glorification of it in one form or another. The war was now looked at much as it was looked at by people in their ordinary life, that is, as a dirty business. A new, brash iconoclasm entered, the contemporaneous cynicism and the gaiety.

I think a great influence was probably Belasco, who was a naturalist, what we would think of as corny because his plots were frightful . . . There were scenes in his plays such as the hero about to be executed and the heroine running onto the stage with the American flag and throwing it over him and the United States Army, about to execute him, could not fire through the flag, naturally. This would be the denouement of the play. However, in making of the productions he was enormously inventive in naturalistic terms. He created volcanoes on the stage; he created waterfalls; and he also created things like Child's Restaurant—down to the flies that settled on the mince pie. It's absurd to talk about it now in one respect, excepting of course that Stanislavski saw it and was overwhelmed by it. He thought Belasco was a very great director. He was aiming always—despite the artificiality of the stories and of the characterizations—he was evidently aiming for naturalism as opposed to the flamboyant, sentimental manner of acting in the past. And he was, of course, outmoded by the subject matter, which was the manners of the life and time at that moment. His subjects were bizarre; they were baubles, but curiously enough, he was directing them as though they had content. And he took them very seriously as social commentaries and moral tales. However, he seized on a tool which the American theater is still using and to much better effect—the naturalistic actor. What was added subsequently was the story whose proportions were closer to the reality as the audience knew it. Robert Sherwood, Maxwell Anderson, S. N. Behrman, Philip Barry, Elmer Rice, George Kelly, Sidney Howard, all began or had their roots in the 'twenties. They brought it of age.

BRANDON: How does their work strike you now?

MILLER: Today a lot of their work seems mild, a bit too play-conscious and even innocent, despite their efforts to break with the older tradition of pose and stage sham. Some of their work is very fine, the workmanship is good, perhaps too good for our current taste. Some of O'Neill seems more valid now, perhaps because we share his neuroticism. Also he wrote more personally. We can see a man through his work. The others were not opening their subconscious feelings on the stage for the most part. They thus appear now too cold, coldly theatrical. O'Neill spoke like a minority man, like us; the others were more public speakers, the majority voice, and lost individuality thereby. We prize the subjective now; they prized craft, wit, comment on manners, iconoclasm. O'Neill is often marred by this same sort of craft, but his inner life remains visible and affecting.

Some of the best work of these men was done in the thirties, but that epoch was characterized for many people by the minority voices, mainly Cliffort Odets and Lillian Hellman. The social playwrights were still trying to be craftsmen, still spoke publicly, but in Odets and Hellman the inner voice broke through in that they personally felt the public anguish of the Fascist years. In Odets a new lyricism, a prose larger than life; in Hellman a remorseless rising line of action in beautifully articulated plays. Both these writers expressed personality, their works identified them, but the symbols were often so tuned to the particulars of the thirties that when that brief cataclysm passed into wartime, their world seemed out of date. It remains to be seen whether this is really so. I am not the one to judge this because I was deeply moved by these plays and remember them with love.

One ought to remember that it was by no means only the "Left" writers who wrote social plays. Maxwell Anderson, Sherwood, Rice, Sidney Howard, even Behrman and Barry were involved with the themes of social and economic disaster, Communism and Fascism. I think it is simply that Odets and Hellman made these themes personal to themselves. That is why it seemed to have been their age. They matured with the Depression, the others before.

The line of development since the forties has been toward more and more intimacy of statement by playwrights and less attention to the older idea of craft, of stage logic. In this sense O'Neill remains the leader, the abiding structure. His work is just as full of ill-digested Freudianism as the others, just as absorbed with questions like socialism, the Negro problem, social justice, etc., and as weighed down as any other with out-of-date slang and mawkish devices and melodrama. But he could not for long be drowned in his moment—we hear his inner voice, we respond to many of its tones. His self-pity, his tortured questing, his relentless doubts, overwhelm his often stagey solutions; the other writers too often were sealed up in their plays.

The forties, and more so the fifties, became an era of gauze. Tennessee Williams is responsible for this in the main. One of my own feet stands in this stream. It is a cruel, romantic neuroticism, a translation of current life into the war within the self. The personal has triumphed. All conflict tends to be transformed into sexual conflict. The sets have therefore become less and less defined in realistic terms, for the society is more and more implied, or altogether blotted out. Its virtue is its ability to intensify the sensual—using that word to mean the senses, feeling.

It has all moved now to a dangerous extreme of triviality. It is a theater with the blues, especially in certain newer writers. Sexual conflict can only embrace so much and no more. It is coming to be a cul de sac of pathology. The drama will have to find its way back into the daylight world without losing its inner life. Every discovery ultimately becomes a convention. I mean that in perfecting itself, it has to repeat and refine itself until it becomes predictable in tone, at least, and often in resolution. The genuine original cry becomes a rehearsed scream or a self-conscious whimper. I sometimes long to see a set with a ceiling again rather than the forced poetics of self-conscious longing and victimization and gauze. Whether it is done through a more overt symbolism or a rebirth of realism in the traditional sense, the drama will have to re-address itself to the world beyond the skin, to fate. And fate is always the others—even if it is you that dies of it.

BRANDON: You seem to be saying that O'Neill was standing to one side of—

MILLER: O'Neill was to one side because the mood of the twenties and the thirties was nonreligious. At bottom their world was rational, his a mystery. The quest for a relationship between an individual and, for want of a better word, fate was not the preoccupation of any other playwright that I know of—as such. That was his central worry, and he hewed to it always. He dealt on one hand with all the conventional problems of modern literature, but he was always calling to the ear of God. He was blessed with an inability to wipe out the Unknown.

BRANDON: Did you see Samuel Beckett's *Waiting for Godot?*

125

MILLER: I've read it. I never got to see it. I admire that play for
the rebellion in it. It is an intimate statement—a very hard thing
to do on the stage, and at the same time an abstract of the time. It
has feeling and it has a brain. I find it necessary, however, to ask
what are its limits . . . the limits of this technique, this form, in
terms of translating a variety of experiences. In other words, its
viability for the future. I feel that desolation is wedded to it; that
such a degree of abstraction, regardless of what lines are being
said, enforces upon us a sense of the desolate. Which is just what
it was designed to do. But I do not think it flexible enough to
embrace other moods, so to speak. That is no criticism of it but a
description. A criticism would be that it is addressed, I think,
exclusively to its own cultural level. That is legitimate and proper.
But, for myself anyway, the challenge is still the Elizabethan one,
the public address on the street corner. To make beauty there. It
is not a question of one being more valuable. There are just
different aims, both legitimate.

BRANDON: I think that you and Sartre are the two most powerful
dramatists today. The difference between you and him, it seems
to me, is that his writings are dominated by ideas . . .

MILLER: There is a great difference between us. For one, I'm
writing in a culture that does not truck with ideas, it has no awareness of what it is doing; it resists knowing what it is doing. This
goes for an ordinary individual and a gigantic corporation. I know
this from my own experience.

In France, to a much greater degree, the people are aware that
if they don't know what they're doing, it is possible to characterize
it objectively anyway; that is, they will concede that *somebody*
knows what they're doing, and that this is a legitimate kind of
work, so to speak. Here, it's a luxury, which a few cloistered people
may indulge in, but it's of no consequence. What the hell is the
difference if you do know? We believe in necessity here; we're
loyal slaves of it. The necessary, here, is mistaken for the right.
But sometimes men must interfere with the inevitable.

BRANDON: Is this partly due to a certain anti-intellectualism?

MILLER: I would like to make clear my attitude toward the
charge of anti-intellectualism in this country. I believe some of this
feeling among Europeans and Englishmen is based on a distortion.

My own feeling is that you people are overly impressed with the fact that we have no sense here of an intellectual *class*. But this fact may simply be a reflection of our unwillingness to name things, to categorize in general.

I am not at all sure, for instance, that there are more people in other countries who understand what an intellectual *does*. But there are more people abroad who have learned to tip their hats to the idea of an intellectual. It reminds me of a barber I used to go to. He'd been cutting my hair for years and never said more than hello and thank you until my picture got into the *Daily News* when I won some prize or other. He was an old Italian who could barely speak any English at all. Then he asked me if I had heard of D'Annunzio. I said I knew his work. From this time the barber's eyes lit up whenever I came into the shop, and when I sat in his chair, he would give me a warm, rather intimate smile, nod his head, and say, "D'Annunzio." Then I would smile back and he would cut my hair—with a good deal more care than before. He knew nothing, really, of D'Annunzio's work, but had attached to "D'Annunzio" a feeling of national pride and accomplishment. "D'Annunzio" made the barber feel more valuable.

BRANDON: You had become an intellectual in the eyes of your barber because you knew D'Annunzio.

MILLER: Writers here have no such connotation for the masses as D'Annunzio had for the Italians. Nor would any writer regard himself—as Russian writers have and many French—as spokesmen for the national spirit or something of the kind. In a word, we have no status excepting that we are makers of entertainment, or sometimes heavy thinkers, or earners of big money.

In the profoundest sense, of course, this is an anti-intellectual attitude, but it is neither hateful nor contemptuous for the most part. The truth is that no other occupation is regarded symbolically as a national adornment, so to speak, excepting, possibly, that of the soldier in wartime. Nor do we have a consciousness of an "American Culture" in the way the French have, and other European nations. But it does not mean we do not value our plays, movies, paintings, music. It is simply that they are enjoyed without being called manifestations of the national spirit. Again, we do not name things, we just do them.

This has both good and bad consequences. Most obviously, it makes the country appear from outside like a nest of peddlers. Denial of public recognition makes some intellectuals take on an unnatural defensiveness toward themselves, an inferior feeling which breeds isolation and hopelessness and weakness. Perhaps the worst effect is that when, as during the McCarthy period, it is necessary for basic principles of human existence to be upheld, the natural upholders—the intellectuals—are face to face with a population that is unused to listening to their advice.

Yet, I ask myself, What good did the much vaunted German adoration of intellectualism do in the face of Nazism? Or the French for five years now in the face of the waste of five years of war in Algeria? Looking at Russia one wonders whether the making of the intellectual into a figure of state does not inevitably make him into an apologist for the state.

In a word, we are not so much persecuted as ignored. But everybody else is ignored too. I doubt there is a single professional class in this country which feels it gets due public thanks or recognition. This even includes businessmen who are always revealing a sense of occupational inferiority, and envy and resent, for example, how artists are all the time being publicly acclaimed!

The benefits, if one may call them that, are not inconsiderable. Without a certain kind of recognition, we are also relieved of a certain kind of irrelevant responsibility. We can write as we like without our works *normally* being transformed into attacks or defenses of the nation by zealous critics. Art here is irrelevant to life, in the minds of most, so it is free to do what it will with life.

BRANDON: Doesn't that depress an artist?

MILLER: Yes. The trouble, of course, is that the artist is hard put to reassure to himself that his occupation is anything but trivial. And this, I think, is the biggest wound the American attitude inflicts. To survive it, an artist has to cling to his dignity with his teeth sometimes, often at the very moment he is being acclaimed, for it is a rare thing to be acclaimed excepting for irrelevant reasons, and this is sometimes a victory that leaves bitterness behind it. But will a public cult of intellectualism really result in a higher understanding of art's relevance to life? If Europe is an example, I wonder. I have heard, in my very limited experience, some of the loudest avowals of pro-intellectualism from some of the most corrupt and unphilosophical people.

The single important advantage of the attitude, I think, is that it presses the artist the more to overcome it. To be dissatisfied with work that does not interpret the common experience. You have to hit them when they're not looking, so to speak; you have to make it real to them the way the subway is real. You can't depend on their embracing your work because it is art, but only because it somehow reaches into the part of them that is still alive and questing. This kind of challenge can almost destroy a delicate art like poetry, but for the drama and the novel it can muscularize them. It can also make them muscle-bound, and strident, and screaming, and sensational. But all I want to make clear at the moment is that the thing is not a dead loss by any means.

BRANDON: How do you feel about such purely intellectual playwrights like Ionesco and Beckett?

MILLER: I think that they are anti-dramatic; I think I know what they reflect. It's much the same thing, it's the cul-de-sac, the end of will, and it's the twilight of the conceptual man. They have driven the "ought" out of art. In other words, life is essentially an absurdity and one is most alive when one is most aware of the absurdity of it. Man and his existence are mortal enemies and a reconciliation is unthinkable.

BRANDON: But Ionesco says that ideology is not a source of art.

MILLER: I believe that too. But such extreme definitions don't operate. I don't believe that the knowingness of a writer is what makes him write, or that it creates his writing. But I don't see any reason why man's subconscious life, which art feeds on and creates art, has to make thought impossible. This seems to be the belief among writers. There is such a thing as felt knowledge. I don't see why what is called idea or ideology is in any way an obstruction to the creative act. On the contrary, I think it can be a stimulant, provided it is not used as a substitute for personal vision. Ionesco's anti-ideology is, after all, another ideology.

BRANDON: Where, do you think, are we moving?

MILLER: One thing the theater will not stand for too long—at least not in this country—is boredom. The blue play is now becoming predictable in mood. We know quite well what to expect; we will expect a pathetic defeat in the play, and the documentation of alienated loneliness. I think they're going to suddenly become quite old hat. Perhaps it is only my feeling, but perhaps life is now less impossible than it was, say, even two years ago. And this is as much a political and social fact as it is a theatrical fact. I mean to say the possibility of the survival of the human race now appears to be a reasonable hope for a person to take hold of. It begins to appear that the two great possessors of the power to disintegrate mankind have been restrained. To be sure, we have an enormous way to go before there is a world community of any sort. But the mere fact that with all the likelihood of war within the last five, ten years, there hasn't been a war—and that certain steps have been taken that would indicate a *rapprochement* of some sort can be made between two civilizations—plus, in my opinion, the spread of technology all over the world, will make war less needful. These things filter down until they become part of the emotional life of people who never read a newspaper, and don't know why it is that it's different now from what it was a few years ago. The lines from the chancelleries to the kitchen are tangled and devious, but they exist.

Take simple things like the draft. When you're drafting every young man of eighteen and interfering with his education for two or three years, this is a pall . . . it awakens all kinds of dormant morbidity. A boy gets the attitude of what the hell is the use of doing anything but wasting my time, because to a kid of eighteen years three years is a lifetime. A sneer creeps into his soul, everything is pointless. The draft has been progressively reduced; I think it will end up with a nominal number of people taken every year. Just that could have a considerable effect on the psychology not only of the boy, but of his parents, and not only his parents but the people around his parents. I mention such a mundane thing as an example; a mood has real causes. These things are of great importance, seemingly unesthetic pieces of realism, but they have enormous importance to the people directly affected, and there are many such people. But the theater as yet has not got the reach, the breadth of vision to see much more than the center of the web in which we struggle.

Sex, Theater, and the Intellectual

I think there are numerous indications that we have a right to state once again that all is not lost. And as soon as that really happens, the black air surrounding many plays may begin to appear unjustified; it will no longer seem the way things are; and the style itself will seem willful and self-conscious.

Beyond Modern Architecture

---

a conversation with
FRANK LLOYD WRIGHT

When Frank Lloyd Wright died in the spring of 1959 the world lost one of the most authentically American Americans. He was not just a creative genius, he was a visionary with a poetic pathos. Like so many geniuses he was an eccentric and like so many eccentrics he was egocentric, and because he was so flamboyantly, so rebelliously egocentric he tended to be tyrannical. But, as everything he did, even his tyranny was in the grand manner.

What was so inspiring about him was his spacious outlook. He not only had a sense of history, but also a vision into the future. Architecture to him was the mother of all arts, and, in spite of his Welsh origin, he put it above poetry and music. To him architecture was the most telling, the most enduring testimony of civilization. What worried him about American architecture and contemporary American civilization, therefore, was that it had contributed little to new yet enduring forms of architecture and too much to the baser comforts of man. "In a thousand years," he worried, "when future generations will excavate the remains of our civilization, what will they find? Bathtubs and dishwashers."

His name probably will not be remembered for his buildings so much as for the new criteria he established for twentieth-century architecture. Epochal ideas in architecture are rare. The Greeks did much to improve the use of the lintel and the Romans in their own daring way contributed the dome, the arch, and the vault. In the Byzantine period the square topped by the dome was added, and in the Gothic period the flying buttress. But until

Wright, as *Edward Durrell Stone* interprets it, new great principles had inspired architecture with fresh dimensions. The skyscraper could be counted among startling innovations based on the development of concrete, the steel frame and the elevator, but it was Frank Lloyd Wright who actually evolved a new principle in twentieth-century architecture, the principle of the cantilever: a beam supported near midpoint with one end held down and the other free to support weight. The principle had previously been used in such minor ways as supporting balconies, but as Wright put it, "My thumb is only supported at one end! It's only support comes from where it joins my hand. This is the twentieth-century way of using steel."

The work "organic" and nature with a capital "N" spelled magic to him. Architecture, he felt, must serve to improve humanity, must therefore be carefully attuned to nature and to the individual. He usually succeeded in blending his houses into the landscape. But like so many architects he injected his own idiosyncrasies into a house rather than those of the future owner.

Even at eighty-eight Frank Lloyd Wright walked erect and confidently and his cane seemed part of his slightly dandyish, slightly theatrical style of dress and make-up rather than a physical support. He always wore a silken tie tucked under a flaring wide collar and as a coat he liked a sweeping, wide cape. His broad-brimmed hat too had a flamboyant quality. It sat squarely on his white dramatic mane which gave his sharp, handsome profile an elegant and distinguished frame. There was some deeper meaning to the modernity of his structures and the old-fashioned style of his clothes. A striving for the new yet an ingrained sense for the traditional.

I met Frank Lloyd Wright in Washington. He had come to the capital, for whose architecture he had little respect, to open an exhibition of his architectural drawings at the Corcoran Gallery and to deliver a lecture for the Institute of Contemporary Arts. Its director, Robert Richman, who has done so much to liven up cultural life in Washington, facilitated my introduction. I had no difficulty in persuading Wright to sit down at my tape recorder right there in the Corcoran Gallery.

He was an ideal person for an interview. He was belligerently *creative, and hence he invited controversy. And because he loved controversy, he not only enjoyed pouring oil on it but also to set it aflame himself. He could afford it. He not only had pride of accomplishment, but he was also so articulate, he had such a gift of phrase, such a command of language that he felt certain of winning every argument. If necessary he would shut you up by an authoritative statement that one could not possibly dare to contradict. Then he was intimidating. But Wright could equally well shrug you off with a mellow, humorous remark. That was the time he exuded greatness to me.*

This interview was the first in this series of "Conversation Pieces." I chose him because he promised the least risk of failure and the best hope of convincing my editor that such a series was a worthwhile experiment. This collection therefore owes a great deal to Frank Lloyd Wright, and so do I.

BRANDON: Perhaps you would first like to define what you mean by "modern" architecture.

WRIGHT: Well, modern architecture is anything built today. It's an ambiguous term, but "modern architecture" does not necessarily mean new architecture. The *new* architecture is organic architecture.

BRANDON: Your organic architecture is really—

WRIGHT: A natural influence.

BRANDON: Isn't it an Oriental influence?

WRIGHT: No—except that the philosophy is perhaps Oriental. It was Tao who declared that the reality of the buildings did not consist in the walls and the roof, but in the space within to be lived in. The interior space was the reality of the building. Now that means that you build from within outward rather than from the outside in, as the West has always been building. In so far as that's Taoism, I suppose the philosophy is Eastern. But somehow only the West has ever built according to that philosophy. And our "organic" architecture happens to be the original expression of that idea. The space concept in architecture is organic, and "organic," as we use the term, means "natural," it means "essential." It means *of* the thing instead of *on* it.

BRANDON: I quite agree there should be a close link between architecture and nature. That's what entranced me about the setting of the Japanese house. But how can you adapt this philosophy of organic architecture to the cities of today? They lack space.

WRIGHT: You can't. The city of today will have to run its course. It's being finished now by excess. Excess is ruining it. When we need a new city we're going to have it on our own organic terms and it will be more an agronomy, it will be part of the ground and it will be pretty nearly everywhere. The concentrations that are now cities are feudal survivals. We've got to go forward and make better use of the ground.

BRANDON: But aren't we going to lose whatever privacy and serenity there is left of our landscapes, of our countryside?

WRIGHT: On the contrary. If we have the right sort of architecture we won't do violence to the landscape as we do now. I would dread to see the kind of architecture that we have in cities go out into the country. But in organic architecture the nature of the thing prompts the fashioning of the thing, and the buildings that would be built would make that country more beautiful rather than less so. Of course, that's a long journey along the line of a culture that we don't have yet.

BRANDON: You've recently been to London. You probably saw that much was destroyed, that much has also been rebuilt. What sort of advice would you have for a city like London?

WRIGHT: London has a dormitory town, London has *suburbia*, and I think for London *exurbia* is important—getting out into the country as far as possible—maintaining the old city, the old buildings, and the old conditions as a memorial. I'm sorry to see the skyscraper about to invade London. I saw it in an illustrated magazine, a high hotel building like an office building, making of the hostelry a rat trap, right in the heart of London. I hope they never build it.

BRANDON: Why are you against skyscrapers? They are one of the outstanding American contributions to architecture.

WRIGHT: The skyscraper is responsible for the congestion, and is making the city of today impossible to use. The skyscraper piles the crowd up high, dumps it on the street, stuffs it in again, and the streets are not nearly wide enough.

135

Paris is so beautiful today because it has that sense of space without the skyscraper. London has something of that, and if it's invaded by the skyscraper, it will lose what it has. I think they should not build up those bombed areas either. They should plant them to greenery. The greenery of London is one of its beauties. Why not extend that and let the people push out into the countryside in becoming buildings in a way that does not damage the country but benefits the invader?

BRANDON: What impression did London make on you?

WRIGHT: I think most buildings in London are worth preserving: they're interesting examples of the old order. But, as compared with what we can build now, they are extremely inutile and will eventually be relics and unbecoming. London is rather far behind in what we call modern architecture and has very few, or no, examples of organic architecture.

See, the architecture we call organic is a natural architecture and it does not use steel like lumber. The steel framing in the nineteenth century was just like lumber framing. They made steel into lumber and used it as beams, as posts and all that. But that's not organic. We use steel suspended in strands for its tensile strength, buried in concrete for its compression strength. The system was invented by the French and we called it ferroconcrete.

BRANDON: Certainly what you have been building is daring and revolutionary. But looking at some of your structures I often wonder what holds them up?

WRIGHT: They hold themselves up. Take my "Mile-High" building. It has a spine with ribs growing out from it. In the Guggenheim Museum the spine is coiled and the ribs or, if you want, the floors, grow only inward. The outer wall is the spine or support and the floor is cantilevered from it.

BRANDON: But is it safe without support on the inner edges?

WRIGHT: My thumb is not supported at the end! Its only support comes from where it joins my hand. This is the twentieth-century way of using steel. But all that is practiced now in our big cities is nineteenth-century architecture—extensive steel frames that are rusting at the joints. Most of the architects we have called "modern" are really wallpaper hangers, papering façades. Posters for whisky, posters for soap.[1] They're not really architecture. They're all right for cities and they're all the cities are entitled to now, but don't call them architecture.

BRANDON: Personally, I prefer the façades of the old buildings on Park or Fifth Avenue. The avenues' majesty, dignity, and sense of proportion will be lost when those old buildings are replaced by these new austere structures of glass and steel, looking all alike.

WRIGHT: This is a matter of taste, and taste is always a matter of ignorance. You taste because you don't know. And if you like the taste of the old, you like the old. If you like the taste of the new, you like the new. But none of it is really architecture. Architecture is a deeper thing. It is the frame of human existence. We must dedicate this existence more to beauty. For if poetic principle has deserted us, how long are we going to last? How long can civilization without a soul last? Science cannot save us; it has brought us to the brink. Art and religion, which are the soul of civilization, have to save us.

Architecture is the only record you can read now of those civilizations that have passed into distance. Water closets, washbowls, and radiators, that's what they would find of our present-day civilization centuries hence. Architecture means *of* the nature of the thing whatever it may be and *for* the nature of the thing whatever that may be.

Most of this educated taste today is an acquired taste. It has nothing whatever to do with certain senses or the beneficial character of the thing tasted; it's only whether you like it or not. And who are you? You are only an artificial thing whose taste may be atrocious. So when we have a taste-built culture; we have a haphazard jamboree of all kinds of things. But if we go back to nature, and make things according to nature, we have a sense of propriety. Not propriety, but proper character in everything.

BRANDON: And you firmly believe that modern architecture will develop in that direction?

WRIGHT: Yes, it will be organic architecture. It was the basis of the present so-called modern. But organic architecture made first a negation and that negation was extremely narrow and affected a great many architects. And they followed the negation rather

[1] Wright was referring to the Seagram and Lever buildings in New York.

137

than going along into the affirmation of which it was capable and which we are now practicing.

BRANDON: Modern architecture was born at a time of scarcity, a utilitarian period. Now we live in an age of greater plenty than, say, twenty years ago. Will this be reflected in architecture, will it make greater use of artful decoration?

WRIGHT: Inevitably it will, but not in decoration as we know it. It will be more like the things we see in nature, in the garden, in the trees, everywhere about. If there is ornament it will be natural to the environment. And if there is a building it will be natural to its purpose in certain senses. It will all have the truth of nature.

Of course, that's all a large order. It's going to take time to reach it. But that's where we're headed for, and architecture is gradually getting a little deeper into nature, which is the mother of architecture, and without which there is no culture.

We Americans have a vast civilization and no culture because we have no architecture of our own. Washington, our capital, does not represent architecture of our own. The Capitol, for instance, represents American history. I do not judge its architecture but respect it for what it is. We have for a long time been flat on our faces, copying nineteenth-century Europe. But now Americans are waking up to the importance of having their own architecture, the importance of organic architecture. Yesterday I gave a lecture on the subject for the International Institute of Contemporary Art, and some fifteen hundred people came to listen. That's encouraging. There is a rebirth of architecture in America, and we're getting our own: organic architecture.

Not for Mere Amusement

a conversation with

HERBLOCK

If any of the offices in the modern, muffled, and somewhat antiseptic atmosphere of the new Washington Post building have the look and smell traditionally associated with editorial rooms, it's Herblock's. It is littered with papers, cluttered with files, and the smell of printer's ink hangs in the air. The drawing table takes up most of the space in his confining cubicle and only an intensive search under some piles of books will bring a chair to light for the visitor to use.

Herblock clearly is not an artist who likes to work in the seclusion of a studio. He wants to be on a par with the editorial writers, he wants to be in the center of life that pervades a newspaper.

Herbert Lawrence Block, to use his full name, is just past fifty, but he does not look his age. His face is pale, his hair thin and blond. His bulging, wide eyes sometimes look at you with the surprise of a new-born baby, sometimes with the pained expression of a man who has seen much unhappiness; almost always there is a quizzical look about them. And if you remember a cartoon he published several months ago that you liked particularly well, he will look almost incredulous. He seems too modest to understand how somebody would pay that much attention to him.

Like so many professional humorists he tends to be serious in conversation. Like Swift he thinks that "mere amusement is the happiness of those who cannot think." This does not mean that he takes himself too seriously. But he cares deeply about the fate

139

of humanity, about human rights, about the need to defend the underdog.

Like any good editorial writer he feels that as a cartoonist he should not simply illustrate policy or somebody else's viewpoint, but that he should have his own strong opinions. At the start of his career cartoonists such as John McCutcheon of the Chicago Tribune (Chicago was the city where he grew up) and "Ding" Darling of the New York Herald Tribune had a major influence on him. He did not agree with all their views, but he considered them excellent draftsmen and, above all, men who expressed their own forceful convictions.

Herblock's first job was with a syndicate. This meant that his cartoons had to be amusing, that they had to appeal to as many people as possible to get the widest distribution, and hence they had to be unprovocative and inoffensive. It not only takes time to develop an individual viewpoint, it also takes time until a cartoonist can afford to express it with authority. And today, although Herblock's views are usually very personal, very partisan, very hard-hitting, his cartoons are widely distributed throughout the United States and widely reprinted abroad.

Working in the political capital and for the Washington Post he draws with an eye to his most immediate audience: the politicians, the officials, members of the government. The editorial page of the Washington Post is one of the best in the country, but when Herblock suffered a mild heart attack in the autumn of 1959 and he had to take a four-month rest, it had lost its main sting. A cartoon idea can strike like lightning, the written editorial can be at best like thunder.

It is not surprising therefore that what worries cartoonists most are ideas. They are haunted by the fear that any day they may end up without one. Many rely on editors or colleagues to help them out. Herblock never suffers from such apprehensions. He is never at a loss for ideas, does not accept suggestions, and does not sit in at editorial conferences. Every day after lunch he presents the editor with several sketches for next day's cartoon. The final choice is left to the editor, and he usually accepts his judgment. He does not act as an independent artist, as David Low does, for instance, but as a member of the staff.

Not for Mere Amusement

Herblock has never studied art too systematically, or paid much attention to such famous predecessors as Daumier and Toulouse-Lautrec. His art is visceral, the political idea rather than the art of drawing is what really matters to him. His draftsmanship is distinctive, but it is not his outstanding quality. He is more a political animal than artist.

Under the sophisticated influence of The New Yorker magazine, American humor has come to walk on thick carpets. It seems almost as if Americans these days feel a little too unsure of their society, as if they are reluctant to make fun of it or themselves too ferociously. Herblock does not suffer from such inhibitions and it has made him America's leading political cartoonist.

BRANDON: In conversation you seem very gentle, very kind, but judging by some of your cartoons, there is a good deal of acid in your veins.

HERBLOCK: I don't feel that I have acid in my veins. Some reviewers have said: This fellow is obviously a kind person who loves humanity. Others have said the cartoons are quite harsh and cruel. This paradox of the political critic reminds me of the story about the teacher who asked the children in her class to give examples of their kindness to Nature's creatures. One little girl told of how a bird had fallen out of its nest and she had taken care of it until it could fly; and a little boy told of how he had taken in a starving kitten on a cold winter day. The next little boy, asked for an example of his kindness to animals, said, "Yes, Ma'am, one time I kicked a boy for kicking a dog."

I think we often demonstrate our love of humanity by kicking boys who kick underdogs. This is largely the function of the cartoonist. I don't think that demonstrates meanness or is inspired by meanness.

My aim is that of most of us in editorial work—to try to say the right thing and to say it effectively. But I don't think this means that you must necessarily be grim. I try to get some fun into most of the cartoons, but the more-or-less amusing presentation is usually a means of expressing a view or making a point.

BRANDON: David Low said once to a friend of mine that his purpose in life was to encourage good intentions.

HERBLOCK: "To encourage good intentions"—well, there's an old saying about good intentions . . . I think we do try to encourage good intentions, which is perhaps another way of saying that we try to "keep 'em honest"—to make it easier for public officials to follow their consciences and more difficult for them to yield to expediency. But I think most of us, including David Low, really want to do more than that. When policies that we think are unwise or dangerous are advocated by perfectly sincere people with good intentions, we try to show that our well-intentioned ideas make better sense than the other fellow's well-intentioned ideas.

BRANDON: What actually interests you the most—the issue, or the issue as represented by a personality?

HERBLOCK: Oh, the issue. There are cases, I think, where the political figure becomes identified with the issue or gets to be an issue, but mostly I think it's the issue itself. And, as you know, it's possible to criticize a person on one issue and feel that he's doing all right on others. People sometimes wonder why you do a cartoon which they feel is rather kind to somebody you've been critical of—or vice versa—and have the idea you must always be "for" somebody or "against" somebody. I don't think so.

BRANDON: Have you ever drawn a cartoon of Eisenhower that you felt was not critical?

HERBLOCK: Yes, but there's no question that most of them have been critical. This is partly because I think it's the function of the Press to keep a critical eye on government; and comparatively few of the cartoons cheer politicians for doing what they ought to be doing. Partly also because during most of his administration I thought President Eisenhower needed more criticism and received less of it than other Presidents I could recall.

BRANDON: Or of Nixon?

HERBLOCK: I think a Nixon or a McCarthy is a case in point where the person, his method of operating, and his public character become a kind of an issue in itself.

BRANDON: Do you draw Eisenhower purposely looking like Donald Duck?

HERBLOCK: No, I've never tried to make him look like that,

MARGARET MEAD

Photo by Cornell Capa, Magnum

Photo courtesy of *ABC Television, London*

PETER USTINOV

Camera Press Ltd.

LEONARD BERNSTEIN

Photo by Ida Kar

BEN SHAHN

Photo by Henry Brandon

EDMUND WILSON

ARTHUR MILLER and MARILYN MONROE

FRANK LLOYD WRIGHT

Courtesy of the Washington Post and Times Herald

HERBLOCK

REINHOLD NIEBUHR

Alfred Eisenstaedt—Courtesy of LIFE Magazine, Copr. 1955 Time, Inc.

RICHARD M. NIXON

JOHN F. KENNEDY

Photo by Jacques Lowe

WALT KELLY

Photo by George Tames

WALTER REUTHER

NORBERT WIENER

Camera Press Ltd.

WERNHER VON BRAUN

Photo by Gjon Mili

ISIDOR I. RABI

JAMES THURBER

except in one cartoon where I represented him as a duck—showed him taking to politics as a duck takes to water—while a campaign manager explained, "Confidentially, he hates it."

BRANDON: I think you are an idealist, aren't you?

HERBLOCK: I suppose in a way . . . But I think the things that are often considered idealistic are really the most practical. Take foreign economic aid. Some people have considered it idealistic, but it's a very practical thing for us and for other countries. Take free democratic government. That's an idealistic thing, really; but I think it's also the most practical form of government. Take the idea of "equal justice" or "equal rights." Ideals like that are never fully realized. But what kind of justice would there be, what rights would any of us have, if we were cynical about such things?

BRANDON: But I think it's not a usual trait in cartoonists to be idealists; their method is distortion . . .

HERBLOCK: Superficially a cartoon is an exaggeration, but I don't think this implies distortion of the basic idea. Quite the contrary; if it's done properly it clarifies issues.

You often present cartoon situations which are like allegories, or parables or fables. Look, let's take something very simple. Suppose a man has lost his job and has had his reputation injured and his career destroyed as a result of anonymous accusations under a so-called security program. You might show him being struck from behind by a masked figure. He has not been hit over the head physically, and nobody has literally worn a mask; but the readers understand this. The exaggeration does not deceive them and is not meant to. It simply illustrates the essential point that the man has been injured without a fair chance to defend himself.

Now, suppose you wrote that the man is perfectly free and nobody has laid a hand on him. This would be completely accurate, but a misleading partial truth—in effect, a real distortion. The signed cartoon, presented frankly as opinion and making the point through acknowledged exaggeration, would be, to my mind, much fairer to the reader.

If you were to sum up journalistic ethics in a few words, I think that's what it would be: playing fair with the reader.

BRANDON: Do you find it easier to draw cartoons with the Democrats in office or out of office?

HERBLOCK: I don't think it makes much difference. The cartoons are independent. They don't follow any line and aren't obliged to support anybody or any party. But I don't believe in the kind of ersatz independence that makes a point of praising or criticizing both sides equally, regardless of who is right or wrong. Of course, the cartoon is a kind of offensive weapon. Even when you approve of what the party in office is doing, you generally support those policies by criticizing the opposition to them in Congress or elsewhere—if the opposition seems important enough.

BRANDON: Do you see a difference between American and European cartoonists?

HERBLOCK: In so far as you can generalize, I think the European cartoonists probably show more individuality. This may be partly because of greater diversity in the publications there, partly because of a more general recognition there of cartoonists as individual commentators.

The other thing I'd say is that, on the whole, the drawing in British and European editorial cartoons is better than in the American ones.

BRANDON: There's much more allegory in the average American cartoon than in a European cartoon, isn't there?

HERBLOCK: I think that in most editorial cartoons there is less of the old-style allegory.

BRANDON: But you do occasionally use the symbol of Uncle Sam, for instance.

HERBLOCK: Yes, at times.

BRANDON: It's been often debated as to whether Uncle Sam is now outmoded and belongs to a different period.

HERBLOCK: The figure of Uncle Sam may be an anachronism, but I don't think there's anything particularly misleading about him, because no one supposes we look and dress like that. I use Uncle Sam occasionally because he serves a purpose—because being immediately recognizable as a figure representing the United States he's useful when you particularly want to show the U.S. or traditional government principles as distinct from government officials, or certain official acts. For example, if I draw Uncle Sam in a box, asking "How did I get in this position?" the figure couldn't be the President or the Secretary of State, who presumably got him *into* the box.

BRANDON: In addition to your own characters, like the one for the atom bomb, do you use any other symbols?

HERBLOCK: Yes. The elephant and the donkey, representing the Republicans and Democrats. You might say that these are also outmoded, that they no longer represent the two political parties, but the parties themselves employ these symbols. And as we use them today people don't think of them in terms of size or character. It is a very simple matter to make either animal look reasonably earnest, or stupid, or comic, as the cartoonist chooses.

A comparison might be made with the characters in animated cartoons. We don't think of Mickey Mouse as a rodent and don't wonder why he's as large as Donald Duck. They are cartoon creatures and are given the attributes and the personalities the cartoonist wishes them to have.

BRANDON: But to come back to Uncle Sam, I mean, doesn't he represent the old rural Yankee who really is more of a sinister figure without idealism?

HERBLOCK: I don't think he's a sinister figure at all. It may be time to put Uncle Sam on the shelf but not for the reason often given that he lends himself to use as a sinister figure by the Russians and so on. Anyone can be made into a sinister figure in a drawing. Uncle Sam can be drawn as a very kindly man or he can be drawn as a Shylock. Actually, the features of Uncle Sam as they're often drawn are very much like those of Lincoln—who was also drawn sometimes as a great and kindly man, and sometimes as an evil or even ape-like figure, depending on the viewpoint of the man behind the drawing pen.

You can do pretty much what you want with symbols. Many countries have used the eagle as a national symbol. But when it was being considered for the U.S. seal, some people—including Franklin, I think—objected that it was a bird of prey. Is the eagle a noble bird and a worthy symbol or isn't it? You could draw it either way.

What I'm interested in primarily is what the cartoons say. If an

Uncle Sam figure or certain animals help to convey ideas quickly, I don't think they're objectionable. If they bother the reader or create false impressions or get in the way of the ideas, they can be dispensed with.

BRANDON: Is Khrushchev a terrifying symbol to you?

HERBLOCK: I don't think I've always made him look terrifying, but I think we're conscious of what he represents.

Getting back to something you mentioned before about symbolizing nations . . . I think a person in Khrushchev's position can be used to symbolize the government—more easily than any figure in a democracy can.

BRANDON: How about the Russian bear as a symbol?

HERBLOCK: I rarely use it, only where it really fits into the cartoon—perhaps no more so than you would use any animal in a cartoon. For example, I did a cartoon using the bear which was a kind of switch on the old idea of having a bear by the tail. This was a cartoon at the time of the Hungarian revolt, which showed the Russian bear with its claws in a fighting Hungary, asking: "How do you let go when you get hold of a man?"

BRANDON: Do you use any symbols as related to England?

HERBLOCK: You mean familiar figures like the old John Bull? No, I can't think of any that I use.

BRANDON: Why?

HERBLOCK: I don't think the old figures serve too well to represent current situations, and in drawing mostly for American readers I hesitate to use symbols of that kind for other countries. There's also a difference in the government structure there. I think the Prime Minister would not remain in power if there were sufficient opposition, would he? Whereas a President may serve out a term long after he's lost touch with a people—or when the people have elected a Congress of another party, or even when he cannot command proper support in his own party. In that sense, the figure of the Prime Minister would serve as a symbol of "the government" there, in a way that a President might not always serve as such a symbol here.

BRANDON: Peter Ustinov said to me the other day—and he's no mean connoisseur of humour—that American cartoons are perhaps the best in the world, but that most American political cartoons are fifty or sixty years behind the times. He said you still feel you are picking up a copy of *Punch* in 1902 when you look at some of them. Everything has to be marked; Uncle Sam is standing there gripping his trousers so they wouldn't get wet, and the sea has "United Nations" marked on it, or the clouds have "Depression" on them, and the bolt out of the blue has "Quemoy" written on it . . . This was a general remark, not related to your cartoons, but there seems to be some truth in this if you look at the average American cartoon.

HERBLOCK: Yes. You know, among his many other talents, Peter Ustinov is a caricaturist, too. I don't think you can generalize too much about these things, or that you can have hard and fast rules saying that a cartoon should not contain any words or labels . . . sometimes they contribute something to it.

You mentioned Low a while ago. He probably uses more words in his cartoons than most readers realize, but he uses them skillfully and artistically so that there is no feeling of clutter or wordiness or banality. I'm inclined to think that we notice the printing more when a cartoon itself doesn't have much to say. But perhaps there is less lettering in European cartoons generally.

BRANDON: Are there any subjects which, as a cartoonist, you consider taboo?

HERBLOCK: I don't think there should be any that are taboo, no.

BRANDON: Anything like religion or . . .

HERBLOCK: Well, religion, of course, is a more delicate subject than most. But I don't know that it's any problem in the cartoons, because you're dealing with issues. If there is a threat to freedom of religion—including the right to have no religion—that's a perfectly good subject. But the issue there would not be religion; it would be freedom. On censorship and other matters on which churches or church people may express themselves, these are also subjects to be dealt with as specific issues, and they are generally issues of civil liberties or civil rights.

BRANDON: Do you think that merely because the audience, say, of the Washington *Post* or almost any American newspaper in any city, covers such a wide variety of political and economic views, that you try to take politically a broader approach in your drawings?

HERBLOCK: Well, I'm not sure what you mean by broader approach. I believe you should say what you think, and that's what I try to do. Many newspapers operate, as someone once said, "like department stores" these days. I don't think the size of the paper really should affect the viewpoint; I think that in its editorials a paper should say what it believes, regardless.

BRANDON: I read the other day in a book that Nixon doesn't subscribe to the Washington *Post* at home because he doesn't want his children to see your cartoons of him.

HERBLOCK: He doesn't subscribe to the Washington *Post*?

BRANDON: Not at home.

HERBLOCK: Oh, really, I didn't know that he gave this as a reason for not subscribing to the *Post*; although I had seen a newspaper story which, as I recall it, told of his complaining to the reporters that one of his children had been teased by a schoolmate because of one of my cartoons. When he was working hard to give the impression that his political opponents were Communists or Communist sympathizers, I wonder if he worried about any of their children? Actually, I think people in politics accept criticism as an occupational hazard, and they all get some of it. But most of them don't try to capitalize on their children, and their children's cocker spaniel.

A Christian View of the Future

a conversation with

DR. REINHOLD NIEBUHR

When I went to see Dr. Reinhold Niebuhr he still lived in the quiet and serene atmosphere of an old brown-stone house not far from the main center of his activities, the Union Theological Seminary. The large apartment was comfortable and tranquil and exuded an old-world charm. It was only one block off Broadway, yet it seemed remote and insulated against the hustle and bustle of New York's noisiest artery. Here Dr. Niebuhr read and wrote and received his friends.

In spite of a severe stroke he suffered a few years ago, his mind has remained sharp and alert and one cannot but be awed by his intellectual powers. He is looked after by his devoted wife Ursula, who is a theologian (formerly of Oxford University) in her own right. He continues to teach, to write books and magazine articles, and to keep up with everything that happens in domestic and international affairs. Only on preaching has he had to cut down. But even within the confines of his apartment and seated at his desk one is well aware, as he expounds his views, of the powerfully dramatic quality of his personality. His imposing figure, his strong features, his penetrating eyes and his expressive hands help to underline it. All this does not make him overpowering or intimidating. On the contrary, his deep, warm voice is reassuring to the visitor and so is his patience and understanding for other people's points of view.

Curiously enough it was his social gospel rather than his re-

ligious philosophy that made Dr. Niebuhr one of the most influential theologians in the United States over the last thirty years. It is peculiar to the twentieth century that so many theologians and philosophers withdrew into their ivory towers. They preferred to live disengaged from current streams of political and social developments. Dr. Niebuhr, however, belongs to the few who not only stood detached on the banks of these streams observing them, but who also waded into them with both feet. At times he shocked people by entering the discussion as a theologian where only sociologists or political analysts dared to tread. As a liberal Democrat his influence was at a peak during the New Deal period. But his voice continues to be listened to respectfully. Among theologians he probably has the deepest understanding of the roots of American religious thinking.

One of his favorite words is "paradox." He talks about "the moral man and immoral society," he calls the United States "the most religious and the most secular of Western nations," and he once said: "Maybe the final evil of civilization will be salvation." In a generally optimistic society he remains a skeptic, often a pessimist. Norman Birnbaum's remark that "the typical American today is, in fact, a Calvinist with neither fear of hell nor hope for heaven" sounds like another Niebuhr paradox because it also illustrates some of his own doubts about how deeply religion is imbedded in the American conscience, how much religiosity is being mistaken for Christianity.

As a Christian realist Dr. Niebuhr comes to grips with all our contemporary problems. He writes about communism, about conservatism, about socialism, about democracy, about the United Nations, and about world government. He searches for answers, but he never pretends to be a prophet.

There is also a paradox within himself. Politically he has been a liberal, at times a socialist, but as a theologian he has always been a conservative. This paradox partly explains why he became controversial, why he is sometimes difficult to understand. Even his own disciples, at times, did not find it easy to solve this paradox within themselves, and as a consequence some availed themselves only of one or the other of his conclusions. But there can be no doubt that his ideas, his relentless search into the relationship between the Christian Church and the world, have helped to stimulate the mind of modern America in a unique way.

BRANDON: The United States is a young nation but with a rich history, and it has been called on to become a world leader, so to say, at a very early age. There is a uniqueness about American Christendom, about American religious life. What is its contribution to Christianity?

NIEBUHR: The unique element in American religious life comes primarily from the degree of our pluralism. We don't have a State Church or anything approaching a State Church; we have separation of Church and State; we've a multiplicity of Protestant sects that Europe didn't have; we, significantly, have a greater Jewish population . . .

I also think it is significant that American religious life has been—at least organizationally—more vital than European religious life. This has developed through two sources: a sectarian church, which conquered the frontier—this is essentially a lay church—and the immigrant church, which was torn out of its intimate relation to its culture into a new culture, and therefore had to provide communities, integral communities, which were as integral as the sectarian community. So the late Bishop Bergraf, when he visited the Norwegian churches, said these Norwegian churches are quite different from what we have in Norway because they all run their own affairs and the laymen are very active.

America may be so religious because it is so secular, that is, it is a highly technical civilization and its communities are bound together. We're a more urban civilization in ethos than you are in England, for instance. In England everyone tries to spend at least a weekend in the country, but we're urban people. We have these urban centers, and they are essentially inhuman. And the religious communities have established communities in which, to use a high-sounding phrase, "Men are completely known and all forgiven"—at least "completely known." And that has given vitality to the religious life of America, which is, maybe not ultimately significant in terms of the history of Christianity, the history of Western civilization, but certainly it accounts for the degree of vitality of our religious life.

BRANDON: Talking about vitality, the Jewish social philosopher, Herberg, said the other day that never has so much been said about religion and so little meant by it as today.

NIEBUHR: That's true in a way. Perhaps my interpreting the significance of American Protestantism in these quasi-social terms might seem to prove that. Certainly, in America there is a great deal of religiosity, faith in faith. President Eisenhower, for instance, never tired of saying, "You must have faith." But he didn't say faith in what? Just have faith. That's religiosity. And it doesn't bother too much about the ultimate problems of human existence; this type of faith is not effective in changing the course of a nation's policy.

Another curious thing in America is the revivalism. We've got a revivalism that grew on the frontier and is a kind of leftover from the frontier: a simple perfectionism—if you bow your head and give your life to Christ he'll make you a new creature, and then you'll be color blind, there won't be a race problem, etc., etc. These are fantastic expressions and irrelevant expressions of the religious faith.

BRANDON: Do you think that Billy Graham makes a contribution to giving religious faith a direction?

NIEBUHR: His kind of faith is relevant to some tortured souls who want some kind of simple, ultimate meaning for their existence, and who want to believe that getting this will also solve the problems of the world. But I don't see how it's relevant in any other way . . .

On a television program, one of the reporters asked him, "How can you justify the religious faith and the goodness of God when so many children die prematurely?" And he said, "I'm not a theologian; but I can only say what the Bible says, and the Bible says: We all die because of our sin." Now that is a rather vulgarized interpretation of the Bible and it's certainly wrong, and it would outrage anybody who had any sense of the natural order and the patches of meaninglessness in the natural order. So I don't think that's a very good contribution. I think it was ironic that in a great city like New York he was supposed to come and "spiritualize" the city. Why, he didn't talk about any problem that had any real relevance, either to the intricate patterns of community or noncommunity, of a great city, or to the problems that we face, the larger problems of our age. There are so many Jews—incidentally, this is another aspect of the religious life of America that we ought to mention—the fact that the Jewish influence is stronger here than in any place, and I think they've made the greatest contribution to, broadly speaking, a liberal, democratic spiritual life of any group.

BRANDON: In the United States the Jews represent about 3 per cent of the population, the Catholics over 20 per cent; the Protestants about 70 per cent.

NIEBUHR: But in New York it's different. Their influence is in the cities; they're a city group. I explain it partly by their capacity for social imagination in dealing with political problems. I've dealt with more Jewish businessmen who were wealthy and who expressed their idealism not in philanthropy but in social policy. I think the first non-Jewish man of great prominence who has done the same is the present Governor Rockefeller. I'm not a Republican, but I'd say that. There you have the history of an early Christian pietism (the grandfather) coupled with buccaneer capitalism and the father turning this into large-scale philanthropy, the grandson to social policy.

BRANDON: An Indian the other day wrote that there is a real irony in that America, which inherited such spiritual legacy from the Founding Fathers and such moral giants as Abraham Lincoln, should base its outlook on materialism while the Soviets, who have been nurtured on materialism, should base their policy on what is called "pure philosophical idealism."

NIEBUHR: That's a good point, but I wouldn't say "philosophical idealism." I'd say they're "moral" idealists, after a fashion. I always find it, not only ironic but a little bit comic, when people talk about the atheists and materialists—when we're the materalists, as it were—and we have been more successful than the atheistic materialists in our practical materialism (we're not talking about the philisophical problem now). But I don't think that the Communists have philosophically turned to idealism; they still profess what they call a materialistic faith. But they have got the ideal of changing the world in some form of justice. I think it's based upon utopianism, leavened by a great deal of pragmatism.

But there is an irony in this that's rather frightening: that the Communist system and ours come together on preoccupation with standards of living. In Nixon's visit to Moscow, in his debate with Khrushchev—significantly in a model kitchen of our exhibition—he talks about gadgets, and Khrushchev either said that they were irrelevant or that they were not available for all people, or that they would have them in seven years. Now the whole debate was on the material success, the technical success of our culture. This is as ironic as to say we were the original idealists and the Communists were materialists.

BRANDON: Do you mean to say that the United States has lowered the debate between the two systems to the Russian level? To the basis of the Communist outlook rather than a more spiritual outlook—

NIEBUHR: I think that's true, but I wouldn't say that the American attitude is purely a spiritual one. I don't think that any collective attitudes are as simple as that. I would say that in the American experiment there were two sources . . . there was a New England source, the Puritans, and there was the Virginia source, Thomas Jefferson. They were both idealistic but also materialistic, because what the Puritans said was: If we're virtuous, we'll be prosperous. And what Jefferson said was (and this is a vulgar interpretation of Jefferson): We can only be virtuous if we're prosperous in a moderate sense.

BRANDON: We are often told that there is a great revival of religion in this country now. Is this correct?

NIEBUHR: I haven't seen any evidence of it, except that church membership continues to grow. I don't know the exact statistics, but in the early nineteenth century I think that only 30 per cent of the population—something like that—was in the church. Now they're over 60 per cent. This growth is partly due to as I've mentioned before: the church and the synagogue have justified themselves in the urban centers. You remember the theologian, Ernest Troeltsch, whose thesis was that religion grows in the simple attitudes of the countryside and withers in the sophistication of the city. I think American history has proved that just the opposite has occurred: that the automobile and everything else has made it wither in the countryside but it has grown in the cities, and I think partly for the reason I mentioned—immigrant churches. This is just a sociological reason; there are more ultimate religious reasons. I know the people suffer pain, frustration, face death in the cities, and in the context of a religious faith find meaning in these horrible antimonies of life which purely rational coherences don't give; that's the religious dimension of it. But one couldn't say that there's a religious revival in a sense that the religious faith, whether it be Jewish or Christian, has taken hold of the country as something impressive to the average person who wasn't previously religious.

BRANDON: You mean there is a quantitative change but not a qualitative one. Is this indicative of a crisis in religion?

NIEBUHR: I don't know about a crisis. Leaving Britain out, you've got this interesting difference; on the Continent a Protestant person is a firm believer (maybe Biblicist in our terms, but a firm believer) and there is a clear distinction between secularism and the Protestant faith as there always has been between Catholicism and secularism. In America I think we've got a more complex phenomena and that is we've got a secularism which is, on the whole, not anti-Christian or anti-religious, except in some intellectual centers but is humanitarian; it believes in the moral goals of the enlightenment. In Britain you have a secularism which has inherited many things from Christendom. On the other hand, you have a greater effort on the part of Christians to come to terms with the scientific and naturalistic culture. I must say I belong to those Christians who do try to come to terms with it and not simply oppose secularism as the source of all evil.

Now that is, I think, on the whole, good. But the bad feature of it is that you may lose the cutting quality of both a vital religious faith and, let's say, a vital secular realism. So there's an overarching sentimentality in American life for which both religious and irreligious people are partly responsible.

BRANDON: It seems to me that in this nuclear age the clouds are not very comfortable for saints to sit on. I wonder therefore how long Christianity can endure in its present form today.

After all, Mohammedanism has lost its dynamism . . . there are these fluctuations in history.

NIEBUHR: If you interpret Christianity just as an ultimate moral idea it becomes irrelevant. But I think, fortunately, Christianity is something more than that. It is, at best, an interpretation of the human situation, that not only is love the law of life but that self-love is a perennial factor in life. I think that the only valid religious faith is one that deals in a significant way with the human situation. So I wouldn't think that the fact that we are living in a collectivist age would automatically make the Christian faith irrelevant, though it would make sentimental versions of it irrelevant.

In what sense is this relevant to the great dramas of history that deal with the rise and fall of nations and the present situation of a nuclear dilemma and a cold war under this nuclear dilemma? That's a moot question. I don't think that Christians and other religious people have asked themselves searchingly enough. I think there's an answer, but it's not a very simple answer.

BRANDON: Would you like to try to go into this answer?

NIEBUHR: Ideally, a monotheistic faith claims that there's a center of meaning beyond all the systems of value that we can construct, and makes this center of meaning the righteousness of God, the justice of God, the love of God, a source of criticism not only for the individual life but for the collective life; certainly the great prophets did this. Ideally, this is the case. But religious people ought to recognize that there's no guarantee that the pious man in his religious experience will make this divine judgment a source of criticism for him. But there's always the possibility that he will make it a source of security for his value.

BRANDON: These growing doubts in our age about religion, about the concept of God, are something of a crisis for Christianity. The question that Christians must face is that the actual course of history has refuted the idea of progress and the perfectibility of man, as you had it, from the eighteenth century . . .

NIEBUHR: And I would say the ultimate religious problem is not whether we can justify belief in God, however defined rationally, but whether we can bear witness to a faith that in some sense has an idea of responsibility for its civilization (our Western civilization, for instance), and in some sense transcends it in the way that Lincoln transcended the Civil War struggle. That is, I think, the ultimate test.

And there it's rather silly for both religious and secular people to be confident that they have the answer. Secularism in the eighteenth century was created mostly by the rise of science, but also by the protest against religious fanaticism. This secularism has produced its own fanaticism, as we know: Jacobinism and Communism. So we're not dealing with a sin of religious people, but we're dealing with the human situation. That is to say, that every man and every nation tends to give a more ultimate significance to its values than it has a right to.

Now, if you transfer this to the problems of a nuclear age, any kind of intellectual discipline which will make us conscious of the fact that we're dealing in this awful struggle, not with a primitive Stalinist despotism but with a new civilization with its own elan, its own self-confidence, as Khrushchev's visit taught us . . . will make us conscious that our democracy, which we can regard as the ultimate norm of human existence, has also a very relative character.

Now any kind of intellectual discipline which will do that has a religious quality—or let me say, an ultimate quality—that transcends any simple religious answers to the question. We need not only the intellectual disciplines, but we also need a profound enough religious faith, something like Abraham Lincoln had in his day, so that people by religious imagination could grasp these two horns of the dilemma: on the one hand, responsibility—what is good in our civilization: on the other hand, an attitude of openness to the civilization which we had abhorred, and I think rightly so. Now this is a test, I think, for both secularists and religious.

BRANDON: Do you think that Christianity can have the kind of influence on Communism, such an impact, that the two worlds could come closer together?

NIEBUHR: I doubt that very much. Christianity might have greater influence than it now has on the Western world so as to make the long path of co-existence more tolerable. But as regards Communism I think it's significant that the Orthodox Church, which was banned by Stalin and then reinstituted by Stalin because it was patriotic in the World War, is still a captive church. And as I see it (now this may shock many Christians) there is no witness of the Orthodox Christianity in the realm of Communism that would have any significance for Communism except the question of life and death . . . there people turn to the Christian faith, maybe. I think they do. But so far as having relevance on changing Communist attitudes, I'm very skeptical about that.

BRANDON: What do you think, then, are the tasks the Church faces in this country today?

NIEBUHR: That's rather a large question. It faces the problem of the urban life, disintegration of the family, which I've mentioned. It faces the problem of race which it hasn't solved very well down South. This is, I think, a deeply disturbing factor. I think the parsons have been heroic but they have to give up their jobs and what not because the congregations are devoted to the Southern way of life. What does that mean? It means that the religious community is deeply imbedded in the mores of Anglo-Saxon pride, and that there hasn't been enough cutting edge of vitality in the Christian faith to dissolve that, a decent Protestantism. The Catholic Church has done better than that.

Incidentally, one might raise some questions about the vitality of pure democracy because the most democratic Protestant sects tend, on the whole, to deliver the parson to the prejudices of the local community, while Catholicism has its monolithic structure, the authority of the Bishop, the authority of the Pope, and they declare that race segregation is un-Christian, and if anybody questions it they simply use their authority to overcome that. I would not say that for this reason liberty and democracy is not valid either in religious or political life. I simply say that there are some limits of getting the absolute authority for the overarching ideal of Christianity through local communities rather than through, let us say, the Christian community. And I think that Protestants ought to recognize, when they tend to become too fanatic about Papal absolutism—which I tend to become on questions of birth control, something like that—that there are certain virtues in a monolithic religious community standing against the prejudices of local communities, at least as effectively as the political community does in its Supreme Court decisions.

BRANDON: There is not enough central direction in Protestantism, you mean.

NIEBUHR: Yes, or sense of a great community that has its own standards against the standards of the local community.

The third problem is: Is there enough vitality and imagination for the Church to contribute to the almost insoluble problems of a nuclear age where, on the one hand, you face a resolute foe who doesn't seem to want to bargain on anything and, on the other hand, you face the problem of a nuclear war. Now, if you say: Is there a Christian solution to this? I think there is a Christian approach, I think there is a religious approach that is valid. But if you say: Is there a Christian solution to this? it always turns out to be, as far as I can see, unilateral disarmament; that is to say, it's the old ethic of irresponsibility. We've got to both hold on, in some way or other, so that we're not overwhelmed by this great power and yet we have to come to terms with it. And that is, I think, a problem so great that all secular idealists and all religious idealists can make their contribution to it modestly by way of intellectual, historic disciplines, on the one hand; on the other hand, by religious imagination that comprehends the terror, the expanse, the depth and breadth of this problem. However much we may hate the foe or, let us say, fear the foe, there ought to be some residual imagination, whether it is derived from intellectual or religious imagination, that at least recognizes we're involved in a common fate, a rather terrible common fate. And the common fate or dilemma is so great that it ought to bridge some gap. Our ability to do this is, I think, the price of our survival.

The only chance that I see of survival is a gradual growth of community across the chasm of this international enmity under the umbrella of a nuclear fear—rather than any provisional disarmament setup.

Positions of Strength

---

a conversation with

VICE-PRESIDENT RICHARD M. NIXON

At the time of writing it was still uncertain whether Mr. Nixon would be the Republican candidate for the presidency. But the purpose of my interview was much broader than to seek simply the views of a potential presidential candidate; it was an attempt to elicit his political philosophy, his ideas about the role of a politician.

Neither friend nor foe will deny that Mr. Nixon is one of the most skillful practitioners in the business of politics. For a man who became notorious for his rough campaign tactics, for the use of the unfair innuendo, he seems to have done well in living down an uneasy past. Whether during President Eisenhower's illnesses or in a clinch with Mr. Khrushchev, he has shown himself capable of handling difficult situations with extraordinary deftness, and as a consequence he has gained in stature and respect. Like a flighty girl who marries well—in this case to the Vice-Presidency—he has settled down and done his best to become a pillar of society. Many still wonder what his moral resources are, what really drives him except the longing for the highest office. He is an internationalist, but his views on domestic policy lack the sweep that animate his thinking about international affairs.

When I first suggested this interview to him, he agreed to it in principle. No time was fixed. But when about three months later it was announced that he would go to England for his first formal visit there, I repeated my proposal and suggested that the ideal timing for the publication of our conversation would be the eve of his arrival in London. Mr. Nixon disagreed. He said he would prefer to do it on his return from London and his explanation was unassailable. "If I gave you an exclusive interview on the eve of my visit," he said, "all other British newspapers would be annoyed by it and as a consequence would be prejudiced against me."

He kept his word. About a week after his return from London a date was fixed and I went to see him in his office on Capitol Hill. I was allowed to enter his office before his return from a meeting of the National Security Council to set up my tape recorder. This gave me a little time to take a look around. It was not much different from anybody else's office on The Hill, except that it seemed tidier than most. There was not a single scrap of paper on his desk. On a side table I noticed a few books; a treasury of Theodore Roosevelt's speeches, Professor Norbert Wiener's The Human Use of Human Beings, and The Ugly American by Lederer and Burdick, a selection that reflects the Vice-President's varied interests. Time and again I was surprised at how much information, how many facts he has been able to store up in his mind.

Our conversation had to be done in two installments, each lasting for about one hour. It was December 1958 and Mr. Nixon at the time was deeply involved in the preparations of the next budget and the drafting of the President's State of the Union message. Each time the interview had to be sandwiched between important and probably quite exacting National Security Council sessions.

For a brief moment at the start he still seemed preoccupied with what he had been doing, but within seconds he managed to switch his attention to me and my questions. He never gave the impression of tiredness, impatience, or lack of concentration. He was always anxious to co-operate, always a little concerned whether he was giving me what I wanted. He was not quite as fluent as I had expected him to be. His replies came slowly and deliberately. He seemed to take the utmost care about the formulation of his responses and, at times, gave me the feeling that he was listening-in on himself, weighing the sound of his ideas. But he also gave me the distinct impression that he had thought about himself a great deal and about United States leadership in the world. He is generally less pragmatic than an English Tory and more conservative in economics. He is more cautious in his advocacy of an accommodation with the Soviet Union than President Eisenhower, but appears to be inclined to use the inherent powers of the Presidency more forcefully.

BRANDON: I assume, Mr. Vice-President, that you had certain expectations, certain preconceived ideas before you went to London—about Britain and British policy. Could you compare those with your impression after you've had a firsthand experience of England?

NIXON: In answering this question I will touch on two or three points on which there was a greater emphasis than I anticipated.

In the first place, there was the concern which most people in Britain in both parties expressed with regard to Britain's relationship with the Common Market. What impressed me was that the concern was not only economic, but even more with regard to the political effects that would flow from decisions made in this area. I had it well impressed upon me by British business as well as government leaders, that it was very important to try to find the solution to this problem which would avoid an impasse and an eventual economic and political division among the nations involved.

In addition to that, I had, of course, a very full discussion of the very knotty problems of Europe. There was more emphasis on this than would ordinarily have been the case because of the Berlin crisis. I was impressed by the arguments that were made very effectively by Mr. Gaitskell and members of the Opposition on the disengagement proposals. I think their approach is sincere, and lacks many of the objections that we think legitimately could be posed to some of the other proposals in this field. But, I believe, there has yet to be set forth a disengagement proposal which would not have the inherent defects of shifting the balance of military security in Europe and of endangering the continuation of the NATO alliance through the necessity of substantial withdrawals from Europe by the United States.

On the subject of our differences with regard to recognition of Communist China, I doubt whether any minds were changed by what I said, or by what those who were talking to me said, but I do believe that there is understanding in Britain as to why we have reached the decision and why our approach to it could, with some reason, be different from that of the government of Great Britain and the people there.

BRANDON: How do you see now the role of the Anglo-American alliance in the over-all American global policy?

NIXON: No one can go to London as I did, even when he has been a proponent of that alliance as I have been, without coming back even more strongly convinced of the wisdom of that view. I say this for two reasons: one, for the obvious military reason with which we are familiar, but that to me is not the primary reason. It seems to me that in the nonmilitary aspects of the world struggle that it is absolutely essential that the Anglo-American alliance be strengthened both in developing a common approach to economic problems around the world, and in developing a more effective approach in what I call the "ideological" struggle. Here we have an area where I came back with a conviction that we should make every effort in developing a more effective grand strategy aimed at winning the nonmilitary battles that are going on around the world. As I pointed out in my Guildhall speech, in winning this battle it's a mistake to say that we are doing what we do economically and ideologically in order to defeat communism. That is, of course, one of the aspects of the problem. But if we're going to win we must put it in the other context, that our major objective is to deal effectively with the problems that exist in the so-called newly-developed countries of the world, the economic problems, the governmental problems and others, to prove to these countries—to help them prove also to their own peoples—that those problems can be solved more effectively in a climate of freedom than in a climate of dictatorship.

Why is it that the Anglo-American Alliance is so important in winning this struggle? Because where ideas are going to be decisive you need the best ideas, and it is here that we must have the exchange of the best thinking that the English-speaking peoples, and our allies everywhere, can produce.

Looking at the next ten years, as distinguished from the last ten years, we're going to find that the nonmilitary area will be decisive. In the last ten years we had to put our emphasis on the military preparedness because if we had not been militarily stronger all over the world than any potential aggressor, this might have resulted in either war or surrender had we been confronted with superior force. I think actually we have won this battle. I don't mean that the danger of war or surrender, which would flow from weakness, has completely disappeared. But I believe that the strength that we have developed and the programs that I'm sure we will continue to support to maintain that strength, has reduced the possibility of both war or surrender to a very great degree, and I am convinced that within the next ten years, if war comes, it will come probably because of miscalculation, and not because of action by either side intended to initiate hostilities.

Having this in mind, then, I look at the next ten years—and I can even say the next twenty-five years—convinced that the area of greatest danger is in the economic and ideological fields. And those who oppose the great ideas for which we stand have already shifted their emphasis from the military to the economic and the ideological. They're still maintaining their military strength, but they're waging a very effective offensive in the other areas. In a nutshell, I want to say that the Anglo-American Alliance will be tremendously important in these next ten years in developing the nonmilitary strength to avoid defeat and possibly assure victory.

BRANDON: Don't you think that the Berlin crisis has been, perhaps, the most serious crisis we've had since the war? I mean, as a military crisis?

NIXON: It's very difficult, when you're in the middle of a crisis, to equate it with others. I'm sure that at the time of Lebanon, for example, we must have thought that was a serious crisis, and going back to the days of Suez, that appeared as a serious crisis because of the implications of losing the resources of the

Near East. The Berlin crisis, of course, potentially could be the most serious crisis because it is in the heart of Europe and it affects the whole NATO complex. I don't want to appear to be Pollyanna-ish, but I am convinced it represents primarily a probing action by the Soviet leaders. It's one which they do not expect and do not want to develop into a war, small or large; it's one which I do not think poses as great a danger of war as many of the observers do, who, incidentally, have good reason for their opinions. The important thing here is that we in the Anglo-American Alliance, together with our other NATO allies, develop a unified approach to resist this probing action. If we do that the possibilities of either war developing out of it, or of a defeat for the West, are very remote.

BRANDON: You made a distinction earlier between the economic struggle and the ideological struggle. It is quite clear how one can fight the economic struggle, but how do you . . .

NIXON: This is a question which we in the West have failed adequately to recognize. Let me put it this way:

I remember when I was in Asia in 1953, some of those who were Asian experts told me that all you have to do to keep Asia from going Communist is to give every Asian another bowl of rice. I think this is a great fallacy. True, the bowl of rice is tremendously important. But I have found in these countries, certainly among the leaders and among an increasing number of people in the growing middle classes and the intelligentsia, that the bowl of rice, the economic approach, is not their sole interest. They want something else out of life than simply a good living from the standpoint of housing, medical care, adequate food, etc.

Now we come to what I call the ideological struggle. I realize that it's difficult to separate economics from ideas because your ideas in the field of producing a good living are, of course, part of the ideological struggle. But what I particularly emphasize is this: we in the West are missing a very great opportunity, and we're giving up a major advantage unless we see that this struggle is fought not only in terms of which system will produce the greatest economic progress but also which system will produce the other aspects of the good life which means so much to us, and which I believe can, and will mean, just as much to peoples in other parts of the world who are having to make these decisions.

I speak, of course, of the basic freedoms which we cherish in the Western world, of the great institutions, for example, that we have among the English-speaking peoples of the common law, the parliament, freedom of expression. It is not that we should say that the system that we have will fit every country in the world. But what is important is for us to see that people of other nations realize that when they choose the way of democracy, they are getting something more than simply an economic system that will produce enough for a good living.

BRANDON: But isn't the rash of military dictatorships that we have suddenly had in the countries that have adopted, at least to some extent, our democratic system, a sign that it is very difficult to apply our kind of ideology in that part of the world?

NIXON: Yes, this is the other side of the coin. Immediately after the War many people in the Western world, and for that matter many of the new leaders in the newly developing countries, were somewhat naive as to how a change in government might affect the future of a particular nation. It was generally assumed that if a nation got independence, if the people were given the right to make their choices at the ballot box, solutions to all the economic and social problems almost automatically follow. In other words, that self-government and independence for a nation, or so-called democracy, was the key which would open the door to the great new future which the people of these countries naturally aspire to have. There's been a lot of disillusionment on that score and this is understandable. Because perhaps the most difficult government in the world to run is a democracy.

We, who live under this form of government, are aware that decisions made with regard to economic matters would be much easier if made by one individual, or a very few individuals, than to have them made by a government which had to be responsive to great masses of people. But it would be naive to assume that exactly the same procedures, the same system of government which has worked reasonably well for us, would work well for a newly independent country which may have an altogether different background and altogether different problems to solve.

But getting to the basic point of your question, there has

been great concern expressed recently about the trend away from democracy in certain countries, in Asia, the Near East, and for that matter, certain countries in Latin America. What should be our attitude? It must be understanding to begin with. Second, we must not deviate from our belief that a democratic system in the long run is the best one to provide not only economic progress, but greater freedoms as well.

I consider the present situations that have developed, for example, in the Sudan, in Pakistan, in Burma, as being not a lasting trend—simply growing pains. I don't mean that we welcome any retreat from the progress toward greater economic and political freedom, but, on the other hand, I think that we have to expect that we're going to have in these countries shifts, changes, over many, many years before there evolves the kind of government which they find is best fitted to meet the tremendous problems which they have.

I mentioned in the United Kingdom that at the present time we're discussing our budget and we think it's a terribly difficult problem. We also have a problem in the United States about what to do with our farm surpluses; we think that's very, very difficult. But none of us can really imagine what problems are until we visit countries like India and Pakistan and Indonesia, countries in which the problems are certainly not surpluses, but deficits; countries in which you do not have a highly literate population, but in which the percentage of illiteracy is extremely high, although it's moving down; and countries in which the economic problems are indicated by the fact that the per capita income in India, for example, today is 1/20th of what it is in the state of Mississippi.

We can only applaud the really tremendous efforts that are being made by the leaders of these newly developing nations to attempt to solve their tremendous problems without going all the way over to dictatorship, and who constantly try to, in effect, make democracy work in areas where democracy may not at the moment, in the form we know it, be the most effective device to accomplish the purposes they want.

BRANDON: You don't think that if we improve the economic

lot of those peoples, the ideological side will come more or less automatically?

NIXON: This is a theory which many have held. I personally cannot go along with that view, although I realize that it's held by very many responsible people. Because when you think in terms of the economic lot of these peoples, how long is it going to take and how many generations are to be denied the basic freedoms which mean so much to life, before their economic conditions are such that these freedoms can be provided for them? It is vitally important that in working for economic progress we do not lose sight of what I call the "Higher" freedoms. To the extent possible, both must come along together. And it is here that I would disagree with the line that some have taken that we put all of our emphasis on the economic side and the other will come along. I'm not sure that will happen. I think we must make every effort to try to see that economic progress, together with personal freedom, can come together.

BRANDON: What means would you use to explain our way of life to them? Do you mean just by what is often called propaganda, or—

NIXON: Well, it's here, incidentally, that I would like to see a far greater exchange of ideas between the Anglo-Americans at all levels with regard to how those methods can be improved, and not only the Anglo-Americans, but other nations who subscribe basically to the same freedoms. I will admit very candidly that we have not done an adequate job in this field, we in the United States. This is new for us, and being new we have to experiment. We frankly don't know what to do. Too often, we put ourselves in a bad light. We appear to be relying primarily on military power rather than upon ideological strength. What we have to do, I would say, is first of all to develop an over-all strategic planning as to how the ideological offensive, together with the economic offensive, the two must go together, can be waged best over the next ten years.

Now, getting to some specifics. I don't believe we should look at this just as a great public relations campaign. Perhaps there's been too much of an assumption that the answer to all of the problems of the West was simply to have bigger radio transmitters, more press releases, more motion pictures, etc., all over the so-called uncommitted part of the world. These are all devices which are effective, but effective only as your policies are effective. In other words, what we do counts really more than what we say. On the other hand, we can do well, but if we don't say it well all we do will be lost. This is our dilemma.

At the moment the area which I think is the surest one, where you can spend your money the best, is in the area of exchange of peoples. I think this can be greatly stepped up, and it should be stepped up not simply in terms of people coming to the United States and vice versa but all over the world. And for that reason I have been a strong proponnet for a new approach in this field of exchange because I don't think we're getting a maximum amount of the type of program that is most effective.

BRANDON: It's been said by students of the American Presidency that there are three different concepts of handling it—the Buchanan concept, followed by men like Grant and Taft and Coolidge, etc., with the President as the chief administrator and conciliator; the Lincoln concept, followed by men like Jefferson and Jackson and the two Roosevelts, which sees the President as the main source of legislation, as the principal political leader who considers parties and politics as creative instruments; and then the third, the Cleveland concept, which swings between the two, but basically sees the Presidency as a defensive function, not to lead but to prevent bad things from happening. Which of the concepts would you think the most effective in guiding the country today?

NIXON: Well, I want to make it clear that I consistently decline to answer any questions as to what I would do in the event that I were confronted with the problems of the Presidency. I think you will see the inappropriateness of my—

BRANDON: It's a question of philosophy—

NIXON: If this is a question of philosophy I would say that, first of all, I do not see as sharp a delineation between these three concepts as some analysts of the American political scene. Part of the difference here is due to the requirements of the times. For example, you spoke of the two Roosevelts: in both those periods the country required and needed the leadership qualities which both of these men gave the Presidency. On the other hand, there are times, for example, speaking of President Coolidge, when the country did not need and perhaps would not have wanted that kind of leadership. One can call it "back-to-normalcy" and other deprecating terms, but this was the mood of the country at the time. The other factor, of course, is the personality of the men involved.

In this last half of the twentieth century, the American Presidents are going to have to be men who have strong convictions; they're going to have to be leaders and men who can make the right decisions in times of crisis and, in addition, win the support of the people for those decisions which might otherwise be unpopular. The United States over a long period of time must continue to have leadership which will help to inspire that will and determination that is required to win the struggle in which we are engaged.

The crucial struggle in the last half of this century will not only be in terms of the world conflict. Within the United States and in other countries around the world, a great philosophical battle will be waged on this issue: Shall we go along with the trend toward increasing substantially the roles of responsibility of government, toward placing more reliance upon government activity, because of the desire of individuals to have government do for them things which they might otherwise have to do for themselves? Or should this trend be resisted, and should we be careful not to let government move into areas which would weaken the responsibility of the individual citizen and diminish his contribution to the national progress we all desire. I believe it would be a great tragedy if the legacy of this generation for the generations ahead, was that we reduced the role of individuals in our society at the expense of increasing the role of government.

At the same time I recognize that if our economy is to be dynamic, if it is to meet the goals that we want it to meet, government must assume the responsibility of supplementing what individuals are unable or will not do for themselves. Government must provide a floor for security, although no ceiling on opportunity, and it has the responsibility in addition to stimulate to the greatest extent possible the maximum growth of the economy.

But I believe that if the American economy is to have its

maximum growth there must eventually be substantial reforms in our tax system, not with the idea of reducing the over-all income from taxes, because we need what we're getting at the present time and probably even more, but from the standpoint of re- forming that system to increase the over-all productivity of the economy.

BRANDON: Do you think Congress is today asserting itself too much in trying to lead the country?

NIXON: No, I would not quarrel with the Congressional leader- ship on this score. I have a great respect for the principle of division of powers within our government, the responsibility of the co-equal branches to make their contribution to government policy. I think very frankly there is room for constructive thinking and leadership on both national and international problems in both the Congressional and the Executive branch of the government. I don't mean by that that the Congress should usurp authority from the executive, because in most instances I think our administration's views will be ones which the Congress will want to endorse as its own.

BRANDON: There is a widespread feeling in the world, especially in that part which depends much upon American leadership, that Congressional procedures are outdated. It takes months for Congressional committees, invaluable time of hundreds of officials, to grind out decisions. Many also wonder about Congress's in- creasing temptation to oversimplify the realities of the crucial issues that will decide the fate not only of the United States, but Western civilization. Do you think there is room for some basic reform of Congressional procedures?

NIXON: There's no question but that the procedures of our legislative bodies must be re-examined from time to time so that they will be adequate to meet the changing problems that con- front us in the world. However, in attempting to get the speed, which we may think is necessary for passage of legislation, we must not deny in the process the time for adequate debate. It is important that in changing rules we don't do anything which would deny to a minority an adequate opportunity to raise its objections.

I believe the Senate, at the beginning of each new Congress, should have the power to change its rules, if it so desires. I've always felt that the present rules were weighted too much on the side of dilatory, filibustering tactics, and not enough on the side of action. On the other hand, I would not go to the extreme, as some have suggested, of providing for a cutting-off of debate by a simple majority of those present in the Senate at any particular time, because I think that might cut off debate before adequate consideration was provided.

In a democracy we believe in rule by majority, but in a democracy it's always important to protect the rights of the minority.

BRANDON: Do you think politics is an art or a science?

NIXON: It's been called worse than either of those two terms, as you are well aware. Those of us who participate in this—shall I call it "the business of politics"—would like to think that at its best politics is both an art and a science. It is a very inexact science, of course, because it deals primarily not with things which are susceptible of being measured, but with peoples whose problems and attitudes are not susceptible of being measured accurately, even by Dr. Gallup with his fine polling techniques.

In this connection I have little patience for an attitude which became quite fashionable during the early thirties when I was in college, the tendency to think that elected officials are generally intellectually inferior individuals who have very little integrity and who are concerned primarily with their personal advancement rather than the interest of the nation at large. I have found myself that those who chose politics as a career are, in the main, honorable, above average in their intellectual equipment, and effective in getting action on problems that less practical people only talk or write about.

BRANDON: Politicians who have a sense of responsibility, I think you were referring to them, are often confronted with a dilemma between fierce public pursuit of their partisan ideas and the ethics of political fair-play. What do you think *are* the kind of rules, or principles, to guide the politicians in our society in the art of politics?

NIXON: We start with the basic cliché, that an individual must be a politician before he can be a statesman. That means, of course, that in order to be able to affect the course of events in a legislative body, or in a nation, an individual must first gain the support of a majority of the voters in his constituency, and then must keep that support by his actions, not only by what he does but by what he says in political campaigns.

Now, in each political campaign each candidate is confronted with the dilemma to which you refer. How can he get his case across, and at the same time maintain the statesmanlike approach? The answer is that it's a question of judgment in each particular campaign. What kind of a campaign is your opponent waging? What kind of a campaign is needed in order to alert the people to the issues? What kind of a campaign is needed in order to sharpen the issues?

As most people are aware—certainly as my critics are very much aware—I believe in vigorous sharp debate in the halls of Congress. I do not go along with a current popular view that the primary aim of a political figure is to be all things to all men, although I realize that no individual likes to be put in that category. This may make him a pretty good politician but he won't be much of a statesman. Today in the United States in the area of foreign policy, and in some of the great decisions that are being made with regard to the future course of our domestic economy, we should have the kind of hard-hitting debate that sharpens the issues, so that the people know what the choice is.

In the course of that kind of debate at times personalities inevitably become involved. I would say that the general rule that should be followed is that the personality of your opponent—his record and his statements—should properly be brought into the debate only when the personality is inextricably tied to the issue, when that is the most effective way of making the issue properly understood.

BRANDON: Actually the controversy about yourself centered around your way of attributing odious motives. Now I am wondering, since there has been talk about the "old" and the "new" Nixon, and so on, how your thinking has developed over the years.

NIXON: With regard to the past, I believe that those who are attempting to evaluate my record should go to the source rather than to those who may have analyzed that record from perhaps a nonobjective point of view. You refer to the motives that I am alleged to impute to my opponents. I have consistently maintained that, where the record that an individual makes, his record of voting, his public remarks on issues, indicates how he might approach an international or a national problem, that record should be brought to the attention of the people. I expect *mine* to be brought forth, and I think it's my responsibility to present the records of my opponents in that respect. Now sometimes a record may be one that is not going to be particularly popular with the people when it is brought forth, but in that instance I have never considered that it is unfair tactics to relate the record of the opponent on all issues if you do it only after you have personally checked it, as I always do in my own campaigns, for its accuracy.

BRANDON: Of late, I think, you have presented a case for a more conservative policy than you had in previous years.

NIXON: In the field of foreign policy, beginning with the Marshall Plan and the Greek-Turkish Aid Program, I have consistently supported our mutual security program. In addition to that, I have always insisted that the nonmilitary aspects of the world struggle are the most critical ones confronting us.

Now let us take the issue of civil rights. Since the time I've entered Congress, I've taken what would be called a strong position on this issue. Part of this is due to my college education, Quaker school, and the like.

As far as my economic philosophy is concerned, it has always been what I would call a conservative philosophy, conservative certainly on fiscal matters, conservative in the sense that I believe that, generally speaking, private enterprise can do a more effective job than government enterprise in any particular field, although I recognize that there are some areas where private enterprise can't or won't do the job and where government enterprise must step in.

The philosophy of the Democrats that the best way to assure social and economic progress was through increasing the government participation in total economic effort and decreasing proportionately the private participation, I termed as "radical."

BRANDON: What do you foresee should be the future course of the Republican party?

NIXON: Well, I would say the Republican party should take a very good leaf out of the book of the Conservative party in Britain. As a matter of fact, I have been studying at considerable length the techniques of the Conservative party in Britain. Of course, the pattern the Conservative party follows will not apply here. But in a nutshell, the Republican party on the organization side has been very deficient.

So our first problem is one of organization, and before we can get organization we have to get adequate financing; in order to get the financing you have to have a new plan. So one—

BRANDON: In terms of Republican philosophy—

NIXON: That's the second one. Once we get the organization, we get the financing to get our case across, we then come to the key point, which is that we must get across to the American people a more accurate picture of what we stand for. Too many of the American people believe that the Republican party works only in the interest of big business, that we work against the interests of the wage earners, that we're not for the farmers, and that the Democratic party is the party of the people and that the Republican party is the party of the so-called vested interests. The fact that those arguments have gotten across is, of course, a tribute to the skill of our opponents, but also it's a condemnation of ourselves that we haven't been doing an effective job of telling the people what we really stand for.

I believe that the Republican party in the international field must take a strong, affirmative position. We must not be satisfied with the obviously sound policies of military strength and diplomatic firmness which are essential to avoid war or surrender. We must make it clear that our aim is not just the negative one of maintaining the status quo in the nonmilitary area, but that we have the determination and ability to develop the strategy which will win that battle. In addition, the Republican party must stand foursquare in our devotion to and advocacy of equality of opportunity in the education, employment, and other fields for all our citizens.

On the economic side, we must make it clear that we stand for fiscal responsibility, for example, that we can and will deal effectively with the problem of inflation. The difficulty too often in the past has been that Republicans in stating their economic philosophy appear to be taking a negative, status quo, reactionary position. We must make it clear that the reason we oppose huge new government spending programs is not because we oppose the goals of the programs but because we know they won't produce what they promise and we must, at the same time, show how our policy can accomplish these very objectives.

BRANDON: It's been suggested that because labor is so committed to the Democratic party that the Republican party should take a definite stand on that.

NIXON: No, I do not believe that the Republican party should take a position against labor; I do not go along with the idea that there should be a Labor party and a Conservative party in the United States. That may work, for example, in the United Kingdom; I don't believe it fits in our system here.

Born into Controversy

a conversation with

SENATOR JOHN F. KENNEDY

This conversation took place over breakfast, between orange juice and poached eggs, in Senator Kennedy's charming old house in Georgetown, that fashionably old-fashioned enclave in the middle of Washington. It was probably the senator's most leisurely hour of the day, for two weeks before the nomination convention his drive for delegates, his efforts to give momentum to his "bandwagon" was nearing fever pitch.

Senator Kennedy apologized for being five minutes late. His own plane, because of engine failure, had reached Washington only at 3 A.M., but now, at 8:45 A.M., he was all dressed, and ready to throw himself into another frenzied day.

The table had been laid on the shady patio. When the senator saw that there was no electric connection for my tape recorder there, he asked his colored valet to serve breakfast inside. We quickly settled down in the soft, comfortable, satin-covered chairs under a gay, airy blue sky of a Boudin painting. There was a quiet, ethereal elegance about the house. White and yellow predominated with touches of red here and there, all unobtrusively matched. The many art books on bookshelves and on various little tables were added proof that in this house Mrs. Kennedy's taste prevails.

After a sip of juice the senator indicated that he did not want to lose any time, that I should proceed. There were no last-minute questions, no reservations, no fuss, no nervousness. It seemed all part of normal business. This was a politician who knew what his duties were and he accepted them not without relish. His answers never betrayed emotion or excitement or irritation. Nor did his face twitch or his eyes blink when I thought I might have touched a sensitive nerve. No question, however personal or wide-ranging, seemed to present a problem. This was an orderly mind speaking. It had sifted every problem in sight and the answers came forth crisp and concise and without hesitation. In spite of the bland, monotonous voice he sounded deeply involved in the great issues of our time. In spite of his casual, dispassionate manner, what he said carried conviction in a sober, reasonable way, yet it was difficult to judge how deeply these convictions were moored in his conscience.

I have known "Jack" Kennedy for a few years, but even now I did not have the feeling that I knew him. Curiously enough, even those who have known him all their life, who have gone to school with him, feel the same way. He is so self-contained, so detached that it is not easy to discern what moves him inside, what inner forces sustain him.

I have always thought of Jack Kennedy as a curious mixture of playboy and earnest student of history and politics. His driving ambition eluded me at first. It was hidden behind his aristocratic casualness. Only a month or so before the Democratic Convention in 1956 when he asked me whether I thought that he should try for the Vice-Presidential nomination, did I realize how high he aimed. Nor did I suspect that he had the ability to master-mind as momentous an operation as a drive for the Presidency. But he is a child of his times. He instinctively knows how to use all the techniques of the modern mass media to his best advantage. He also knows his weaknesses. He does not try to hide them, he meets them head-on.

His candor and his intellectual curiosity are probably his two most attractive traits. They may be the reasons why intellectuals are eager to work for him. To them he represents a new generation in politics, a new type liberal, a man with "growth potential." Essentially he is a pragmatist, a tough-minded realist, a utilitarian humanist. He may lack warmth, he may be cold and calculating, but those eager to work for him suspect or at least hope that he would follow up ideas with action. Here is a man, they think, who

178

*not only knows how to gather good brains around him and knows
how to pick them, but who also has the talent to create an
effective political machine.*

*The interview ended as abruptly and as casually as it started.
There was an urgent meeting on the Hill and he dashed out and
into his convertible and drove off. As I closed my tape recorder
and got ready to go, I noticed that while I had gobbled up
everything on my breakfast tray, he had hardly touched the eggs
or the bacon or the toast . . .*

June 13, 1960

BRANDON: When did it first occur to you to try for the Presidency?

KENNEDY: I suppose after the Vice-Presidential race for the
nomination at the 1956 Democratic Convention. I began to play a
more active part in the 1956 campaign more as a national figure
than just merely a Massachusetts figure. And then after Governor
Stevenson was defeated in 1956, in early 1957 I began to consider
the prospect very strongly.

BRANDON: Was it because you felt there was an open field, or
was it because of some compulsion?

KENNEDY: Well, I think there were two reasons. First, in a sense,
there was an open field and, therefore, there was the opportunity
—there were indications that my name was being considered along
with other candidates. The most important part, of course, is that
it's quite obvious that the Presidency has become the key office.
I've been in Congress now for fourteen years, and while the Constitution makes us an equal and co-ordinate branch of the government, the pressure of events and the change in circumstance give
the President a predominant influence. This is essential—particularly for the successful conduct of foreign affairs. Therefore,
I really run for the Presidency for the same reason that I ran for
the House fourteen years ago and for the Senate eight years ago:
I'm strongly interested in the direction in which the United States
goes and the role it plays and the responsibilities it meets, and the
Presidency is the center of action.

BRANDON: What do you think are the basic qualities a President must have and that you feel you have?

KENNEDY: Well, I think a President certainly must have, we would hope, character, judgment, vigor, intellectual curiosity, a sense of history, and a strong sense of the future. Many other qualities would be advantageous but I would say these qualities were essential for any successful President.

BRANDON: It has been said that your youth and your Catholic religion are against you.

KENNEDY: Yes. Both of those factors were regarded strong on the debit side; but they were not wholly debit. Youth—I've come on to the political scene at a time when the leadership is old. The President is old, his health has been affected, his leadership is not wholly successful, and therefore I think there is a desire to turn a new page and start with a newer leadership, fresher, and we hope more vigorous. I am not sure that youth has not been a real asset, even though it has its debit side too.

My religion is a matter of great political concern and has made me a controversial figure. In that sense I was evidently born into controversy. But I don't know whether it wasn't advantageous—looking at the situation as it was in '57, '58, and '59—to be controversial in one way or another.

BRANDON: It makes the whole country aware of you—

KENNEDY: Well, I think you have to look at the way it turned out. I think the prospects of my being nominated are good—and my religion and my youth are with me—so I can't say that they were wholly obstacles to be overcome, in the political sense.

BRANDON: Do you think now, after your victory in West Virginia which has only 5 per cent Catholics, that religion is still a key issue in American politics?

KENNEDY: Yes, it is, but I think it's far less. For a while it looked like it was the only issue and that was, of course, most unfortunate. Now it is an issue among many issues—but it is an issue. The whole fight for religious freedom, the whole struggle of the Reformation, the whole character of the United States, all these things make the prospect of a Catholic President a matter of serious concern to a good many Americans. The majority of these Americans want certain questions answered, and when they're answered in a responsible way I think they are then prepared to move on to the other serious problems facing the United States. Some will never accept any answer—

BRANDON: One's always heard about the opposition among protestant voters, but do you think there is an opposition to you among the Catholic hierarchy?

KENNEDY: Some—but I would hope that those that are Republican would support a Republican candidate. The corollary of the desire not to be voted against merely because of my religion is also the hope that those who are co-religionists will not vote for me because of my religion. So if there is opposition among the hierarchy, I would hope that it's confined to those members of the hierarchy who are Republican.

BRANDON: There have been signs . . . for instance, in the statement on birth control and some of the editorials in *Osservatore Romano* that, in one way or another, were critical comments on your candidacy.

KENNEDY: I don't hold that view. I don't think my candidacy was in their minds. That may be a good or a bad fact, but I think they have a longer view than the 1960 election. They, therefore, were not really thinking of the implications of their statements on my candidacy, and I think that's probably just as well. If the hierarchy ever began to bend its statements to suit my candidacy, then the charge would be proved that there is an improper, or unwise, connection between Catholic politicians and the Catholic Church. My point is that there is not, and the very fact that these statements have been made, which have had in some ways a potentially harmful effect on my candidacy, indicates that they're not engaged in a Popish plot.

BRANDON: I've heard it said that one of the reasons why the Catholic Church would not like to see a Catholic President in this country is that the United States is one of the few—perhaps the last country—where the Church can still gather new members, where there is still a fairly wide field for the missionaries, and the figures prove the Catholics have made great gains in this country in the last few years and that more gains can still be made, but that with a Catholic President perhaps this would not be quite so easy.

KENNEDY: Well, I don't know who holds that particular view, but

I don't hold it at all and I don't feel that it would be wise for Catholics to withhold themselves from the office of the Presidency in order to affect the policy of the Church in the United States. I can't believe that view is held seriously by many members of the hierarchy and, if it is, I disagree with it. I can't believe that the religion of the President is going to affect the decision by many Americans as to which church they're going to embrace. If it does, then their conversion is not very soundly based. I don't know what President Eisenhower's religion is—what is he, a Presbyterian?

BRANDON: Yes.

KENNEDY: I'm not sure he has many converts, has he? Or prevented many from moving into the Presbyterian church?

BRANDON: Well, I think they're not in the same—conversion "business" are they? (*Laughter*)

KENNEDY: They all follow the desire to spread their message. I hope they do.

BRANDON: Well, if, as a President, you've got to contradict the dogma, don't you think that would create difficulties for the Church?

KENNEDY: What dogma?

BRANDON: The idea, for instance, that as the *Osservatore Romano*, the Vatican mouthpiece put it, although members of the Church enjoy a "wide autonomy," they should allow no split between "the believer and the citizen."

KENNEDY: It seems to me that the position of the Catholic Church in the United States is quite clear in support of the Constitution—in support of the separation of church and state; I strongly support it. If one held the view suggested in the question, it seems to me really I shouldn't be a United States Senator because I take the same oath the President takes in regard to defending the Constitution.

BRANDON: Well, take the issue of birth control—

KENNEDY: What about it?

BRANDON: I mean, if the Church says "This is our position," and you contradict it, you don't think that would create problems for them?

KENNEDY: The office holder is bound by his oath of office which he takes to defend the Constitution, which he swears to in an oath or affirmation, an oath he swears to God. It would be an extremely serious offense to violate that oath. The separation of church and state provides for the President to exercise his best judgment as to what is the way the Constitution can best be defended and the United States can be defended.

In my opinion there is no conflict. If there were, then, of course, you would say that no man of my religion could take that oath. Catholic judges grant divorces every day, even though they, themselves, do not believe in divorce. You have to make a distinction between your private obligation and then your public duty as a public official. I find it not difficult at all to make this distinction.

It seems to me the point is belabored. If you accepted the view that a President was unable to fulfill his Constitutional oath of office because of his religion, then you'd really have to say that a senator or a congressman of that religion was unable to fulfill his oath of office. The principle is the same. We've worked all this out quite successfully in this country. Two chief justices of the Supreme Court have been Catholics, for instance. I don't think we've found it difficult to make a distinction on the whole between what is Caesar's and what is God's.

BRANDON: Politicians who have a sense of responsibility are confronted with the dilemma between fierce public pursuits of their partisan ideas and the ethics of political fair play. What are the rules that guide you in the art of politics?

KENNEDY: Well, I think a breach of the canons of fair play usually ends in defeat. I think there are self-regulators in politics as there are in other areas of life. I think the most successful politicians rarely transgress.

BRANDON: It is often said about the father-son relationship that sons either rebel against their father or, on the contrary, they are a chip off the old block. How do you see your relationship to your father?

KENNEDY: I would say that the great majority of cases of father-son relationships really don't fall into either category that you describe. There are many disagreements. In my particular case there are many disagreements on policy and have been for a great many years. He has a wholly different view of what the role of the United States ought to be in the world than I have had in the fourteen years I've been in Congress. And on many domestic matters he has substantial differences of opinion. But it's not a matter really of discussion. We do disagree and therefore I'm not going to attempt to convert him, and he does not attempt to convert me, so it's outside of our personal relationship which is very satisfactory.

BRANDON: Is perhaps his pride in a son who might become President greater than his desire to see him agree with his own ideas?

KENNEDY: No, I don't think it's that at all. I think it's merely that he feels he has a large family, that they should determine their own lives and make their own decisions. His responsibility is not to impose his political views on his children. It makes a much more successful and lasting relationship, I think, when a parent does not.

BRANDON: If it isn't the father, then, who, or what, influenced you in your political thinking?

KENNEDY: Experience and my own observation, pragmatic judgment—all these. In addition, I think the world around us influenced me and my judgment. Now he may see the world from a different perspective. But I can't believe that all sons fall into either echoing their father's view or being rebels. I would hope that for the great majority the relationship would be comparable to mine. Living in a different generation, facing entirely different problems, they make their own decisions—but their personal relationship remains harmonious.

BRANDON: Arthur Miller said to me the other day that if an international crisis sufficiently intense gripped the United States, McCarthyism would recur, because it was the conservatives that defeated him, not the liberals or the left, not the people who knew what he was about. Do you agree with this?

KENNEDY: Well, I'm not sure that any historical period repeats itself in the exact same form. I do think the words "appease" and "soft on Communism" and all the rest have been thrown around with some vigor in the last month or so since the U-2 crisis. Senator Scott of Pennsylvania stated that it was necessary for Governor Stevenson and myself to come and relieve ourselves of the suspicion of being "appeasers" because we didn't happen to agree with the way the administration handled the U-2 flight. Now, it does indicate that there are those in the United States who would be glad to take the ax off the wall if political pressures sufficiently disturb them and go back to the old techniques.

BRANDON: Would you take a much stronger position in future than you once took on McCarthyism?

KENNEDY: I don't agree with the technique, if that's your question, nor did I ever.

BRANDON: It used to be Churchill's definition that Britain's foreign policy is based on three circles with Britain in the middle: one, the Anglo-American Alliance; the other, Europe; and the third, the Commonwealth. I think this basis has become somewhat obsolescent. I am wondering how you see the role of Britain in the world today.

KENNEDY: I would say the three circles are still there. The Anglo-American Alliance is certainly a basic element in the foreign policy of both countries. The Commonwealth tie is pre-eminent. The area of recent concern, of course, has been the third circle, the relationship between Great Britain and Europe. As the power of the United States, the Commonwealth, and Europe have developed, of course, it has affected the relative position of Great Britain, but she still remains a connecting link between the three circles.

BRANDON: Do you think Britain should actually join the Common Market?

KENNEDY: That's a decision that Britain ought to make. It's not for an outsider to recommend any trade policy toward a country with all the complex problems that Great Britain faces. Her people are better judges whether she should do that or not. Perhaps the British could have taken a more affirmative policy in the last three years toward that whole development, but I'm not sure it would be wise for us to attempt to advise her at this point.

BRANDON: Would you like to see a supra-national authority in Europe? I mean, a development in that direction?

KENNEDY: Yes, I would. I think we can go ahead in trade and we can go ahead in other areas. But I think there is a quite obvious limit beyond which, at least in the near future, it won't proceed.

BRANDON: Sooner or later the United States will have enough

185

ICBMs not to need bases in Europe. Do you think this would lead to a policy much more independent of Europe?

KENNEDY: No, I think that the ties are very basic between the United States and Europe, and the need for co-operation will persist, perhaps even more strongly. There are many areas that we can approach on a common basis. I don't think that our need for bases abroad explains our interest in the development of the resurgence of Europe in the last fifteen years at all. I think a vigorous, free Europe, with expanding economies, playing a proportionate role in assisting the underdeveloped world, playing its proper role in the defense of the West—these are great common objectives which transcend the location of military bases.

BRANDON: You mean that NATO would survive this development?

KENNEDY: Well, NATO in the sense of military guarantees of Western Europe against attack—in the sense that there's a pooling of military effort—that would certainly survive, and I hope would survive in a more vigorous form in other areas so that the energies of Western Europe and the United States can be more effectively pooled in the newer areas of responsibility. The military situation may change, but I think the basic tie will remain which can be expressed through NATO.

BRANDON: When you say "military," you mean the question of American troops in Europe?

KENNEDY: No, I mean the bases. It certainly would be wise to continue American troops in Europe even when we may no longer need the air bases. Those troops are there not merely to defend the air bases, but also as a guarantee of our determination to meet our commitments under NATO and to West Germany and to Berlin. As long as Berlin is in a state of inflammation, I would think the troops would remain regardless of whether the bases would be needed or not.

BRANDON: In view of the fact that Germany will remain divided for ten years—maybe more—will it be possible to maintain the present situation in Berlin that long?

KENNEDY: I don't think anybody can say what's going to happen in the next ten years. I would say that the United States could not afford, nor could Europe, nor could West Germany, nor Berlin, afford to see West Berlin's freedom lessened. I would think that would continue to be our objective. I don't know what the situation in Germany is going to be or what the situation is going to be in Berlin; I don't know what the policy of the Soviet Union is going to be for the next decade but, at least, that basic premise must remain in our hearts.

BRANDON: Do you think we could maintain a free Berlin with the help of the United Nations?

KENNEDY: Though the main burden for the freedom of West Berlin will continue to rest on the United States, Britain, France, and the Germans themselves, nevertheless, the participation of the United Nations in their guarantees would be advantageous.

BRANDON: If you look in a broad sweep at American-Russian relations, say, for the next ten years, what do you forsee?

KENNEDY: I envisage it as a continuing competitive struggle with periods of relative warmth and periods of bitter cold. I don't imagine there will be a sharp enough change within the Soviet Union itself, or within China, in the next decade to cause a complete reversal of the present policies. The tempo may change; the goals will not. I say this with some degree of hesitation because the world has changed in so many ways the last ten years, certainly in the last fifteen years. But I would judge—based on the information we have at present—that the competitive struggle will continue and will be affected in its vigor by the actions that we take.

BRANDON: De Gaulle seems to think that sooner or later we may be able to bring Russia onto the side of the West in defense against the Chinese. Do you think it would be impossible to—

KENNEDY: There isn't any doubt that there seems to be some difference in outlook and in philosophy between the Soviet Union and China. But I would think it would be some years away before you could expect there would be a greater community of interest between the Soviet Union and the West than there is between the Soviet Union and the Chinese Communists.

BRANDON: Do you think it will be possible to keep the Chinese as much excluded from the world community, from the United Nations, as at present?

KENNEDY: I would think if their policies would change, if there would be some indication they wish to live in harmony with us and with the countries to the south, that they desire to work out the problems of the areas on which there is disagreement, then I would think the relationship would become more harmonious. But I think anyone's naïve to believe that under present conditions, by bringing the Chinese Communists into the United Nations they would relax their vigor, their outward drive or inward drive.

BRANDON: Do you think the U.S. could afford to give up Formosa?

KENNEDY: In exchange for what? Or for what reason, or under what conditions? It might be possible that Formosa would be recognized as an independent country, and so on, but it would depend a good deal on what the relationship was between the United States and Communist China—how vigorous they were in carrying out their present Stalinist policies—how hard they were pushing against India and Burma. I think that the United States should attempt to encourage the Chinese Communists to come into the present negotiations at Geneva on disarmament and nuclear testing. If they are successful, we can possibly get other areas of negotiation on problems which may divide us: the admission of newspaper men, travel, and so on, and begin to lay a foundation for a more satisfactory relationship. But, under present conditions, I'm not optimistic that the Chinese Communists are at all desirous of paying a price they would have to pay—at least in relaxing their aggressive intentions—by entering into harmonious relations with us or by meeting the conditions which are set for admission to the United Nations. I think they're far more determined, far more ruthless, and that they in some ways rather like the present condition which permits them to pursue their objective with little restraint.

BRANDON: And how do you feel about the offshore islands?

KENNEDY: I think it was unwise for us to draw the line at Quemoy and Matsu. They're not essential to the defense of Formosa and they are rather difficult to defend. I objected at the time of the Formosa Resolution to their inclusion five years ago, and I said on several occasions that this was not the place to draw the line. Formosa we should defend, however.

BRANDON: What kind of lessons do you draw from the summit fiasco?

KENNEDY: Well, I think we should realize how tentative are the signs of *improvement* in the relations between the United States and the Soviet Union. They can always turn cold again and we should maintain our strength in every area of national life so that if the negotiations are successful, we gain; if they're unsuccessful, we have the means of protecting our security and our commitment. That's the first.

Secondly, I thought it was unwise to have the U-2 flights so close to the summit. I thought the lack of executive co-ordination and the lack of preparation for this engine failure contributed to the disastrous summit meeting.

BRANDON: Would you want to resume the U-2 flights again?

KENNEDY: No, I think they're gone as a method of gaining intelligence—it would be far too provocative and dangerous to continue them.

BRANDON: And how do you feel about going to another summit meeting?

KENNEDY: Not unless there had been some reasonably successful action at the secondary level, either at the foreign minister level or the ambassadorial level or at the United Nations so that we had some reason to believe the summit would be successful, that the Russians were genuinely interested in it.

BRANDON: You've done so much in promoting aid to India, have you thought about an approach to the African problem?

KENNEDY: Well, it's somewhat different because, in the first place, there are many countries and few of them are in the advanced state of development which permits the kind of effective assistance which I think we could provide for India. You have therefore a lower level of economic development in the free African nations which requires a different kind of effort by the United States than India does. Teachers, economic assistance, grants, educational funds, medical exchanges—all these we can do usefully. And, I think, we need to have a more sympathetic attitude toward their aspirations.

BRANDON: In your Algerian speech in July 1957 you used a phrase: "The Western house must be swept clean of its own lingering imperialism."

KENNEDY: Well, I think an impressive job has been done on

that. There are still areas where the Western house isn't clean, and there are people who are compelled to maintain their ties to Western Europe unwillingly. But I would say that great progress has been made in the last fifteen years in freeing Africa from the remnants of Western imperialism.

I don't think there's any doubt at all that Africa is going to be free in another decade. The big problem now is going to be what will happen in those free countries, whether they will be able to maintain a free society. Are they going to be able to solve the staggering problems that they face? As people hope more and more that life will be more generous to them, the great problem is making the benefits of life shared more generously. That's going to be a great problem for the African leaders and for us who have a stake in free Africa.

BRANDON: You know, the British have been trying to meet the African problem, or the African people, more than halfway, and I think they've come to the conclusion that there is no more halfway.

KENNEDY: Well, democracy is a very sensitive plan. The desire for political independence is, so to speak, the tide that is sweeping Africa. Building something on it, particularly building democracy on it, I think is going to be extremely difficult.

The Africans are determined to take the road to freedom, and it's proper they should take it. The most challenging days for Africa are still ahead. And one of the problems is that there is a great area of ignorance here and lack of interest about Africa. African policy is a matter of great debate among the British parties and there's a good deal of discussion in all the political periodicals of Great Britain. There's comparatively little information about Africa here in the United States. It's not a political issue. There's no strong feeling. It is still the Dark Continent from the point of view of information.

BRANDON: A lot has been written about the waste of American wealth for the production of unnecessary goods. How should the United States use its affluence wisely to live up to its global commitments and to enable her to lead Western society?

KENNEDY: I do think that if we're going to play our role as a great defender of freedom—to meet all of our commitments, to prepare ourselves for a population which is going to be double what we have today—we have to continue to maintain our "capital structure." We have to develop our natural resources, build schools and hospitals, homes and recreational facilities and all the rest. And that requires a public effort, not merely a private satisfaction of our needs. That requires the local, state, and national governments to meet their responsibilities. And that's always a struggle because it requires draining off from private consumption, which is immediate, funds for public consumption, which is less obvious to the individual.

BRANDON: But how are you going to persuade people to produce, say, fewer television sets?

KENNEDY: I'm not suggesting really that they produce fewer television sets—

BRANDON: Well, washing machines—

KENNEDY: Well, washing machines—I don't think that is particularly affluence. I think that the washing machines and television sets contribute to our life. Washing machines relieve heavy burdens and television does open up a window to a lot of people. I would say that we must persuade people that there are certain expenditures in the public sectors that must be made—that this is a commitment which must be met. With what remains—with everything the government is not required to appropriate through the taxing powers—the people themselves shall determine how they shall spend it. They can do a better job on that perhaps than we can. But I do think that the needs of the public services must be met.

BRANDON: You are really talking about regulation by taxation rather than by rationing.

KENNEDY: The purpose is not regulation. The purpose is to secure sufficient tax funds so that we can fulfill these public commitments that must be met so that we have a harmonious life for our people. We're not attempting to direct tastes. I don't think we've come to that yet and I don't think we're particularly equipped to do it in the government.

Laughing at Oneself

a conversation with

WALT KELLY

When some years ago a newspaper strike deprived New Yorkers of their daily diet of comic strips Mayor La Guardia went on the air and read the "funnies" to his citizenry to keep it happy and up-to-date on the latest exploits of Dick Tracy, Li'l Abner, Terry and the Pirates and all the other heroes Americans grow up with and keep a lifelong companionship. This humane gesture, at the time, was received with relief and profound gratitude.

It was, perhaps, the most flamboyant proof that comic strips are part of the American social scene. To follow them is like walking up and down the escalator of the American "way of life." Do they reflect a nostalgia for youth, since most of their readers are grownups, or are they just a convenient escape from the front-page news? Perhaps they are simply an addiction like smoking. American newspaper editors see them as one of the most important circulation builders, because the acquisition of one good comic strip, some say, can make enough of a difference to shift the balance between their own papers' circulation and that of the opposition. Readership surveys certainly prove, if you can believe such surveys, that sixty to seventy per cent of the people who read a newspaper also read Little Orphan Annie or Blondie. And even though, again according to the surveys, Walter Lippmann is read by only half the number of people, he can be considered to be doing well under the circumstances. European newspapers have lived and survived without comic strips, but in the United States they still have a special place in life and society.

Laughing at Oneself

Some time ago, out of curiosity, I went to a luncheon given in honor of a score of comic strip cartoonists. I wanted to meet some of these artists whose work gets so much attention from the American public. To my surprise they all looked disappointingly normal. You would hardly have suspected them of being artists. They sported neither goatees nor corduroy trousers—even their ties were conservative. All gave the impression of being goodhearted, well-fed, jolly fellows, "regular" guys, not eccentrics.

Walt Kelly, the creator of Pogo, is one of them. His studio is in one of those mammoth office buildings on Madison Avenue and it is as impersonal as hundreds of other offices in the building. It consists of two small rooms without much direct daylight. Mr. Kelly uses one, his business manager the other. Both were prosaic and conventionally furnished and on first sight you would not have suspected this was an artist's studio. Mr. Kelly sat behind a tallish, old-fashioned desk with a roll top and next to it, somewhat hidden, was a simple drawing board with a strong artificial light above it. It was much more a one-man factory than an artist's studio.

Mr. Kelly was jovial, likable and friendly. His wistful look and easy charm were undeniably Irish. And like any good Irishman he goes for inspiration to Tim Costello's bar, which he calls "the Establishment for the Arts."

Mr. Kelly holds strong views, but he likes to express them gently. He is neither a moralist nor an idealist. He does not want to impose ideas on others; he only wants to make everybody feel a little guilty. This is his way of keeping Americans safe, he says. His satire is neither biting nor bitter. It is impish, and a little mischievous, and almost always an air of bewildering innocence hovers over his kind of Disneyland, which he calls "Pogofenokeeland," an imaginary swamp land, where sooner or later everybody sinks in up to his ankles or even up to his knees, but never quite deep enough to suffer fatally or to lose his sense of humour altogether.

His strip, which he calls Pogo, is not a continuous story; it is more a running commentary on the contemporary scene. It moves at a sort of unpredictable speed into various unpredictable events. His characters get involved in Little Rock's school segregation, in Mr. Khrushchev's visit to the United States, in Presidential elec-

tions, television scandals, etc. Some five hundred newspapers carry Pogo and to facilitate the distribution Mr. Kelly keeps Pogo about six weeks ahead of himself. This is a relatively short margin. Other comic strip cartoonists told me they sometimes stay as much as six months ahead of the distribution date which enables them to take long vacations. Such a work schedule plus the high income these cartoonists can earn convinced me that there is definitely something rewarding about the "funnies," certainly for their creators. But I dare not be flippant about them. They are part of American folklore and one day they may prove to be as important a source for social historians as the Egyptian hieroglyphs were for our archaeologists.

BRANDON: I think there are today forty million—or is it more—American readers of comic strips.

KELLY: We have about fifty-five million circulation in newspapers in this country, and we sort of assume that anybody that reads a newspaper reads a comic strip. But this is not quite true.

BRANDON: I heard of some poll which even showed that the majority of American newspaper readers begin with the funny page rather than the front page.

KELLY: I've heard that but, again, I would doubt it judging from my own experience, and I don't think I'm too different from most people. I usually read page one first—read at it—and then I usually turn to the sports page and from sports I might go to the comics. I think that's a general trend.

BRANDON: Why do you think comics are so popular here?

KELLY: Well, it's probably the same sort of desire for relief or escape—and I prefer the word "relief"—that most people have everywhere. Some people chew—what do they call them—betel nuts and other people take opium. Here we take comic strips.

BRANDON: Some people even read books.

KELLY: Some people read books and some people look at television and I regret that they look at television, but on the other hand it's not too dissimilar from our business. I think the picture story has always been an engrossing sort of way of delivering a message; it captures the attention of almost anybody.

BRANDON: But in Europe, for instance, you find that there are very few newspapers that carry comic strips. It is primarily an American phenomenon.

KELLY: Yes, and I'm not sure why that is. Of course, if you go back into the origins of comic strips you'll find that they started along about the early part of the nineties as a result of various attempts on the part of newspaper proprietors here to increase their circulation. Comic strips, as a matter of fact, in this country are really the result of an accident, the desire to put color into the Sunday papers. It wasn't until about 1905, I think, that we tried daily strips. The daily strip then, for some reason, got even more popular than the Sunday one and people began avidly following them. At that time the strips were not syndicated on a national basis; they were local. But after a while the syndicate proprietors, the people who sell features, and, in fact, a group of publishers banded together to form a syndicate to distribute feature material to each other more cheaply. For example, if an artist were to make a hundred pounds a week, he would make one pound from each of a hundred papers—rather than make a hundred pounds out of one newspaper. It was for this reason that the syndicates were formed.

Now *why* we like comics, I don't know. Our taste earlier ran to such things as what we call dime novels, the penny thriller, that sort of thing. And we did a great business in that all through the last half of the last century and the early part of this one. You experienced that sort of phenomenon over in your own country.

But why we like comics, I'm not sure. I think it's partly a matter of distribution and the selling of them. It's possible that their popularity is quite overrated; I don't think anyone has ever quite tested that.

BRANDON: Weren't they originally for children?

KELLY: They originally were, yes.

BRANDON: Then you could, perhaps in an overly facile way, come to the conclusion that Americans are very childish.

KELLY: I wouldn't be the one to leap at that immediately, but I think there is a good deal in that. I think that this is a part of the growing up of this country. I heard the other day about a man who was going to psychoanalyze a whole Mexican village, and he's not going to psychoanalyze the people in it, he's going to psychoanalyze the village. I think if you were to psychoanalyze the United States, you would find it still in the growing pains of an adolescent country. A lot of the things that we went through since the last war are indications of how youthful we are—not youthful so much as young—abominably young many times, too many times. Our trouble with McCarthy, our fear of spies was, in fact, due to this.

We are a young people and this is part of the reason that we look at comics. I think you might be quite right. We are somewhat amused by childish things: we like to draw mustaches on posters in the subway and so on. And you won't find just children doing this, you'll find rather elderly ladies doing this sort of thing.

Our obsession with motion pictures, our desire to have not a good car but a new car—all these are manifestations of our continued growing process. And, of course, if we don't grow a little faster, the Russians will have grown up before we have. They'll own the moon and we won't have anything but ourselves. What a pity.

I guess comic strips are an indication that here in this country, at least, we are still delighted and obsessed with a picture story. Now in my own comic strip I have tried to go a little differently and present not so much picture as word. I try to give them some thought. There are probably not more than three or four men in the country who care that much about their work. I don't say that we care more; I think that we're just a little more self-conscious than some and not quite as willing to take the money and not worry about what we're doing for it. We might even feel a little guilty about getting paid so much money for doing so little . . . why some of us even spend time working on what we want to say.

BRANDON: Was your comic strip the first serious comic strip?

KELLY: I don't think it's entirely the first. I think Al Capp has always tried to put into his some sort of satirical—if not philosophical—comment and very often political parody gets into his work. He's done that now for twenty-five years. There was a comic strip here called Krazy Kat which ran many years ago. The man who drew it, George Herriman, died about 1944 and he had done it since 1915 or 1920. His underlying philosophy was that the gentle will survive. He was serious to that extent. Capp, on the other hand is serious to the extent of wishing to make fun and poke holes in people who are a little too pompous. My strip does the same thing. It is a continuous allegorical expression, which doesn't particularly make it a good comic strip but it certainly does what I want it to do.

BRANDON: What is your basic philosophy?

KELLY: That life goes on in spite of everything we do . . . we can't keep it from going on. We manage to survive despite ourselves. No matter what we do to enhance our position or to make it worse, we remain just about where the good Lord intended us to be at the moment.

BRANDON: Don't you encourage the idea that there isn't really very much we can do about ourselves—

KELLY: I'm not sure that I don't . . . I think you're right. I think this might be my philosophy. And this is not a philosophy of weariness so much as it is one of knowing that we are what we are, and that we can always try to be better. But very little that we do will actually change the kind of people we are. We can always expect the "boob", as we call the fool in America, to show up. There were a number of little children waiting for a school bus to come along the other day and some damn' ex-convict who had stolen an automobile charged into thirty of them and killed three or four. This sort of accident comes up constantly—the fool or the boob—upsetting all the best-laid plans of mice and men—a continuing discouraging manifestation. Not that I'm weary or that I think people should be weary, but I don't think we should be too upset if something comes along to upset an applecart, or our children. We can expect a lot of this.

BRANDON: But you said earlier the American people, you think, are very youthful and in the process of maturing.

KELLY: I would hope they're in the process of maturing. We do seem to be gaining some sense as we go along. We do show signs of improving. We probably would not go in again for a McCarthy, and I doubt whether we would drop again the atomic bomb; I think there might be a little sentiment against that sort of thing.

BRANDON: But, I meant whether it is part of your aim in your comic strip to bring this home and to help this process of maturing.

KELLY: I think it is. It is not only my aim, it is my obligation to remind us not only how youthful and how brainless we are, but also within the same framework hold out hope for the future. I don't mean there's no possibility of any hope. I merely like to state over and over again that we shouldn't ever expect too much of ourselves because we're very frail and we're inclined to break— very easily. And I think my philosophy is not unlike that of the Reverend Dodgson. I think his trial scene is one of the greatest pieces of satirical writing; it certainly fits our whole McCarthy period. The poem that the White Rabbitt found and read is a great piece of work—absolutely meaningless and yet accepted with the greatest respect by the court. And this is exactly what we did! We did this for about the last ten or fifteen years . . . we only stopped doing it about four years ago. And the reason largely was because McCarthy, in our country, finally got in trouble with his own private court, the Senate. It wasn't that he had caused others to suspect well-meaning citizens; it was that McCarthy had over-stepped particular house rules in the Senate; he had been a whore to his fellow members. And this annoyed the Senate. His crime was not against the American people; it was against the club, and that's exactly why he went down; he didn't go down for any other reason.

This, I think, is great comedy material. So, I parodied that in my own way in my strip. I think Mr. Khrushchev's visit here was hilarious and I treated it in the strip that way. And all these people in our country who are rushing over there to see Mr. Khrushchev, just as they did in your country, the big political candidates, busily checking in with the bear. They must go over and check in with Khrushchev before they can run. Nixon went over, Hubert Humphrey did, and a few others. And you, of course, had Mr. Macmillan go over and the Labour party leaders—this is all pretty funny stuff. In order to run for office in your own country you must check in with Russia! I don't see anything in it but that all these people think this will bring them page one attention in the newspapers; this is the big reason they do it. I'm sure that Mr. Eisenhower doesn't have that in mind, but I'm sure Mr. Nixon welcomed it and Mr. Stevenson has already been there.

BRANDON: I'm sure you feel the weaknesses and the strengths of this country better than most. We've talked mainly of the weaknesses; what do you think are its strengths?

KELLY: I think it was quite manifest when Mr. Khrushchev came here, that without any instruction from anyone in particular our people just turned out and looked at him as if he were a curiosity, and they stood back and, in fact, did not treat him with discourtesy so much as they treated him with apathy. They were not really impressed by him; but they were curious. I think therein lies two of our strengths.

First of all, we are curious and we will continue to probe for those things that we think we want. Secondly, we are not too impressed with other people's strength at this moment. We are certainly, and almost with alarm, finding ourselves in a position of strength, of real strength, of world leadership. And I think we are taking it rather well, and we are not too pompous about it. I think there's a quiet feeling about the strength rather than a feeling of being able to intimidate anybody or threaten anyone. I think we're amazed at finding ourselves in this position because we had felt that you people had that position for so long and that within my lifetime—forty-five years—this position has changed. And, I might say, much to our regret! We would rather be where we were—having you out front.

But now we find we're there—we're taken aback—and yet we feel quiet about it. We really don't want to have any trouble. At the same time we don't intend—I think we showed this at Khrushchev's visit—we don't really, despite whatever weapons they have, we don't intend to have anybody push us around. Whether we intend to let anybody push other people around, I don't know; I'm not sure about that.

BRANDON: Do you think Americans are basically people with a sense of humor?

KELLY: I think they are generally. I think that any group of people who are on the way up have room within their minds to laugh at themselves. For all too damn' long we laughed at other people, and now we are beginning to find ourselves rather funny. I think the British developed that style of humor, of self-expression, to a high degree, and it's still going on. I think we're just beginning to get at that. We can work in innuendo now and suggestion and with more subtle grace than at one time. We don't have to hit a man on the head in order to get a laugh. I think we still have room, and your people still have room, to laugh at themselves. And I suppose we may not see any sign of it here and there, but I suppose the Russians have room to laugh at themselves. I think, however, that they are more inclined to take themselves rather seriously. The thing that I've always liked about the Chinese, for example, is that they can always laugh at themselves, even in the worst situation. The Indians, on the other hand, I don't think have a very great sense of humor. And I think that these things *do* run racially.

I hesitate to be racial about anything, but numbers of us are inclined to take ourselves seriously and others are inclined to find room for laughter. I don't think we have any bitter laughter in us because we haven't lost that much yet, whereas the Mediterranean people have quite a bit of bitter laughter; they've lost so much so often.

BRANDON: Therefore, what kind of humor do you think has the main appeal here? Slapstick humor or—

KELLY: Well, the exaggerated, incongruous form of humor . . . and one of the forms has been here what we call the "shaggy dog" story, which is a greatly exaggerated story usually involving an animal. There is the story about the man who came into a bar with the mouse and the frog, and the mouse stood up and sang and the frog played the piano, and the bartender said: "How can that mouse sing like that?" And the fellow said, "Because the frog is a ventriloquist." You see, this sort of thing. It doesn't really mean anything; it actually has no point to the story, but it goes from one exaggeration to another and the second exaggeration is supposedly an explanation of the first. I think we like that sort of joke but it is not our only diet.

BRANDON: Is this the reason that you chose animals for your strip?

KELLY: No, I chose animals largely because you can do more with animals. They don't hurt as easily, and it's more possible to make them believable in an exaggerated pose than humans.

BRANDON: Do you see yourself as Pogo?

KELLY: The characters in the strip are all unfortunately representations of me, I guess, all of them. I would guess that myself as the cartoonist here, as the artist, as the commentator—you might consider me to be Pogo, sure. But the other people are also me and, unfortunately, my friends find this all too true at times. But, as I say, we actually have no heroes as such in the strip because I don't believe in heroes. We have no good, we have no evil, because I don't believe in either. My villains eventually get to be almost like other people and it's a real effort to keep them from becoming rather tiresome.

Labor and the Inner Man

a conversation with

WALTER REUTHER

When I said to Walter Reuther that in Britain he would have a real chance of becoming Prime Minister, I admittedly threw out a bait to test his own political ambitions, but I also meant exactly what I said. A man of his success as a trade union leader, of his sharp and lively intellect and of his arresting power of oratory would be almost bound to reach the top of the Labour party in Britain and hence would have a real chance of the premiership.

With his upbringing, family traditions, training and talents he almost could not have failed to become an outstanding trade union leader. His grandfather was an active member of the Socialist party in Germany, and his father, who came to the United States as a child, made a rapid career as a labor organizer. And by organizing his four sons into debating teams every Sunday afternoon he gave them the best training for a career in the trade union movement, or, for that matter, in politics.

At the age of fifteen Walter Reuther became an apprentice tool-and-die maker. He got his education at night school and through world-wide travels. In 1935 he began to organize the automobile workers and his union today is the largest in the world.

He is no doubt an able organizer, a shrewd negotiator, and an aggressive thinker. And he has fought consistently against Communist influence in trade unionism. But it is indicative of the political prejudices against labor that neither the Democratic nor *the Republican party have thought it advisable to run a labor leader, even of Reuther's gifts, for high political office.*

I went to see him at the newly built Detroit headquarters of the UAW (United Automobile, Aircraft and Agricultural Implement Workers of America). His office was spacious and modernistic and, though one had clearly the impression that it was the boss's, it was not pretentious. Nor was it warm; on the contrary it had a certain antiseptic atmosphere.

Reuther's boyish looks, his almost too neatly combed sandy hair and his unbounded energy give you the impression that he is fortyish instead of over fifty. He is slender, of medium height and his ready-made plain-colored suit, white shirt and matching tie made him look more like a superior bank clerk than a labor leader.

It would perhaps be incorrect to refer to our talk as conversation. Reuther, even in conversation, talks as if to a large audience. Like any orator he sometimes tends to overelaborate an idea or to use high-sounding catch phrases. The problem was not to make him talk, but to make him shift subjects at the right moment. He doodles while he talks. When we began he had no writing pad in front of him to doodle on. Suddenly he felt compelled to get up and fetch one, explaining that doodling helps him to concentrate.

Reuther may or may not be the most powerful trade union leader in the United States, but he is certainly the most brilliant among them. He is not merely content to occupy himself with current problems but to think ahead, think about the future. And it was this distinction which made my conversation with him so rewarding and thought-provoking.

BRANDON: You know, what puzzles Europeans most about the American trade union movement is that it has not tried to create its own political party to advance labor's own interest. Trade unionism here seems to have as its main function bargaining for higher wages. How do you explain that?

REUTHER: To begin with you need to understand the structure of American society. It is, I think, more in a state of flux than is the case in Europe. A Labor party, as such, in America, could not possibly succeed because a political party to succeed in America has to have groups that go way beyond the question of labor as a group; you've got to have farm groups, you've got to have small businessmen, and therefore a Labor party, as such, would not represent an effective vehicle for the implementation of a political program.

The American labor movement is essentially trying to work within the two-party structure, but to bring about within the two-party structure a basic realignment so that the two parties really stand for distinct points of view. And I think that this process is happening very rapidly. I think more and more the Democratic party is becoming a party that reflects the kind of programs and policies that the American labor movement can support because they are part of programs that deal basically with economic and social problems, while the Republican party more and more becomes the party of big business.

BRANDON: But didn't a lot of labor people vote for the Republican party in the 1956 election?

REUTHER: Well, some . . . but I think in terms of percentages it was a small percentage. In the Detroit area, the surveys here indicate that about 21 per cent of the vote was Republican but only for the Presidency, because Eisenhower could give us greater assurance of world peace. That obviously had some impact upon working-class groups as well as upon people generally. The same thing is true in Britain. Not every worker votes for the Labour party candidate.

BRANDON: Well, almost.

REUTHER: Well, I don't think that's true. I think that they lose also, but they lose less than we do because you've had a longer time to develop a political understanding than we've had.

BRANDON: But if it is possible in England for a Labour party to get enough support from a broad section of the public, why shouldn't that be possible here?

REUTHER: Well, I think America is quite different from England. In England you've got a much more rigid class structure. The middle class is less important in England than it is here, but here the labor movement is developing a whole new middle class.

Last year the average automobile worker's income was more than $5000 a year. Well, a political movement has to reflect these kinds of economic and social realities. If I were in England dealing with the kind of rigid, narrow class structure which you have, which came out of your past, I would be for a Labour party, but in America I'm for the approach that we're making because I think it's more realistic.

BRANDON: Perhaps the reason that the labor movement has not been able to create a broader political base here is that it has no real ideology apart from bargaining for higher wages.

REUTHER: I think that there is developing an ideology. I agree that the original labor movement was basically pure and simple trade unionism—bargaining for wages and for hours and for working conditions—and that the people who conceived of that labor movement didn't consider that it ultimately would have to broaden its essential function in society and become a social movement.

But the labor movement cannot carry out its historic mission if it continues to be no more than that. As the problems of our modern society become more complex and interwoven, as our technology becomes more productive, their solution cannot be economic or political—the solution has got to be economic *and* political.

Take the question of unemployment. Can you solve unemployment at the bargaining table? The answer is No. You can make a contribution toward the solution of unemployment, but unemployment is a broad social question and its answer must be found in the economic, the social, and the political fields.

If the labor movement is to deal with problems such as unemployment, it must act economically at the bargaining table and it must act politically. For example, a few years back, in 1945 and '46, we had a strike with the General Motors Corporation and it lasted 113 days. The auto workers had raised a new demand—it was a demand for higher wages without higher prices. We said that the labor movement had to take into consideration the impact of its wage demands upon the price structure, because the price structure may determine the general economic climate and may have an impact upon employment opportunities. Well, in 1945 when our union raised that demand—and we raised it not theoretically, we raised it in a practical sense because we had a 113-day strike to implement that demand—we were criticized by corporation executives, by people in government, and I think by 80 per cent of the leadership of the American labor movement, who at that time took the position that prices are no concern of labor, that the question of prices is an exclusive managerial responsibility. Well, 1945 is not too far back in history, yet today—only a few years later—I think that 90 per cent of the leadership of the American labor movement now accepts the basic concept in respect to the relationship of wages, prices, and profits that we advanced in 1945. Why? Why has there taken place this tremendous change in the attitude of the leadership of the American labor movement about the relationship of wages, prices, and profits? Because they have come to understand that all of these things are inseparably woven together in the basic economic pattern of America.

Now the same thing is true about other things. The AFL, which I think more or less represented the basic concepts of pure and simple trade unionism fifty years back, has moved a long way toward accepting what we would call the beginning of the American trade union ideology. In 1932 the AFL for the first time went on record in favor of unemployment compensation. Until then they were against any government action that bore upon the economic position of the wage earner. They wanted to have a monopoly; they wanted only the unions to deal with this. Therefore when the government talked about minimum wages, or unemployment compensation, the government then was beginning to intervene in the area in which they as pure and simple trade unionists felt the labor movement should exercise a monopoly. Now why did they do this in 1932? Well, unemployment had become so overwhelming that they knew they couldn't cope with it by pure and simple trade unionism, and therefore they turned to government action. I cite this to merely indicate that gradually we are getting away from pure and simple trade unionism, and we're beginning to take on these new concepts, new ideas, and this is the beginning of development of a trade union ideology. Now it is not being borrowed from anywhere.

It isn't based upon Marxism, it's not based upon any other preconceived, thought-through philosophy; it's a special American trade union philosophy born of the problems of America.

BRANDON: But it is still very closely related to the direct interests of labor—it has no real political content.

REUTHER: Well, the price question is certainly not something limited only to labor because when you deal with the impact, you deal with the impact of collective bargaining upon the wage-price-profit equation, you're dealing with a broad economic and social problem that goes way beyond the limits of trade unionism. As a matter fact, we complicate our collective bargaining problems because every time we become the advocates of a strong position in opposition to higher prices, or, in fact, in favor of reduction of prices of cars, we obviously don't win friends across the bargaining table with the people we have to represent. Now why do we do these things? Because we happen to believe that the industry has been pursuing an administered pricing policy. They have been unwisely inflating the prices of cars which in turn penalizes our own people, the consumers, and the economy. They are not only hurting the automotive industry but steel and rubber and so forth, the whole economy. Therefore we have advocated government action that will begin to deal with this problem.

BRANDON: Why did you think in '46 or '47, that there was a need for a third party?

REUTHER: Why did I think that?

BRANDON: Yes.

REUTHER: Oh, it goes back further than that. At that time we hadn't made as much progress inside the labor movement itself, and I was influenced in believing that if we had our own party it would be a more effective vehicle for getting broader participation than through the labor movement itself. Another thing that influenced me was that the Democratic party in the earlier periods was essentially a party in which the major industrial states were controlled by machine politics. The result was that the labor movement was having little influence upon the policies of the programs of those machine-controlled state organizations. We have made considerable progress now. The old machines are falling apart, new leadership is coming up, which more nearly reflects the kind of programs and policies that we think are adequate to meet these new economic and social problems. These are the reasons that have influenced me.

BRANDON: Influenced you that the third party is not necessary—

REUTHER: That's right. For these reasons we felt that instead of trying to create new political instruments through a third party—or labor party—that we ought to help accelerating the realignment that was taking place.

Ten or twelve years ago I argued this issue with Wayne Morse at an educational conference in Cleveland. He then said he disagreed with my philosophy which was that in order to bring about a realignment we must get the liberal forces in one party and the conservatives into another. I pointed out that without this no party will ever have the kind of clear-cut policy and the kind of leadership to translate policy and implement policy, because the power of the party will be diluted on basic questions and the parties will never develop sufficient internal discipline to be effective instruments for carrying out policy. And I tried to convince Wayne Morse that he ought to be in the Democratic party! He couldn't see that. He said he was needed in the Republican party because by keeping liberal ideas alive there, he raised the challenge within the party. Well, he got over that. He finally understood the futility of this and he came over to the Democratic party. He recognized that this was the party most nearly in line with his thinking.

BRANDON: How do you foresee the relationship between the labor movement and the Democratic party?

REUTHER: Well, I would be opposed to the labor movement trying to capture the Democratic party. I think that at the point the labor movement captures the Democratic party, you then destroy the broad base that is essential to make a political party an effective instrument to translate sound policy into governmental action. It may be hard to do but the essential problem for the labor movement is to learn to work with a party without trying to capture it.

The Democratic party adopts a good policy, a good program at every convention—just as advanced as the Labour party in Britain. As a matter of fact, in some cases we are ahead of the

Labour party, because, I think, we're more realistic about the necessary adjustments to modern technology.

BRANDON: But in Britain a man of your caliber and your oratorical gift would have a good chance to become Prime Minister. You haven't got that in this country—or do you think you have?

REUTHER: I suppose that the day will come when a labor leader could aspire to the top job in America . . . I personally do not aspire to that. I mean, I have no political ambitions whatsoever. This, again, is something that my opponents have not understood or accepted. The facts are that I made a decision a long time ago that what little contribution I could make I would make inside the American labor movement, trying to get the American labor movement to mature philosophically and to essentially change its basic character from a pure and simple trade union group dealing with narrow economic issues to what I hope ultimately will be a social movement. This is exactly why I'm subjected to more criticism, I presume, than the rest of the leadership of the American labor movement combined: it's because I am unwilling to waste my time being the leader of a pressure group.

BRANDON: To European ears American trade union leaders sound often like capitalists when they praise the free enterprise system, yet they often act like socialists.

REUTHER: I think the important thing is, first of all, motivation; and secondly, policies by which you attempt to translate basic motivations into specific and tangible action. The American labor movement is as radical on basic things as the European labor movement, but we don't dress our things up with socialist slogans because we are not essentially committed to a socialist philosophy.

We are pragmatic; if a thing will work, we are for doing it— if it's radical or conservative, we're for doing it. We are committed to the free enterprise system because by and large it has worked. Now it has a lot of defects, but instead of trying to overthrow the system and substitute in its place a nationalized economic system, where we have to bargain with the government, we prefer to bargain with the private employer. But we prefer to make him more responsible. We sit down together and we talk through and think through what are the basic deficiencies in the free enterprise system, what can we do economically and politically to overcome these deficiencies and make the system work more in the interest of the common good. That's why we've come up with the guaranteed annual wage. This didn't come out of the socialist labor movement; it came out of a free enterprise labor movement. That's why we came up, too, with a privately negotiated pension plan to supplement the governmental plan.

When this was first raised some of my socialist friends in the European labor movement thought that we were going to destroy the government system. We said, "No, this is a simple way by which we can use the special leverage that we have at the bargaining table to facilitate greater progress through governmental action." For twelve years under Franklin Roosevelt and the New Deal, we had a favorable governmental climate to make progress as regards pensions and social security. But we made no progress whatever. We did not increase the level of social security payments one penny for twelve years. Then we said: "Okay, we've got to use our leverage at the bargaining table to try to facilitate greater progress through legislation." And within forty eight hours after we adopted the Ford pension system, where we required the employer to pay the total cost of the private pension, as contrasted to the worker paying half and the employer paying half in the public system, we got action out of Congress—in forty-eight hours action that we were unable to get in twelve years.

Now the socialists said that the minute you begin to deal with matters as basic as social security in the private sector of your economy, rather than through governmental action, you're going to destroy the whole public system. We said: "No, why can't we use the private leverage at the bargaining table to accelerate governmental progress." Thus our private negotiations did more to accelerate progress and to make stronger our public social security system than anything we ever did through governmental action. This is a peculiar kind of American phenomena, and the American trade union movement is constantly probing for pragmatic, practical ways to make free enterprise work better, instead of trying to overthrow it.

Labor and the Inner Man

BRANDON: It seems to me that something akin to a corporate structure has developed in this country. You have industry, which set up a very strong position in order to counter labor, and labor, which set up a very strong monopoly position to withstand industry. It makes government intervention, for instance, in a recession more difficult.

REUTHER: First of all you've got to recognize that in our age of technology big corporations, big industry are inevitable. You can have small companies in a relatively simple, technical situation; you cannot have small companies in a period of automation and electronics and down-the-road peaceful use of the atom. As our technology becomes more complex, as it takes greater and great investment capital to provide one job for one worker, industry is going to be more and more concentrated, that is an inevitable development.

I think the old liberal concept that bigness was evil and that smallness had a natural virtue is a lot of nonsense. You can have small tyrants as well as big tyrants. Now big labor is also a by-product of the same technological facts of life as big industry. You can't have small unions dealing with General Motors; you've got to have big unions, strong unions.

The question that arises is not: Do we want to escape from a world of bigness, big corporations, big unions and big government? They are, I think, an inevitable by-product of the world in which we live. The question is how do we live with bigness and make it responsive to basic human needs. How do we avoid the human individual getting lost in the shuffle, in the wilderness of bigness?

Well, this is a matter which needs a great deal of careful thinking through. And this is an area in which our union is working. Inside of our union, for example, we have created something which I'm sure the European trade unionist would find very hard to understand. We have created what we call a Public Review Board, to which we have designated seven prominent leading citizens, and given them constitutional authority in our union to review and to modify, to affirm or to completely reject any decision that we make with respect to the individual who has a grievance within the union.

In other words, we are willing to have an outside, public group of prominent citizens review our stewardship of the internal workings of our union because, in effect, we believe that we have taken on responsibilities and power that makes us sort of a quasi-public organization; and that, therefore, we have to be prepared to have our basic decisions subject to public review, based upon the standards of public conduct that we would expect a government official to meet. That's one thing we're doing in the union—voluntarily—to help meet this problem of bigness, so that a worker who belongs to a union like ours, which has one and a half million members, will not get lost in the wilderness of this bigness.

BRANDON: Now what about big corporations?

REUTHER: Well, we proposed before the Kefauver committee that what we ought to do is to give consideration to creating a governmental mechanism that would be the sort of public watchdog on the price structure.

If a corporation in any given industry that is responsible for 20 per cent or more of the total production of that industry—now this would not affect too many companies—that company would be free to set prices, but it could not increase its price except by prior notice to this governmental agency, and the governmental agency would than hold public hearings. This industry, this company, would then be required publicly to defend the economics that it believed supported its need for a price increase. If it came there and said higher wages were responsible, then the trade union that was demanding higher wages would have to defend publicly its demand. The union could still go on and fight for higher wages, or the company could still raise the price, but it would have done it in a fishbowl, defending its position before the public. Now I believe this is the kind of voluntary mechanism in which the government facilitates the public hearing but does not make the decision. It's this sort of thing that needs to be developed so that we can make private decisions more publicly responsible. The only other way to do this is to have the government do it, and you have no assurance that government decisions will be responsible either. When the government does it, they don't have to account to anybody, and this is the point. The more we make private decisions responsible, the less we create the vacuums in which public decisions will have to be made to meet the responsibilities that private decisions fail to meet.

BRANDON: But aren't you contradicting yourself with what you said previously that you'd like to avoid government interference as much as possible.

REUTHER: That's precisely why I propose the kind of mechanism in which the government does not make the decision but merely facilitates a public discussion. Now there are some areas in which the government has to move. You take the whole question of technology. Does anyone really believe that the government knows *all* the answers to all the technical problems? No one has that much wisdom.

I think the real problem in the field of technology, as automation and electronics and the peaceful use of the atom develop, is going to be that industry is too compartmentalized. General Motors, Ford, Chrysler will know all about automation and the future impact of technological development upon the automotive industry, they know that. General Electric, Westinghouse, will know the same thing for their industry. Du Pont Chemical, they will know it for the chemical industry, and so on down the line. The problem is that no one is in a position to look at the total economy and the total of our society in terms of the accumulation of these separate impacts.

You take the question of atomic power. If you trace the industrial development of America—and this will be true, to some extent, of any other country—you will find that essentially the pattern of industry grew out of and reflected the sources of power. When coal and steam were the source of power, then you had a gravitation of industry around the source—coal. And when hydroelectric power became a more economic means of developing power, you then had a gravitation to the sites of big hydroelectric power plants. And therefore the industrial pattern was developed essentially around the sources of conventional power—coal, hydroelectric power. Now with atomic energy coming in, you can put the plant anywhere, because a truckload of atomic fuel will operate a big plant for several years. So you will be able to ignore the normal economic reasons that determine

213

the industrial pattern of a nation. And that means that we can now begin to plan: we can arbitrarily decide to have an industry anywhere because the source of power is no real economic problem. You can build it where you want it.

Now, what should be the role of government? Well, we don't want a big bureaucracy that sits in Washington pretending it has superior wisdom, pretending that it knows all the answers to these complex problems. What we want is a governmental clearing house, a place where you can have a top group periodically sit down and evaluate, and based upon their recommendation have the private decisions then attempt to translate and implement these broad policies. The private group would have the right to make a mistake, but if given these facts it would seem to me that we could have some rational approach. Some people will say: Isn't this kind of a supra-planning board? Well, call it what you want, the difference being that it does not make the decisions, it makes recommendations, it makes available information, it's a clearing house where you can come to find out what rational answers are there to problems of this kind.

BRANDON: You mentioned automation . . . Now it seems to me there are two serious problems for the future of the trade union movement. One is the impact of automation and the other that white-collar workers are now outnumbering blue-collar workers.

REUTHER: Well, the problem of automation is actually the problem of learning to live with abundance, and the only way you can learn to live with abundance is to learn to manage it, and the only way you can manage it is to share it. There are really two basic questions. Number one: We've got to learn to distribute the abundance that we know how to make. Number two: Ultimately we've got to find a way to give people a more rational means of choosing between gadgets and leisure. I mean, how much do we want to improve our living standards in a material sense?

How many cars should a family have? How many television sets? How many bathrooms do we need in an ordinary house? Ultimately, when we have reached that plateau of economic living standards, where the law of diminishing returns sets in very rapidly, we've got to give people the educational background, the stimulation so that they would be interested in another kind of consumption. And that means the ability, the desire, and the willingness to spend a larger portion of their time, not making gadgets, but in the pursuit of constructive and creative leisure.

In the face of automation, I think, we will be confronted with this very real problem, that we may overfeed the outer man and starve the inner man.

The thing that bothers me is that the fellow working in the Cadillac Motor Company making the Cadillac motorcar can be a part of making that Cadillac, and yet when he looks at it he gets no sense of creative achievement. And this is, I think, a very serious problem. In an earlier technology, a craftsman—no matter what he made, he finished doing something—there was a little bit of him in what he made. There was a sense of creation. And when God made us in His own image, He also gave to each of us some creative capacity. That is being starved. An automated factory does not give a worker any sense of creative expression. And we have to find a way to satisfy man's need for creative expression during his leisure hours. And just having two more television sets in the house to sit and look at does not meet that need. We've got to begin now in our education, in our community activities, in our trade union activities, in our church groups, to stimulate people to achieve a sense of creative expression in our leisure hours.

BRANDON: But we may then have your—let's call them "tycoons of leisure"—go fishing and learning how to paint, how to garden while the working class of the professionals, the scientists, teachers, doctors, civil servants will be working long hours. I'm wondering whether this will not spark off a new kind of class war between the "haves of leisure" and the "have-nots of leisure."

REUTHER: I think that we're going to have to shift more people into these categories. We obviously need more doctors. There are thousands of young people with the potential capacity to make wonderful medical people but they don't have the economic resources to get access to medical education. So our society has a part of this whole question of working out a proper balance between gadgets and between leisure, has also to work out a proper balance in the area of human services—teachers, medicine, music, etc.

This again, you see, is a matter of working out a proper relationship between competing values. You have to pay for everything in life and if you want more medical care—and we want more medical care—then we have to see to it that we make medical education available to more young people. The same thing is true of schoolteachers. We need more schoolteachers—well, we have to make it possible for schoolteachers to make as much as a sweeper does in an automobile factory and then we'll get more schoolteachers.

The point is that all of these things are essentially a matter, first of all, of deciding what we really do want. What kind of society are we trying to build? Are we trying to build a society so that every kid of eighteen has a sports car and that every room in a house has a built-in television with standard equipment, and that we have so much plumbing in the house that you need three plumbers on every block to keep it going? Is this what we want? Is this the sort of thing our advancing technology is going to give us? Or are we really trying to find a way to essentially satisfy man's basic economic and material needs, and, having taken care of the outer man, we want to find a way to facilitate the growth of the inner man. Is this what life is about? I happen to think that it is.

I think we can all agree that culture is the product of leisure, and having satisfied man's material needs we can now give the great mass of people access to culture and learning and the opportunities to facilitate the growth of the inner man.

Now the trade union movement is important only as it facilitates these long-range objectives. Automation is important only as it provides the tools of economic abundance that we can use with social responsibility to create the economic base upon which the mass—having had their material needs satisfied—can then have access to what only the few have had access to in the past. This is the way I see it.

BRANDON: But the satiation point of the minority is necessarily far above the satiation point of the majority and to the minority there are two types of satisfaction available that could never be made available to the majority: One is expenditure on direct personal services—scarce amenities—and certain types of housing, professions requiring special skills . . . You could never, I think, make all these amenities available to a majority.

REUTHER: In our kind of society, where success essentially is associated with the acquisition of material wealth—and, in a sense, I think it's associated in the outward sense with conspicuous consumption—if you can consume a lot of things you must have the money to make it possible to consume a lot. Ultimately in the kind of society that I envision there's going to be a shift in these values. I think that once everyone has all these things, the fact that somebody has an extra one is not going to impress anybody. "Conspicuous consumption" can be only an outward measurement of success as long as other people can't match it. At the point everyone has all the things that they need essentially, then the values that get associated with having three Cadillacs are going to go. And in its place we're going to develop new and more fundamental values. And in that kind of context the sort of thing you're talking about will change radically. Sure, there will be one fellow who prefers to get more personal services. There will still be women who will want to be fussed over by beauty parlor attendants; there will be other people who will want something else. There will be a man who will want to spend most of his time going fishing. But there will be a great body of people whom I believe will be essentially the reflectors of a society with these new values, in which people will develop new appetites, new interests, that will be quite different from anything we have in this present day. I don't want to say exactly what it will be because I don't know. It'll be different, that I do know.

BRANDON: I think it is very difficult to raise the standard of living by mass producing more material things without raising also direct personal services and scarce amenities.

REUTHER: There's going to be a shift in the next twenty-five years. The number of people in personal industries is going to increase tremendously. And this is going to bring about quite a difference in the structure of our whole society in terms of economic groupings.

BRANDON: But what is this going to do to the trade union movement?

REUTHER: It's going to change its character. The trade union movement will obviously have to change in order to reflect this new relationship, and if it doesn't it obviously will become less and less important. If it does, it will become more important. This is precisely why the trade union movement must not stay wedded to narrow economic concepts, and it must more and more and more think in broad terms. Only as it thinks in broad social terms can it change its basic structure that will integrate it in this broad social scheme.

BRANDON: How do you think it should reflect this change?

REUTHER: I think more and more it has to fight for economic policies that reflect the needs of our whole society. I think the UAW is trying to do that in a limited kind of way—we're making a beginning.

You take this profit-sharing idea. This has frightened a lot of people because they don't understand why we propose this. The profit-sharing idea was not a demand, it was a mechanism. In the profit-sharing scheme we're trying to find a rational means by which free labor and free management, sitting at the bargaining table, can attempt to work out in their relationship practical means by which you can equate the competing equities—in workers and stockholders and consumers. So we have said that what we ought to do is to work out the equities in two stages: you work out a minimum package, that we call our basic minimum demand, and you make that sufficiently small so that you know that it will have absolutely no inflationary impact.

BRANDON: To come back to the way you pictured the future. Don't you think that the shift of people into the professional classes, that the impact of automation will have a serious effect on the future of trade unions?

REUTHER: Well, the industrial membership of the trade union movement proportionately will decline as automation makes it possible to produce more with fewer workers. But the membership of the movement in these other fields will increase.

BRANDON: But you haven't been very successful so far to enroll white-collar workers.

REUTHER: That's because our industrial revolution had its first impact upon the industrial workers and the second phase of it will have its greatest impact upon the nonindustrial worker. There's no question about it, automation is going to have a greater impact upon the clerical worker in an office than upon the factory worker, because you can standardize office procedure routine—you don't come out with a new model every year. And as the impact of automation becomes more apparent, you're going to find these workers organizing in order to protect themselves against these problems.

BRANDON: Since the appearance of Sputnik, some of the more thoughtful people have been asking whether the American ability to turn out consumer goods, its generally spectacular capacity to produce, is still one of its greatest elements of strength, for in this thermonuclear age all-out war would be very brief—there would be no time to convert industry to war use. The question asked is, therefore: What sort of a gap lies today between ordinary industrial productivity and the achievement necessary to cope with the problems of this nuclear age? Are the long, shiny cars and the splendidly finished refrigerators a waste of resources and a drain on security?

REUTHER: Well, I personally think that America and I think, in a sense, the whole free world, has not fully comprehended the dimensions of the challenge that we face in the world. That accounts for a kind of a "business-as-usual" attitude, "diplomacy-as-usual" attitude. I don't think this is a matter of choosing between having nice motorcars and having these other things. I think we can have both if we fully utilize the productive potential of the American economy. I think our problem, primarily, is that we need to put more effort into education. The answer is to find a way to get the American people to put into the educational system a larger percentage of our gross national product. And here again it isn't a matter of taking that away from something else; it's a matter of realizing the potential.

Between 1954 and 1958, for instance, we lost roughly 96 billions of dollars in gross national product because of under-utilization in both manpower and our industrial capacity. Now, things you're talking about could have been paid for out of that 96 billion.

Our trouble is not that we are inferior to the Russians; we're not incapable of meeting their challenge—our problem is that we are not trying. We have really not worked out what I call a set of national priorities in which we put first things first, and then commit our industrial capacity and our economic and human resources to the achievement of these priorities. We really don't know what we're fighting for.

The tragedy is that we're still essentially moving based upon negative reflexes; we're still fighting *against* something. And the free world cannot, in my opinion, meet the challenge nor can it really comprehend the dimensions of the challenge, as long as we shape our policies and our programs in the images of our fears and our hatreds.

I happen to think that the Russians, knowing essentially what we know about the H-bomb, have made a decision. I don't think there's going to be an H-bomb war unless some mistake is made somewhere—somebody just pulls the trigger. The Communists have been compelled to re-evaluate their dogmas and to come up with a decision that they can't take over by destroying the bourgeois state by force of arms—that since the bourgeois state has the H-bomb and they have the H-bomb there will be no world to inherit. So I think that they're going to concentrate on economic penetration and political subversion.

That's the area in which we're either going to win or lose. I think we've got to be strong on the military front to check aggression or possible aggression, but we've got to realize that the real challenge is on the economic and social fronts.

BRANDON: What should the U.S. do on those fronts?

REUTHER: We're going to lose India if we don't move. It would take so little to help save India in terms of what we're spending for military purposes. The great tragedy came home to me so clearly—when I was last in India. I was up in Northern India where they're building this huge dam, and they were using equipment made by the members of our union in Peoria, Illinois, in the Caterpillar Tractor Works, huge earth-moving machines and they were shifting the mountain. They had three or four of these, and behind the big earth-moving machines there were hundreds of workers with little straw baskets. They'd fill these baskets with wooden shovels and women and children would carry them away on their heads.

And I asked the chief engineer that if they could get more of this machinery from America could they complete the dam earlier in order to harness the monsoon rains one season earlier? He said yes, they could do that but they couldn't afford to buy these machines. We had 19,000 workers in the Peoria plant—their number dropped to 12,000 during the recession and they were working three to four days a week only. If India had one week—not of the production—one week of the production that we were then *losing* by unemployment, it would have given them enough machines to finish these dams and roads and irrigation projects.

In India we have an opportunity to demonstrate freedom's superiority. The great tragedy in America is not that the Russians are better than we are—they're just doing better because they are trying and we aren't.

Human Machines and Inhuman Games

a conversation with

PROFESSOR NORBERT WIENER

Professor Norbert Wiener looks and sounds like Sir Thomas Beecham—except in a very different key. In his voluble yet gentle way he tried to make me feel at ease in his office at the Massachusetts Institute of Technology in Cambridge—he showed not the slightest concern when I prepared my tape recorder for action. Thoughts and words are no effort to him. Professor Wiener used to be a child prodigy; now he is sixty-four. He came to Harvard (where his father taught) at the age of thirteen and graduated at eighteen. He has remained a genius ever since. And it is he who developed the idea of a new science which he calls Cybernetics, "the study of messages as a means of controlling machinery and society, the development of computing machines and other such automata, certain reflections upon psychology and the nervous system, and tentative new theory of scientific method." He has written several books, the best known among them is The Human Use of Human Beings. *For relaxation he writes novels. Professor Wiener has lectured in England (also studied at Cambridge), Germany, France, Switzerland, Italy, Spain, China, Japan, Mexico, Canada, India, Israel, and Norway, but MIT has been his center of operations since 1919.*

In spite of the complexities of cybernetics he was easy to follow, though sometimes his insights into machines gave me a creepy feeling about a realm beyond comprehension. Sometimes he sounded like a prophet in the biblical sense and I felt like

*touching him to make sure he was still with me and all human.
It was therefore most reassuring when, after our session, I asked
whether I could take a photograph of him and he replied: "Certainly, but may I comb my hair first?"*

WIENER: I've found that it has always been an uphill fight to
do the things that were natural for me to do. I won't say an
uphill fight in my own career over the people close to me—no.
But in general, it isn't easy not to conform.

BRANDON: What were the roots of this fight?

WIENER: They're mixed. For a long period in this country the
economic and social development of a new country that had to
be opened up took precedence over intellectual activity to a
large extent . . . There were exceptions to that—New England
had a certain culture of its own that developed fairly early, but
there was a tendency in that to be an exclusivistic culture
reserved only for people of the right origin and people of the
right families . . . Coming in from a foreign group, a Jewish
group, there was much more shoving to the outside then than
there is now—many, many times more—I wasn't on the inside
track . . . On the other hand, there was no particular group
that I did associate with; I was relatively isolated. The really good
contacts that I had were people who, in an environment that
wasn't labeled an aristocratic or cultured environment, did retain
a great deal of cultural interest.

That was a very interesting thing in this community. Our
community of Ayer where I went to high school was a railroad
town. It was originally Groton Junction, and Groton was a
farming town later settled by well-to-do people; this was a working town. I think the people in it had a great deal in common
with certain elements in England, the North of England, which
has a deep culture of its own without a tradition of long position.
It had a simpler—when it was cultured—more natural mode of
life than that of the people of position. As a matter of fact,
I think there is a great deal in common between some of these
people, who represent the best of the mill towns here, and your
North-of-England people.

223

BRANDON: Do you think this situation has now changed, or is there still a lot of anti-intellectualism?

WIENER: Yes, but it has taken a different form. At that time it was a general feeling that it was American to grow up with the development of the country, with business and so on . . . At the same time, in scientific circles, this anti-intellectualism at that time did not penetrate very deeply. Because we were a minority, because we were different, we could keep a certain attitude of our own. Now, with the very success of science and business, the attitude of hurry and climbing has come into science itself and it is not nearly as easy now to keep the good side of the ivory tower as it was then. I think there are too many people who have gone into science now for success. It means, then, that the fight is within ourselves and therefore a harder fight than it was in my childhood.

BRANDON: The nouveau riche of the scientists—

WIENER: The nouveau riche of the scientists . . . I mean, previously there was a contradiction; if you were a scientist you had to take a loss and therefore it was much easier to become consecrated to science than it is now. But the very success has introduced into the scientific circles the anti-intellectualism that was not previously found in them although it was found in the community.

BRANDON: But there is still a great deal of anti-intellectualism outside the scientific community.

WIENER: That is true—but the point is that it hurts more inside.

BRANDON: In what sense?

WEINER: Because when one is dealing with a colleague—and now I'm not talking about my immediate colleagues here with whom I am on excellent terms, but people whom I find every now and then—one has to watch one's hat and coat. There is a tendency for exploitation; there is a tendency to put personal advancement above intellectual communication and it can be a very painful one.

BRANDON: May I switch the subject now to your scientific work?

WIENER: Please.

BRANDON: Would you just for the record explain what cybernetics means?

WIENER: Cybernetics as I've defined it: The science of control and communication wherever it occurs, whether in the living organism or the machine.

BRANDON: You have worked on the idea that the brain functions very much like a machine and you have applied your theories in many new and provocative ways. How does the human brain differ from the machine?

WIENER: I don't think there is much of a difference. I mean, there's nothing that a machine couldn't do, although we have to step it up many times and that isn't easy. I think that the chief difference is in the means. In building the machine we depend on parts that are made with high speed and high precision but we can't have very many of them when we compare them with the number of cells, units, in the brain. In the brain we must work with what we call a self-organizing system; it means that the actual use of the brain tends to create its organization to a large extent. We have a large number of parts, many of which are not too specifically assigned at the beginning, but by the use of these parts they pool themselves together into an organization which becomes effective largely—not entirely—but largely through its own experience. This question of how a system of a large number of not too specific parts by its continued use can increase its organization is a fascinating one, and it's the one that is concerning the neurophysiologist very much. I think that the study of self-organizing machines, which are no more and no less deterministic than the others, but more flexible, is one that is going to develop a great deal in the next few years.

BRANDON: What would be the primary application?

WIENER: The primary application would be to actually make machines more flexible, to make a machine work itself into its final state by being used for certain purposes, to make the memory effective in changing not only the data of the machine but the mode of operation. Now for that—for what we will call programing of a very high type—the brain is far superior to any manufactured machine. The ability, in other words, to make itself into a new machine by being used, by rewards and punishments if you want, is going to be a very important thing in automatization in the future.

BRANDON: Your research in the extent to which machines are going to take over from man has led you to believe that machines might gain the upper hand over man.

WIENER: The chief point now is the way in which the machines have developed. The original machines for control were what we call "first order" machines. That is, the programing—the record by which the mode of performance of the machine is determined—was done humanly. We knew pretty much what they would do operationally although perhaps not socially. At present we are getting machines which are more remote from the people who control them than they were before. The programing of machines is being itself programed. In other words, we make machines to achieve certain ends, and by setting the ends we often know relatively little of the means by which they do it. The fact that a person has made a machine does not mean that he fully understands it . . . and with machines of this sort there is a much greater tendency than there was before for the person to conform to the machine rather than the machine to the person. It's the Samuel Butler stuff at the level at which Samuel Butler did not think at all. Samuel Butler did see that people could conform to machines, even machines as he conceived them at that time. But the idea that the machines could themselves develop policy which was incompletely understood in its detail by the person who was using them was not anywhere nearly true to the same extent that it is now.

BRANDON: Could you give me an illustration?

WIENER: Yes. We have an automatic milling machine. In the form in which we originally made it, it was essentially a larger Jacquard loom sort of thing for working metal and not cloth, working by punch tape as the Jacquard loom does. Then the work concentrates on the punching of a tape; now we are developing ways by which—knowing the general thing to be done—we can program the punching of a tape. In other words, we have a "second order" automatization. When you do that, you are going to be regulated more by what the machine can regulate easily than by a thorough thinking through the problem as such. It's much easier to be dominated by a machine, where the detailed performance is not fully understood, than it is by one where the detailed performance is understood. Or let's take another thing, a chess game; let's take a chess-playing machine. Chess-playing machines exist now; they won't play master chess, but they will play a surprisingly good run-of-the-mill chess.

BRANDON: A full game?

WIENER: Some of them have played a full game, but most of them don't. But let's consider such a machine from the point of view of the opposing player, and let's put the opposing player in a position where he's not impressed by seeing the machine in front of him; let's play correspondence chess by such a machine in order to make it a fair comparison. If you play chess with an opponent—and it doesn't matter whether it's a machine or a person—your playing the game will give you the impression of the personality of your opponent, a game personality. If the machine has an absolutely set policy, you get the impression of a rigid personality. That is the present state of chess-playing machines, but they are rapidly developing to another state, in which instead of merely storing the previous moves of the game itself they have a record of previous games played and the evaluation of position depends on the success or failure of moves in previous games; they have a long-time memory, the second auto-memory. Now when you play such a machine you will find that gradually the machine will get onto your tricks because its storage depends not only on what it has played but on what you have played and on the evaluation of both moves. Such a machine would be far harder to size up as a machine—if you were playing against it. You would find that as you kept playing, sooner or later the tricks you had applied at first wouldn't work any more, and the machine was learning. Now that definitely is developing not only in chess-playing machines but in all sorts of machines. In dealing with a machine of that sort, in other words, you have the same type of problems coming up that you have in dealing with a person, and just as you can conform to a person when you play with him long enough, with a machine with a long storage you can also begin to conform to the machine. Now if that is done in political and social things, you see, the machine can really begin to dominate.

BRANDON: Well, how would you apply it to political and social fields?

WIENER: The problem is very much the one we have in folk lore concerning magic, namely, when you have agencies that act as powerfully as this, whether you call them magic or not is a matter of terminology. Now all the magic stories have just these cautions on them. Take, for example, *Der Zauberlehrling,* the magician's apprentice: When you have a magic power, you'd better be sure that you ask for what you want and not what you think you want. When the magician's apprentice asked the broom to carry water, he'd better be sure that he wanted it to carry water! You've got a beautiful example of that in the story of *The Monkey's Paw.* The point is that the first machines are approaching the monkey's-paw stage. Now when you ask for things—and particularly when you ask for them socially—you must be sure that you ask what you mean and not what you think you mean.

BRANDON: Well, where do you think that could lead—

WIENER: For example, if you are running a factory as part of the community at large, and you're merely asking for efficiency as a factory, you shouldn't be surprised at the consequent unemployment problem—it can be very serious. The machine won't pay any attention to unemployment unless you make it pay attention, unless that is built into the machine's consideration or there is some feedback from the social consequences of the machine. So long as the machine is technically competent but not integrated into society, you can't expect it to work automatically in a beneficial way for society. It is important not only to use the machine but to decide when and how to use the machine. Consequences other than direct mechanical ones must be taken into account, and if we don't we're in a very dangerous situation. With the power of the present machines and with the ability of one factory to upset a whole industry . . . you can get very, very serious consequences. In other words, you can't expect a machine to answer questions that you don't ask of it, that you don't give it the data to answer.

BRANDON: You really mean that the human intellect should set a certain limit on the use of the machine.

WIENER: It should set a certain question as to when the machine is to be used, and in that it should consider consequences of the machine other than the immediate manufactured consequences. You are playing too powerful a game now for laissez faire. The point is that laissez faire, when you can upset a whole industry by a single factory, does not have the checks and balances that laissez faire used to have and the philosophy of it no longer works.

BRANDON: I discussed not long ago automatization of factories with Walter Reuther and he said that the way to deal with the abundance that is created by automatization is to give people more rational means of choosing between gadgets and leisure.

WIENER: Without any doubt, but that's what I say . . . the whole policy of automatization must take account of those choices and this cannot be done by merely introducing automation—I hate the word "automation," I prefer automatization, "automation" is a barbarous form—introducing it merely as an adjunct to a social economic system as it now exists.

BRANDON: Do you think American society has begun to struggle against the machines?

WIENER: It has not begun to formulate questions like the need for leisure, the employment of leisure, enough. It has begun to, yes, but it has not gone very far along that path.

BRANDON: Well, do you think it has gone far enough in relation to the advances made by the machines?

WIENER: No, because the advances made by the machine are likely to come so rapidly that unless the adjustment is a little bit in advance of that—the adjustment to the way of thought— we're likely to be left high and dry. One of the surprising things with modern technique is that every apparatus, every method is obsolete by the time it is used. Techniques are developing so rapidly that we cannot, unless we are going to have a large period of chaos, allow our thinking to lag behind the techniques and the possible modes of development.

BRANDON: Now, Walter Reuther also pointed out that automatization causes an atrophy in the creative desires of man and that that is also very serious.

WIENER: That *is* very serious. I mean, when you degrade the skilled worker to a machine hand, you are not only making a change in efficiency for the particular job, but you can to a considerable extent destroy him as a human being; this is just the sort of thing I'm talking about. I don't think Reuther and I are at cross purposes here; I think we are using somewhat different language to talk of the same things.

BRANDON: Well, what advice would you offer—

WIENER: I would give the advice that society at large and the government should be sufficiently informed about its own social purposes to be able to use these new tools for the certain consideration of these purposes instead of as purely technical devices where the whole ideal is massive production. I think that the factory system, as we know it, is taken by many of us today too much for granted, as belonging to society in general instead of to a very recent period in history, and that in judging automatization we are combining it with the state after the First Industrial Revolution rather than finding how we can act in society in general and interpreting society sufficiently deeply to make the proper use of it. In other words, the combination of the nineteenth-century factory system with automatization—unmitigated nineteenth-century factory system with automation—I think is devastating. We cannot ignore social effects like that with respect to pure economic effects and expect to avoid chaos.

BRANDON: One of the problems is really how to relate this to the constant need of industrial expansion, one of the cardinal problems in this country.

WIENER: It is, but I might point out the following: That a constant expansion of any sort is unstable; that constant expansion cannot keep up indefinitely; that we've got in the habit of taking the growth of nineteenth and early twentieth century as a normal phenomenon when it cannot be a normal phenomenon, and that we will have to—if we wish to survive, merely survive—adopt some attitude which looks forward to some sort of stabilization of humanity or we shall change our environment so rapidly that we cannot accommodate to it and push ourselves off the earth.

BRANDON: Well, one reason for the pressures here for expansion is that the Russians are expanding, that they are coming more and more under the same influences that the United States has already been under. I mean . . .

WIENER: This is perfectly true, but if this keeps up indefinitely it is destructive to both. That is, sooner or later we shall be faced with a need for some sort of stabilization, and if we don't achieve this it's just too bad.

BRANDON: Now in the kind of society that the Russian represents, do you think it is possible to inject these intellectual restraints?

WIENER: You've got to make a very sharp distinction between Russian official policy and Russian individuals—quite as sharp as here. I've been talking to a good many of the Russian scientists recently and the problems and attitudes of the individual scientists —we don't talk politics together, naturally not—are just about the same as here. This question of over administration bothers them just as much as it does us. While the official Russian attitude is extremely rigid, I don't think that in the long run it will be any more permanent than the dogmatism of early Christianity. I mean, we've been through states like that before in the world. Now, if you say, it may be rigid enough so that either we will have a destruction of society or a temporary long-time destruction like the Dark Ages, I won't deny it; we may very easily have that. But if society is to survive and if we aren't going to go back into a permanent Dark Ages condition, in which, by the way, Communism as it exists at present *and* Western society will both go under—I think there will have to be some change and some flexibility as to our ideals—taking into account other things than merely increasing productivity. The productivity spiral cannot go on indefinitely without being quite as dangerous, or more dangerous, than the inflation spiral.

BRANDON: Did you get the impression from this session with the Russians that the social forces could become strong enough to restrain the dogmatism?

WIENER: To some extent: to a slight extent that has already begun, I would say that. For example, I'm going to take up a personal matter here which is not very deep, but nevertheless it is interesting. This whole idea of cybernetics was at first reproved as anti-Marxian, and very severely reproved. First they said it was a pseudo science, they spoke of me as a slave of the capitalist warmongers—not only that but a cigar-smoking slave of the capitalist warmongers, which seems to be a particular insult in Russia . . . I ran into some of the Russians in India about five or six years ago and I said to some of them: You'd better be careful how you talk with me, I'm a dangerous man; *Pravda* said I'm not only a "slave of the capitalist warmongers," but a "cigar-smoking slave." I said: Have a cigar? (*Both laugh*) Now about two years ago in Russia they changed their attitude. The Russian Academy voted that cybernetics was really a science and not a pseudoscience, and they've gone into it in quite a big way. I found that one of my Russian acquaintances from my trip to India has become head of an important cybernetic institute in one of the Soviet republics. He was here the other day and we had a certain amount of discussion of the possibility of my making a lecture tour in Russia in a year or so. This isn't the important thing. The important thing is that I could see very clearly that a considerable amount of the old dogmatism against cybernetics and myself has broken and that some of the scientists, at any rate, are in a more receptive position.

Well, at any rate . . . now you may say that they adopted this for purely economical reasons, but I've heard also that a good many of the scientists have gone back to my books which have been published in Russia, including *The Human Use of Human Beings*, although with a preface which points out that I'm not ideologically dependable and with some of the sharpest passages taken out—but not most of them—some pretty sharp passages were left . . . this has become a rallying point of the more liberal group of scientists there; this is what I've heard from several sources. As a matter of fact, an article recently came out in a Soviet journal on the new cybernetics institute in which the author stated that the neglect of cybernetics had been criminal and damaging to Russian development. The thing that I wish to emphasize is that there are books outside of the Communist frame which are being read in Russia now even though they are being read with a certain label "dangerous" on them. They are being read in the same way that the orthodox read books on the Index, but they do read them.

BRANDON: Well, how do they explain the reasons for the change in attitude?

WIENER: Simply that the intellectual class is developing more, that scientists are becoming more and more important—economically and socially as well as scientifically—and these people cannot be neglected. Therefore an opinion is developing among them which, while it may be dominated in action by the official opinion, is showing some signs of being an opinion of its own. I mean that people think in ways that are not too rigidly along the frame that they're supposed to think, even though they have to burn incense before Caesar.

BRANDON: It occurred to me a little earlier in the conversation, when we talked about the chess machine and all that; whether in the near future, for instance, the machine could determine—given certain facts—who would win a war between the United States and Russia?

WIENER: Provided the people programing it were sufficiently far-sighted to have well defined what we mean by winning a war—that is, if you don't put into the machine all the things that you mean by winning a war—certainly. You may well find out that winning the war has given you nothing but complete destruction.

BRANDON: Now we say that the machines on both sides have created a "balance of terror." Is it possible—even approximately— to measure that?

WIENER: Not at all easily and for this reason. I saw an article recently by a French general who wrote that we've gone far beyond the point in an atomic war with the terrors balanced; that is, we seem to have come to the point where either side can give substantially complete destruction to the other system. Under those conditions doubling the bombs does not double the terror. We've gone to the point, in other words, where if the thing starts at all both sides will go under. And under those conditions a balance of terror—if you do it simply by a linear counting of cities destroyed, and so on—ceases to have meaning.

That means in order to balance the terror we've really got to balance what we are valuing—and what we are valuing is not the question of the number of people killed by the bomb but whether enough are destroyed to make the continuance of civilization impossible. I think we've been too much influenced by considering all conflicts in terms of the formalized conflicts which are our own games. And here I can say something which is quite interesting—I can give you an illustration of that. You know how the world was shocked by the way that prisoners of war were used in Korea and other places like that. Do you realize that that could have been anticipated by anybody who intelligently understood Japanese chess? In Japanese chess the pieces are not shaped like our pieces here but are wedges with characters on them. When you take a man, one of the possible moves is to put the man back on the board that you've taken as your own man—pointing him in the opposite direction and counting him as your man in that way. Anybody who plays that sort of a game could be counted on not to take a prisoner of war as something out of the game. That could have been anticipated! Or take Chinese and Japanese Go . . . the object of that game is not to take pieces but to surround pieces. It is closely associated with traditional Chinese military theory. Their books on strategy and tactics are far ahead of any ancient European books. Their ancient books and the tactics and strategy are based on this sort of a thing, not so much removing pieces as controlling pieces by surrounding them. I may say that one might as well pay some attention to that now. "Victory" was a well-defined term when the wars were sufficiently limited so that somebody could really get advantage out of a war. I think the last war when that was definitely the case was the Franco-Prussian War; the last great war. In the eighteenth century it was regularly possible because of the limited game. The War of the Nations has not been possible, although it might have looked so at the Napoleonic time. The last one where there was any possibility of it was the Franco-Prussian War . . . the First World War showed that the percentage on the house of the gamble was too great, and at present the percentage on the house, which means on universal destruction, is so enormous that a war at present is like a revolver duel in a gas-filled cellar. Perfectly easy to kill your opponent, but not without blowing up the cellar.

The Age of the Flying Grandmothers

a conversation with

DR. WERNHER VON BRAUN

I asked the corporal who drove me back to the airport after my talk with Dr. Wernher von Braun, then the Director of the Development Operations Division of the Army Ballistic Missile Agency, how people on the base felt about him. "Look what he has done for this place," he replied. "In 1950 it had 16,000 inhabitants, today it has 50,000 and the payroll has gone up to 100 million dollars a year. We're proud of him."

Dr. von Braun received me in his spacious wood-paneled office overlooking the sprawling base. He sat behind a large, cluttered desk with two secretaries at his elbows. He looked like the head of a big private industrial combine who had made a rapid career, either because of his outstanding abilities, or because he married the boss's daughter. The confidence, authority, and self-satisfaction he exuded would support the first assumption, his striking handsomeness in a Teutonic way could lead one to the other. Tall, broad-shouldered, blond, blue-eyed he radiated strength. He was clearly a man of action and determination and a man who knew how to take care of himself. He spoke an American-English with a strong German accent, but he spoke it with remarkable fluency and with a rich vocabulary of American slang. His slightly heavy yet urbane old-world charm, his informality and wit quickly relaxed the atmosphere. The tape recorder did not bother him, except that once or twice he asked me to shut it off when he was not quite sure whether he was violating security or not.

Dr. von Braun is a man with a remarkable history. He was born in Germany and his "skyrocketing" career began at the age of eighteen with his joining a group of inventors who formed the German Society for Space Travel. Two years later he began working on rocket development for the German military establishment. Five years later, when he was twenty-five, he became technical director of the Peenemünde Rocket Center where the V-2 was developed, which caused some of the most grievous wounds to the British Isles. Fortunately, it became operational too late to have a decisive influence, but in the war's closing days Dr. von Braun, with more than 100 of his fellow scientists, surrendered to General Patton's Third Army and was shipped to the United States to resume research in rocket and missile development.

I had gone to see the builder of the V-2 flying bomb for Nazi Germany with mixed feelings. Was he an adventurer, a technocrat, or a mercenary? It was only after our tape-recorded conversation had been concluded, the instrument shut off, that we began talking about his past under the Nazis. Not surprisingly this subject made him a little uncomfortable, though obviously it was not the first time that he was being questioned about it. He attributed his past simply to bad luck and the unfortunate destiny of having been born in Germany at that particular time, of having grown up under the Hitler regime and of having become, as a scientist, the prisoner of the military whose orders he had to obey.

With unmistakable pride and satisfaction he showed me a cable of congratulations from Britain's then Minister of Defense, Duncan Sandys, sent him after the launching of Explorer I, America's first successful satellite. It said in part: ". . . you and I have had some differences during the war. I am glad we are now working together for the same cause . . ."

Today Dr. von Braun's main aim, he says, is the exploration of space. But he has learned from his experience of working for the United States Government that it is easier to obtain the necessary funds for military rather than civilian purposes. He has therefore appeared several times before Congressional committees pleading the cause for more money for rocket and missile development. He received much publicity with his warnings that unless the United States was willing to spend more, it would fall dangerously behind Soviet Russia's rocket achievements, and he has been proven right.

BRANDON: Can you give me any idea of how many millions of pounds of initial thrust it would take to fire a man to the moon, or for a trip in a satellite, assuming that he would have enough supplies with him to subsist in space for several days?

VON BRAUN: I think this depends entirely on the scope of the objective. If the objective is to get a man into a satellite orbit, a single man, leaving him there for a few orbits and then retrieving him safely to the earth, this is about the minimum sustained space flight that you can achieve.

By "sustained" I mean as compared to, shall we say, a ballistic missile flight, where you know in advance the thing comes back into the atmosphere fifteen or twenty minutes after you have fired it. If you get him up in an orbit, you could keep him there, if you wanted to, as long as you wish. But you may plan the experiment in such fashion that you say: I don't give him even some food, and I give him only an oxygen supply for two days, because I want to get him down, say, after ten orbits or fifteen, that's the minimum sustained space-flight objective.

That can most certainly be done with our ICBMs, like the Atlas, as boosters, and it can be done also, if you squeeze a little hard, with our IRBM. I would say the minimum that you need to do this is between 150,000 and 200,000 pound thrust, and it is simpler if you have twice that much. But you don't need a million to do that. With a million-pound thrust you can get two men in orbit, sustain them there for a substantial period of time, give them all kinds of equipment to make observations, physical measurements, you can equip them with lavish telemetry to check on the physical well being of the people and all that. *And with a million pounds you should most certainly be able to get one or two men in a trip around the moon with a landing back on the earth, but not including a landing on the moon itself.*

The moment you include a landing on the moon, you have to make additional allowance for the fuel for the retardation maneuver, for the landing itself, and the fuel to depart from the moon again. And all this fuel, of course, must be brought up to the moon to begin with, so the initial rocket is substantially larger. In addition to this, in order to land people on the moon, if they are to do more than just walk importantly around the landed rocket there, you have to equip them with some, say, transportation and housing and exploratory tools and equipment to do something useful. And all this costs weight.

BRANDON: What is really the problem in producing a million-pound thrust?

VON BRAUN: I would say the main problem is the dollar—money. You can get a million-pound thrust in the simplest form by clustering existing engines—do what you do with airplanes; you take four engines and make a four-engine plane out of it and you get four times the propeller thrust or pull. When you come to very large units, where you will have to use too many of these engines in a cluster, it pays off to have bigger units to begin with. That is why both must be done. I think that up to a million pounds there's no reason why you can't cluster engines existing today, but once you go into the multimillion-pound thrust class, it would be advisable to begin with a single unit of a million pounds each, so that you put 4 or 6 or 8 together to get a four or six or eight million-pound thrust.

BRANDON: It isn't anything more than an engineering problem.

VON BRAUN: Precisely. Nothing more than that. And very straight-forward engineering, too. It's just costly because it involves large test facilities and you burn up a lot of fuel making the tests.

BRANDON: How much would you estimate was the cost of the Russian propulsion unit for their Sputnik III?

VON BRAUN: One unit, after the development had been paid by somebody else?

BRANDON: Yes.

VON BRAUN: In terms of American money, after the development has been paid for, maybe two million or three million.

BRANDON: But when you were saying that a million-thrust engine is a question of dollars, you were also thinking of the experimentation that goes into it?

VON BRAUN: Yes, that's what I meant. The development of such a new engine today, until it can be flight certified—which means you'd be willing to put a man into a rocket powered by such an engine—is a question of, oh shall we say, to give you a "ball park" figure, one hundred million dollars.

BRANDON: You mean the clustering of existing engines alone is

238

not good enough. You then have to test how they work together.

VON BRAUN: Yes. And in order to do that you have to build test stands, you have to operate test stands over an extended period of time, and you have to have crews there with measuring gauges, and data deduction teams and all this. You must study, for example, the vibration level . . . it may be that you get such a terrific vibration in that tail that you get bursting ducts for your fuel lines, or something like this. I mean, these are engineering problems; they are relatively straightforward and, once you run into trouble, you can usually do something about them, but unless you take a very painstaking approach, you can run into sudden, unexpected catastrophe. And how dangerous these things can be is best attested to by the famous Comet incident in England, where one phase—which at that time no one considered very critical because Britain was pioneering in this field and was the first to stick its neck out in commercial, high-pressurized jets—nobody was aware of a hidden danger, and all of a sudden you had disaster. It turned out it was nothing but a window frame that caused all the trouble. But look at all the repercussions it had. It almost broke the BOAC's back, didn't it? And that's why you can't be careful enough.

BRANDON: Are you aiming at an engine of, say, one million-pound thrust, or something at least closer to the kind of rocket motors the Russians are using?

VON BRAUN: I can tell you that the Advance Research Projects Agency only a few days ago has given us here at the Army Ballistic Missile Agency the assignment—and on a high priority—to construct a liquid-propelled booster engine with an approximate thrust of 1.5 million pounds. We will use motors similar to those used in the IRBMs or ICBMs, already existing motors, and cluster them into a single unit. This is the quickest and least expensive way of going about building such a big engine.

BRANDON: There are a great many serious scientists who say that it would be a waste of time and money to work now on sending human beings into space, that plenty of new scientific data about space can be obtained simply by instruments and that that is a much cheaper method.

VON BRAUN: There are lots of things you can measure and determine with instrumentation. We are doing just that with our Explorers, so I'm certainly not against this approach. And as more and more weight becomes available in satellites—and space probes— the equipment, scientific equipment, measuring equipment that we can send up there can become more sophisticated and our measurements can be refined. Now here, in a way, we have already done just that with the Explorers. For example, Explorer III carried a tape recorder to record cosmic radiation data throughout the orbit and play it back over a receiver station upon command from the ground, whereas in Explorer I we had only information on the cosmic rays impinging on these Geiger counters while the thing was in direct radio contact with a ground station. Now in Explorer IV we even put four different counters—two scintillation counters and two Geiger counters. Some of them were shielded with lead, others not, to distinguish between the energy levels of these particles. So we refine our instrumentation as we go along. And of course, as more payload becomes available, we can do even better. The Russians' big Sputnik III is a flying laboratory. Their weights enable them to put a lot of instrumentation into these things that we couldn't afford to bring up yet.

But now, when it comes to the role of man, I think we should realize that there are certain areas where instrumentation just isn't so suitable, especially areas where judgment is needed. When you build an instrument to measure cosmic radiation, you are actually after an effect for which the human body hasn't even a sensor. By exposing a man to the conditions of outer space, you will never be able to tell what energy levels these particles have; you have to send instrumentation up there. But let's take a hypothetical case of a space ship landing on Mars. I wouldn't know how to design an instrument to radio me back from the surface of Mars as to whether there's life there and what kind of life. Of course, you can send a television camera up there, but that information will be very, very limited. In order to analyze such problems, to analyze the improbable, shall we say, there's nothing like the human brain.

The study of life begins with the question of soil bacteria, it goes all the way through the flora that a planet may have, which may be anything from lichen to mosses and trees and grass and what have you—even forms of plant life that we are not familiar with on earth. And when it comes to animals, you may run into anything from fleas and ants to big animals. There's nothing that can really match the human brain when it comes to evaluating a rather unexpected and, in a way improbable thing and correlate observations that have very little to do with each other. If you want to study—to give you an example—a phenomenon like the hibernation of certain animals in the Arctic world . . . it wouldn't be very difficult to put some instruments up in the polar region, but I couldn't even think of any instrumentation that could furnish us some information on phenomena like that; you just have to send expeditions up there to observe things on the spot.

BRANDON: A lot has been said about the advantages and disadvantages of liquid and solid-propelled missiles. How do you feel about this?

VON BRAUN: Well, this is a very interesting question and can't be answered in a sweeping statement either way. In order to throw a certain weight, say a military warhead, over a given range, you need a total impulse—the product of thrust and burning time. Now today for warhead, weights and ranges, as we have them in the Jupiter or the Thor, there's no solid rocket available anywhere that can do the trick. And if you would build one it would be such an awful monstrosity as far as transportation is concerned, you couldn't airlift it and even its transportation on shipboard would be an awful thing. So, such solid rockets (a) do not exist and (b) if they were built would be very awkward to handle.

About reducing the payload weight as it has been done on the Polaris, you can reduce the missile's weight—after all, it's only a transportation agent, a means of transportation for the warhead itself—and by cutting the warhead weight down you can do the same thing with a smaller missile. Now in the case of the Polaris, and this is a very important thing, the Polaris *is* the first IRBM that has ever been built as a solid rocket. The firing base is a submarine. As a result, the submarine provides the transportation, and the submarine is loaded for this Polaris and munition in the harbor by means of big harbor cranes or in open sea by means of fleet tenders, which have heavy booms to put new missiles in, and so under these conditions rather heavy loads can be handled relatively conveniently, but the moving platform itself is the submarine.

Now we are, as you probably know, presently developing a solid-rocket missile that is called the Pershing, which will be a longer range Army ballistic missile; this will also have solid propellants. But this missile is broken down into individual components that are so light that the thing can be airlifted.

The fundamental advantage of the liquid rocket is that you can ship it empty and you can load it up with five-gallon containers, if you wish. The solid rocket always comes as one big unit—the advantage is you needn't fuel it, but your disadvantage is you have to ship the whole unit in one piece. When you go to the very big units, it's like shipping the Leaning Tower of Pisa through the countryside, and that's where the limitation comes in.

BRANDON: Mr. DuBridge, the president of the California Institute of Technology, once said that space platforms from a military point of view are not very useful. Are you thinking of the space platform mainly for scientific purposes—because he said it is about as difficult as getting one human being back to earth as it is to project a bomb back to earth—it is very difficult to land it in exactly the right place.

VON BRAUN: I don't like that word "bomb." Because it is quite obvious that you can't drop a bomb from an orbit at all. I mean, if you try to detach it from its shackle in a rocket plane or a space station, it simply wouldn't fall down because it has the same speed and is also suspended in the orbit. What we should be talking about is launching guided missiles from such a space platform and the technique would be to provide them with a relatively small— probably solid—rocket charge and fire them in the direction opposite to the orbital movement. In this case, you upset this delicate balance of centrifugal force and gravitational pull to retard this missile, actually, so the gravitational pull gets the upper hand and pulls the thing tangentially back into the atmosphere. And once it gets into the atmosphere you can control it again—aerodynamically—like a very fast guided missile.

BRANDON: But it would have to be guided from the platform—

VON BRAUN: It's guided from the platform and the important thing is that the angular velocity of the missile around the center of the earth remains approximately the same as that of the station, so as the station goes around the earth the bomb also goes around the earth and so the station sees the bomb—the launching space station or space vehicle—sees this bomb, or this missile, all along and the earth merely seems to rotate underneath. And finally the target comes into sight—swings over the horizon—and there is still that missile going down. So these men can virtually establish a line of sight contact between target, missile and station, and the problem is very much the same, although much simpler actually, than that of an antiaircraft guided missile where you have to establish an intercept between the missile and the enemy airplane that may even conduct evasive maneuvers. So it is essentially the other way around.

BRANDON: The space platform has to be manned, I presume—

VON BRAUN: Yes, in this case it would be manned. But when I say "space platform" I don't necessarily mean a doughnut-shaped, huge thing with a hundred or two hundred people inside. It can actually be a hypersonic plane equipped with, say, twenty such guided missiles, but this hypersonic plane would be temporarily, at least, in an orbit. It can go in orbit three times around the earth, fire these missiles, and then land again. It can even make slight changes in its orbital path in between, so as not to be too much of a sitting duck for antisatellite missiles that the enemy may shoot at them.

BRANDON: Does such a plane exist?

VON BRAUN: It doesn't exist today. There's still some argument about the military value of all this and very often these things only develop as you go along. My personal feeling is that this unfortunate tendency of making things into weapon systems too early—just in order to get the big money rather than the small available for research and development projects only—forces people to make all kinds of statements as to how to utilize such things for military purposes before they even know how to survive up there.

I consider this whole business of putting a man into space and getting him back alive and how to observe from space and so forth, as a research and development problem in essence. But there is a kind of vicious mechanism involved: to get the big money support, you have to make a weapon system out of this. And for that reason quite a few people make bold statements on exactly how to wage space warfare because they have to spell it out in much detail in order to qualify for the financial support. But I am convinced that these ballistic missiles, these guided missiles from an orbit have a very great military potential. And if people say they can't see why they should get it up in the orbit to begin with, you might as well say there's no point in carrying a bomb up to 40,000 feet in order to drop it to the ground again.

BRANDON: But if you can send an ICBM over 5000 miles, why do you need to—

VON BRAUN: Well, in the first place, the ICBM has its drawbacks. The ICBM is fine and good when you know exactly where your target is. But the Russians don't publish the geographical co-ordinates of their atomic plants and the like, as we do. Here you can go into a filling station and get a road map and find the most secret plants on the map. In Russia we don't know of the existence of the big factories and maybe even of big cities. However, such targets may be discovered from an orbit by just seeing the thing —you have the possibility of just hitting it without knowing where it is. It's very much like with an airplane. When you see a target underneath, you may not know exactly where you are but you say: Here am I and there's the target, so let's drop a bomb on it. The moment you use artillery, you have to know the co-ordinates, and this is a great difficulty. Even determining them from photographic reconnaissance with the necessary accuracy isn't so simple—this is point one. And point two is, of course, the question of moving targets, because the ICBM is completely useless against the fleet. And suppose you discover a moving fleet in the wastes of the Pacific—well, no ICBM or IRBM will do you any good whatsoever. You have to get in there either with planes or with submarines or with other cruisers or aircraft carriers, or something, and knock it out. Whereas when you have a space station with missiles that you can aim at sight, you don't even care where they are exactly, you just shoot them down with the line-of-sight method.

BRANDON: But if you have a reconnaissance satellite—I'm talking about the first point—you can then pinpoint your target, can't you?

VON BRAUN: Yes, but a fleet is moving, you see?

BRANDON: Yes, that was your point two. Your point one was that there are a lot of targets that are invisible to us, or we don't know where they are.

VON BRAUN: Yes.

BRANDON: Now, couldn't you pinpoint those targets by a reconnaissance satellite?

VON BRAUN: And then tell the ICBM to get it, you mean?

BRANDON: Yes. I think once we've had the few reconnaissance satellites in the air we will know where those targets are, in fact.

VON BRAUN: Yes, this is to some extent right for stationary targets but for the moving target it doesn't help you a bit, because even if a reconnaissance satellite determines an enemy fleet moving through the Pacific Ocean or the Atlantic Ocean, that thing keeps moving. By the time you get an ICBM there, it may be twenty or fifty miles away.

I would also mention one more thing. This may sound a little fantastic, but I believe that even this has a future. I believe with these guided missiles, launched from a satellite, you can even get after airplanes, after high-flying bombers. Bombers flying at 40,000 to 50,000 feet are well above the clouds, but from the vantage point of this space station, you will see these bombers crawling over the cloud cover, or whatever it is, like bedbugs. And you can get after them with these missiles. On the homing phase of these things you can even get planes down, say over the polar wastes or so. And I believe there's a much cheaper way of getting planes down than having permanent guided missile sites on the North Pole—not nearly as cold either.

BRANDON: You prefer the space platform to the moon platform?

VON BRAUN: I believe for the time being any attempt to justify trips to the moon for military means is too far-flung. I believe the most military application of space is, of course, the reconnaissance and probably very soon thereafter with the bomb-carrying orbited vehicle, but the moon so far is an exploratory challenge, like Antarctica. Now whether the moon will have a military importance a hundred years from now, nobody can tell—it might.

BRANDON: Do you consider yourself a scientist or an engineer?

VON BRAUN: I often wonder about that myself. In our field it is hard to tell what exactly the difference is because in engineering alone you don't get very far, and in science alone you don't get very far either. I heard it said the other day: A scientist is an engineer who likes poetry. Maybe that's the difference.

BRANDON: What is it really that is the driving force in your work?

VON BRAUN: I got in all this as a kid when I was interested in astronomy. When I was fourteen my parents gave me an astronomical telescope, so as a youngster I spent many hours during the night watching the skies and looking at the moon and the planets. Then I saw a little booklet on astronomy, and there was an announcement in the book that Professor Oberth had written on the attainability of the planets by means of rockets. And I got that booklet and, of course, I was startled by the mathematics it contained, then I worked my way through it and—well, ever since that day rockets have been my life.

BRANDON: Are you, yourself, yearning to get into space?

VON BRAUN: Oh, yes.

BRANDON: You are? So it's really the exploration instinct in you, is it?

VON BRAUN: Yes. I think—let's look at it realistically. I think by the time we can put man into space, they'll probably pick some younger men—test pilots and so forth—to make the first exploratory trips. But if you look at aviation, the clientele of the airlines these days, you'll find they're mostly grandmothers and children that fly the transatlantic lines. This is the age of the flying grandmothers! It may be that by the time I'll be a grandfather, grandfathers on the moon or on space stations will be a very customary sight.

BRANDON: It's not just the desire for technical accomplishments?

VON BRAUN: No, I think it is just curiosity—I like to know what it's like out there on the moon and I think curiosity has always been my main motive. I think curiosity is what makes a scientist—I guess I'm a scientist—but if it takes engineering means to do it to get there, then I probably am an engineer.

BRANDON: You are European educated. Why do you think it is that Europeans seem to be better equipped for scientific and engineering work than Americans?

VON BRAUN: I don't think that such a sweeping statement can be made. My own observation has been that—at least in the engineering field—the tendency in American education is to produce more specialists and to narrow our fields. In Europe, apparently, people try first to acquire a broader background before they specialize. We find it very simple in this country to get excellent high-frequency engineers, or gyro specialists, or aeronautical engineers. But it is relatively difficult to find people with a reasonable working knowledge in several fields so that they can co-ordinate efforts together. For example, in the aeronautical field, it's very typical. When you simulate the movement of a guided missile through the air on the electronic simulator, you need a man who knows a little about aerodynamics, a little bit about mechanics, a little bit about mathematics, and a little bit about electronics. You get fine experts in all these fields but we always find it very difficult to find a man who is, shall we say, seventy per cent equipped in all of these fields rather than one hundred per cent in one.

BRANDON: But your work *is* a very specialized work . . .

VON BRAUN: Yes, but it goes into many fields. You see, even in an American hospital you can see this. By the time you are through you have been in touch with twenty different doctors—one is a heart specialist, one is a brain specialist, one is just for the spine, one for nerves or kidneys . . . and you get a wonderful report about yourself but in all this experience you haven't met one good old-fashioned house doctor who tells you what's wrong with you. And I think this goes in our own field also. Maybe my views are very old-fashioned in this respect, but I still believe in the old house doctor, and I think in engineering and scientific work this helps, too.

BRANDON: And where do you think the Russians have been able to get ahead of us? I mean, apart from the fact that they have almost unlimited means at their disposal.

VON BRAUN: I don't think they do. The Russian effort in engineering and science is just as limited by their total resources as it would be in any country, but it's a question of emphasis and priority. And for some reason or other the Russians decided to go into this rocket business maybe a little earlier than the decision was made in this country, and as a result they are a little bit ahead of us right now. Something else probably has suffered from this. Maybe they don't have a Strategic Air Command comparable with ours, because they said in this field we can win the race anyway, so let's jump over this whole phase and go after rockets. I don't know. But it just goes to show whatever you decide you want to have, you can get within the resources of a country and it's essentially a question of where does the priority go.

Of course, with their customary disregard for consumer goods and personal conveniences that has been the hallmark of Russia since back in the Czarist days, they throw more of their resources into armament and the buildup of heavy industry and things that make a country strong economically as well as militarily. In this country the decision to go ahead with the development of a ballistic liquid rocket of more than 100-mile range was made in 1951, when we got the assignment to develop the Redstone. That was six years after the war was over, and the Jupiter and Thor missiles—in other words, the IRBMs—were approved only in 1955, which was ten years after the war was over. Now based on the technology that existed at the end of the war, in particular as regards the V-2 program in Germany, many of these things could have been done years earlier.

The Russians apparently decided to go after this a little earlier, and you can't buy back lost time with any amount of money.

BRANDON: How much of an edge do the Russians have?

VON BRAUN: Well, my personal analysis is that they simply have these big ICBM-type rockets flying—and reasonably reliable—things of the Atlas class—that are still in the experimental stage in this country. But before you weigh the relative strength of the two nations you should look at the over-all situation. For example, even if the Russians have an ICBM that is reasonably reliable and could drop bombs on New York or on Washington they know that if they tried, the entire Strategic Air Command would be unleashed, and within a couple of hours all major Russian cities would be in ashes, they still would not shoot. And for that reason I believe it's unrealistic to say, well there may be a year or two when the Russians really have the edge on us because our Atlas isn't ready and theirs is. This isn't true as long as there is a Strategic Air Command in existence. Of course, it would be quite different if at the same time the Russians had an antiaircraft missile which would make the operation of the Strategic Air Command impossible. I think as they improve these weapons it may be increasingly dangerous to fly missions over Russia with jet bombers.

BRANDON: Well, don't you think they must have built up an antiaircraft defense by now?

VON BRAUN: Yes, but absolute antiaircraft defense, in my opinion, is the kind of a thing that is, shall we say, impossible. It is impossible to protect a large country completely with aircraft missiles. You can pick out certain vital areas, like the Moscow defense area, or the New York defense area, for that matter, and give them an almost airtight protection there, and make it very dangerous to attack those heavily defended areas. Well, whether the Russians have done this—and can do it—for all their potentially vital targets, I don't know, but the consensus of opinion of the experts in the Air Force is that the Strategic Air Command not only constitutes a very formidable threat to the Russians and could fly wherever they wanted to be, but also that the Russians know it.

BRANDON: How far do you think we've gone with the development of the antimissile missile now?

VON BRAUN: I would say the antimissile missile is recognized today as feasible, limited to certain defense areas. It is not the kind of thing where you say once we have an antimissile missile, no point in England or no point in the United States can be hit at all by a Russian missile. But it appears to be entirely feasible to provide a means of defense for, say, the city of London or the city of New York. It's not available today. It is feasible to build it and, well, a great effort is going on in this area, but I think it's a question of several years.

BRANDON: Would the suspension of nuclear tests delay the antimissile missile development?

VON BRAUN: That's a hot one. I think this is a loaded question. Of course, as a scientist I must say that there is little doubt that you can make progress better if you are able to go on experimenting. But the question you asked me is of much bigger scope. It therefore must be decided on a much broader basis by people who can assess the implication of the entire problem.

How Far Ahead Is Russia?

a conversation with

DR. ISIDOR I. RABI

I went to see Dr. Rabi at a crucial moment in history. The Soviet Union had just sent its first Sputnik into space and the challenge it represented to American scientific and technical leadership had suddenly dawned on Americans with a vengeance. They were stunned, indignant, furious. Outrage reverberated across the country. "How did the Russians manage to get ahead of us?" Everybody asked. And everybody was searching for explanations, for scapegoats, for remedies.

Dr. Rabi was at the time still chairman of President Eisenhower's Scientific Advisory Committee and he seemed to me the best person to seek out for the answers: a great scientist, a Nobel prize winner in 1944, an experienced teacher, and a man close to the crucial governmental decisions in this field. The question was not only what problems Russia's achievement in space posed for American scientists, but also what were the long-term conclusions to be drawn from it about the American system of education which got a good deal of the blame for this setback.

Dr. Rabi saw me in his office at Columbia University on 24-hour's notice. He received me calmly, like a man who knew exactly what he wanted to say. In spite of his short, delicate figure, his little feet and narrow shoulders, he seemed capable of carrying, so to say, the world on his shoulders. Behind his shyness and restraint there was bite, often passion—passion for humanity. What interested him most were the wider political and social implications of scientific progress and their influence on the outlook for the future of our civilization.

Dr. Rabi came to this country from Vienna, Austria, at the age of three. His father had a grocery shop in New York and life as a student was not easy for young Rabi. But forty-three years after his arrival in this country he won the Nobel prize in physics for his discovery of molecular beams. He has been Higgins Professor of Physics at Columbia University since 1950 and ever since the war he has been closely associated with the American nuclear defense program. He was a member of the General Advisory Committee to the Atomic Energy Commission and he remained chairman of President Eisenhower's Scientific Advisory Committee until Dr. Killian became the President's principal scientific advisor.

In President Truman's days in the White House, Dr. Rabi participated in an historic conference whose purpose was to decide whether or not to proceed with the development of the hydrogen bomb. The Truman administration at the time was rent by conflicting views, and the scientists had failed to come up with an agreed recommendation. Mr. Truman at that conference, facing his key advisors, asked one simple question, according to Dr. Rabi: "If we don't do it, could the Russians build it nevertheless?" The simple answer he got was: "Yes, they could." Mr. Truman's very simple conclusion followed: "Well, then, we must proceed with it." And that settled it.

BRANDON: Russia's launching of two satellites was a great shock to the Western world. Do you think American scientists or the government were to blame for Russia's being ahead of the United States in this field?

RABI: Of course, there's not so terribly much science in Sputnik. It's chiefly a matter of engineering. We need to make headway in exploring new fuels, and in improving electronic guidance systems and engine designs. All this is not basic science. It does not mean that the Russians are ahead in basic science, but they are probably well ahead in rocketry. Our progress does not depend on scientific decisions, but on whether we will employ more money and more people. It is a decision for the government. With more money and greater effort we could go ahead much faster. Of course it would be done at the sacrifice of something else—teaching and research in other fields—but we can do it.

BRANDON: I have been told that the United States has many blueprints for space projects but that the hitch is a shortage of space engineers.

RABI: I don't think this has been proved yet, but we are in the habit of indulging ourselves by going off in many different directions at once. I rather think that if we focused our efforts we would find we have plenty of personnel.

BRANDON: Are there space faculties at any United States universities, and have the Russians any?

RABI: I don't know of any here, but the Russians have all sorts of things. I met some Russians, for instance, who were professors of television. Russian scientists are generally more broadly trained than either Americans or British.

BRANDON: What will have to be done in the West to win the science race with Russia?

RABI: Fundamentally the general public must first of all learn to appreciate the importance of science as an element of culture. If that happened, it would result in a revision of the curriculum of secondary schools, and public and grammar schools in your country. More time must be spent on mathematics and science. When science is considered as valuable as language has been in the general part of our education, our troubles will be over. We must also teach science not as the bare body of fact, but more as human endeavor in its historic context—in the context of the effects of scientific thought on every kind of thought. We must teach it as an intellectual pursuit rather than as a body of tricks.

In Russia science is considered essential to a general education. As far as I can see the Russians are getting a twentieth-century education, whereas in the United States and England young people are getting a mid-nineteenth-century education.

BRANDON: In Russia scientists come from part of the élite that includes industrial managers, generals, and prima ballerinas.

RABI: Yes, the Russians have orientated their revolution toward science, even though it is sometimes pseudoscience. Nevertheless, that's an important part of the image which has been a stimulus to young people. In the West the scientist has been a late-comer and has not had the same social acceptance. That acceptance is gradually increasing. Today, if a man has no feeling for art he is considered narrow-minded, but if he has no feeling for science he is considered quite normal. This is a fundamental weakness of our whole civilization. Right now it's the thing which may bring its destruction.

BRANDON: I have often heard scientists blame the traditional anti-intellectualism of this country for their lack of recognition.

RABI: Yes, we are very rich, and rich people become intellectually lazy. However, today, professors in the United States have a very high standing. They are extremely important in their communities and in the government, much more powerful and significant than in any other country. But the general public myth remains, and it is the public myth about the social handicap of being a scientist which still decides what young people go in for.

BRANDON: Is this public myth still influenced by memories of McCarthyism and the fate of Professor Oppenheimer?

RABI: It is still too early to judge the long-range effects of McCarthyism, but the exclusion of Professor Oppenheimer, a man who accomplished so much for his country, is indication of the failure of the country and the authorities to value correctly such contributions, both intellectual and substantial, to the welfare of the United States. Only when he is returned to more active government service will it indicate that a change of heart has occurred. It will be a source of encouragement to the whole scientific community. Nevertheless, there has been a tremendous upsurge in American interest in science. We were not beaten by the Russian developments for lack of interest. I think the chief criticism must be not that we are not contributing vast amounts but that we haven't contributed as much as we could and should.

BRANDON: Is the West handicapped by its free enterprise system? Our scientists are much more under pressure to show results and success, something that is particularly hard on the pure scientist.

RABI: I think this is more true in England and on the Continent, but in the United States there has been a tremendous support from the government, from private industry and from foundations. Of course that does not mean we could not use more funds, or that we should not make science as a profession financially more attractive. Another great mistake is that our universities have expanded at the expense of professors. Their funds, instead of going into the salaries of professors, have gone into building expansions to increase the number of students.

BRANDON: What kind of advantages have the Russians gained from launching their two Sputniks?

RABI: I would say, at least from my point of view as a scientist, that science is a very worthwhile activity in itself, for the delight and knowledge it gives you in exploring the world in which you live, the universal matter, the universal laws of nature and so on. So the advantage they have is that they are acting like human beings and are learning about the universe. And I am sure that most Russian scientists take it in that way. If there are certain side advantages, insofar as military applications are concerned, and, of course, general prestige, that's true of many other endeavors. But the real thing is that there is space and that we must learn about it.

BRANDON: Will it enable the Russians to get to the moon ahead of us?

RABI: Certainly. Just as great attempts were made to reach the South and North Poles when I was a boy, so we will have realistic attempts to reach the moon.

BRANDON: Do you have a yearning to get to the moon?

RABI: None whatsoever. But there are people I know who would volunteer to go to the moon even if it were the last thing they did.

BRANDON: What would be the advantage of shooting a rocket or a person to the moon? The accomplishment of spectacular achievement?

RABI: Yes, it makes you feel good.

BRANDON: It makes scientists feel good?

RABI: The whole world. I think the whole world was inspired by the Russian achievement. It was a very worthwhile thing.

BRANDON: I could have done without it. It's not the kind of thrill I get excited about.

RABI: Well, we could have done without our civilization. Our ancestors, ten thousand years ago, did without many things, and they lived and died. You could also do without the poetry of T. S. Eliot . . .

BRANDON: I think that rather than being thrilled, this country is in a mood to redouble its efforts to match Russia. Maybe this is the time to call for sacrifices.

RABI: I agree. Better now than later. But I also think that it will require more than sacrifices. It will require a certain amount of intelligence.

BRANDON: What do you mean?

RABI: I mean a policy which is more suitable to the times than the policy all countries have been pursuing for the past ten years. It has become a truism to say we are headed for destruction. But these wise statesmen both in the East and the West keep on heading for it.

BRANDON: You don't believe in the deterrent power of these weapons?

RABI: Oh, I think they certainly are very deterrent to rational people; but do rational people make war? The worst of it is that as the deterrent grows, the result of a single mistake becomes more and more terrible. The deterrent is nothing but a psychological thing, and I don't know whether anybody knows enough about human psychology really to place a lot of faith in it. A policy of mutual deterrents will ultimately lead to universal disaster—but that's my view.

BRANDON: Has your committee suggested to Mr. Eisenhower the need for much closer collaboration between American and British scientists, and do you think the atomic energy law should be repealed?

RABI: Certainly, and the President is very sympathetic to close collaboration. It would strengthen our whole effort. As regards the atomic energy law, I think it need only be changed. We still need a protective law, just as we have protective laws about drugs. Some of the information protected by it involves the fate of the whole country.

BRANDON: The number of atom bombs, for instance?

RABI: That's the last thing I would want to keep secret. I think if I had the deterrent I would like people to know its full extent. But that's not the kind of information I am talking about. I mean weapons and devices and one's new discoveries in that field. But there is a great area where our exchange of information needs improvement. We could beat the Russians by having a much closer relationship.

BRANDON: And how long do you think it will take us to catch up, to safeguard our long-range future?

RABI: Oh, a generation. You know how long it takes to change a cultural pattern. The growing general awareness of this need will help us, but nevertheless we will have to work hard to succeed in a generation.

The Tulle and Taffeta Rut

a conversation with

JAMES THURBER

Remembering the melancholy end of James Thurber's story
The Interview, *I approached an interview with him not without*
trepidation. Would mine too end with pencil and notebook
thrown out of the window? Or, worse still in my particular case,
would the tape recorder be flung out into the street?

What made me even more nervous in my eager expectation
was the fear of an anticlimax. Everybody thought that Thurber
was a "natural" for my type of conversation piece. Yet at the
back of my mind I remembered how often I had found profes-
sional humorists to be disappointingly unfunny in conversation.
Finally, knowing from his writings how much he hates gadgets,
I wondered how he would react to the presence of my tape
recorder.

It was with these anxious thoughts that I knocked at the
door of Thurber's suite at the venerable Hotel Algonquin, the
old haunt of the literati, right across from the offices of The New
Yorker *magazine, which owes so much of its reputation to*
Thurber's funny, quiet desperation with humanity. The Algonquin
is his habitual pied-a-terre *whenever he comes to town from his*
retreat in Connecticut.

My anxieties, however, were quickly dispelled by Thurber him-
self and his dedicated wife Helen. They made me feel at ease
in no time, even though Thurber's gaunt figure and his flat,
commanding voice were a little intimidating at first. This was
not the "little-man-what-now" type trapped between the "hard

257

covers" of life, this was a man who knew what he wanted, who had learned and obviously succeeded in overcoming many vicissitudes of life. He had read an earlier conversation piece of mine with Leonard Bernstein and, obviously impressed by Bernstein's performance, wondered aloud whether he would be able to do as well. Now it became my turn to reassure him, to put him at ease. A human situation in the best Thurber style had evolved.

Helen quietly left after a while and Thurber without any prodding began to talk about himself, about his ideas. The interview did not begin with a question: it just happened. We were talking and I switched on the tape recorder . . . My earlier fears proved completely unfounded. Not only was Jim a relaxed conversationalist with a humor that slays with the touch of a feather, but he also seemed completely unconcerned about my tape recorder. At least that was my impression that afternoon.

However twelve hours later, and in all fairness to Jim, I must mention this; he sent a three-page, single-spaced letter to my room which began as follows: "In the watches of the night I began remembering recent verbal assaults I have made, when in a bad mood, upon the craze for interviews. My opposition lies in the fact that offhand answers have little value or grace of expression, and that such oral give and take help to perpetuate the decline of the English language in my country and yours . . . While lying awake around dawn this morning I began polishing some of the things I told you. Since I rewrite everything all the way through from five to twenty times it is hard for me to think of my conversational replies being used as my final considered opinions and judgments. Maybe it will come out all right, but here are a few written thoughts . . ."

I sat down immediately and listened to the tape, then compared it to his letter. There was no doubt in my mind that the tape was much better than the content of his letter. And in the end he agreed.

Thurber is one of the oldest members of The New Yorker staff, and his stories and fables have made him perhaps the most important writer of serious comedy today. His humor has a universal quality because it springs from the inadequacies, the

pathos, the inevitabilities, and the tragedies of the human situation.
Nothing is more difficult than to make you laugh at the truth.
But that is Thurber's great gift. He also makes you think. There
is always something serious, something moving hidden between
the lines. It is a humor touched, often soaked, in melancholy.
It is devastating in a quiet way and so are his drawings of the
bewildered human race. Since his first book, which he wrote with
E. B. White, Is Sex Necessary?, he has written some two dozen
others, his latest being his reminiscences of Harold Ross, the
fabulous character who founded The New Yorker.

The total blindness which has enveloped Thurber for some
years now has made it impossible for him to continue drawing
his whimsical cartoons. Today, the only thing he can still draw
in a sort of mechanical way, is his dog. He showed me how.
He placed the fingers of his left hand on a paper in an obviously
well-rehearsed position and then he led his pencil carefully from
one finger to another. The connecting lines between the fingers
surprisingly added up to a perfect outline of a dog's head. But
in order to place its eye in the right spot his wife had to come
to his aid. He lives now in a diffusion of light. But the eyes
of his mind are sharper than those of most seeing people. Thurber's
real secret however is a warm heart and an angry mind.

THURBER: . . . One of my great English friends was the late
Paul Nash, your great painter and critic. Paul came over here
in 1931 as one of the three foreign judges of the Annual Carnegie
Museum of Arts Painting Show, of all places in Pittsburgh, and
I had lunch with him at the Century Club, not realizing that
the forefront of American art would be there, all the great
American painters. Nash had never heard of any of them. I'd
only been drawing for about two years but he came to me and
said: "You're Thurber." And he insisted on having me put at his
right, whereupon I got so nervous I grabbed a bottle of Scotch
from the sideboard and put that on my left between us. Then
he said to a distinguished bearded connoisseur of art across the
table: "Do you know Milt Gross?" And the man said: "Never
heard of him."

Of course, Paul was what I call in one of my pieces, Admirer-in-Chief of American comic art. In this piece I tell about one incident in London twenty years ago . . . I had a one-man show of drawings to my own amazement. Nash, of course, came around. One wonderful thing was that two of the drawings were stolen; the gallery boys were frantic about this but I was pleased mightily that anybody would risk arrest or, at least, reprimand for stealing some of my drawings. After all, if you have your drawings stolen, you're made.

Nevertheless *The New Yorker* turned down a series of mine called "The Patient"—about ten drawings of a man in the hospital. Shortly thereafter they were printed in a London magazine no longer in existence called *Night and Day*. Do you remember *Night and Day?* I sent the prints to Ross, the then editor of *The New Yorker*. He then decided that definitely I was just a passing fad—"the fancy of the English" as he said, but he became very proud that the English knew about *The New Yorker*.

Nash had said in one piece in the *New Statesman* about comic art that "Thurber seems to start drawing with nothing in mind—just scrawling as in the early style of Henri Matisse." Word of mouth changed this into the fact—the supposed fact— that Matisse admired my drawings. He happened to be in London, the old gentleman, in '37 or '38, when I was, so they called him up to see if they could arrange a meeting. But the gallery man who called up his secretary came back pale and stammering and said: "Mr. Matisse's secretary says that he had never heard of Mr. Thurber OR *The New Yorker*." That delighted me no end and I innocently sent a telegram off to Ross that Matisse had never heard of Thurber OR *The New Yorker*. Ross had never heard of Matisse, so that evened things up.

BRANDON: What does really inspire you to sit down and draw?

THURBER: Well, actually, it was a thing just like lighting this cigarette, I think . . . it was a form of relaxation after writing, or when I got stuck on a piece of writing. A great many of the drawings I did, I was unconscious of doing. It was only in 1929 when I shared an office with E. B. White at *The New Yorker* that he began to pick up my drawings—pencil drawings on yellow copy paper—and then, I think in April 1929, sent one to *The New Yorker* art meeting. I'd done it in about thirteen seconds—a seal on a rock gazing at two distant specks and saying: "Hmm—explorers."

Well, Ross thought it was a gag—Rea Irvin, our art editor, drew on my drawing, up in the corner, a head of a seal—Rea being a professional artist and great draftsman—and wrote under it, still on my drawing: "This is the way a seal's whiskers go." Andy White promptly the next Tuesday—we had an art meeting every Tuesday—sent it back with a note saying: "This is the way a Thurber seal's whiskers go." They still rejected it.

Then White and I wrote *Is Sex Necessary?*—a burlesque and parody on the flocks of sex books coming out at the time. We took the drawings to the publisher and laid them out on the floor, and three members of the firm of Harper's stared at them and said: "These are, we presume, a rough idea of what you'd like a professional artist to do for the book." And White said: "No, these are the drawings that go in the book." Well, that really shook them—they almost brought the book out quietly.

But then, to everybody's amazement, including Ross's, it began to sell, and he heard about it—and about the drawings—and he came into my office and said: "Where's that damned seal drawing you did—several months ago—that White sent in." And I said: "Where is it? You rejected it, so I threw it away." And he said: "Don't throw things away just because I don't like them—or think I don't. Do it again!"

Well, I didn't do it again for two years. And when I did do it again, by sheer accident, it became the best known of all my drawings. In trying to draw the seal on a rock again with pen and ink—and the seal was just the same as ever with Thurber seal's whiskers—the rock looked more like the head of a bed. So I finished the bed, put a man and his wife in it and had the woman snarling at her husband: "All right, have it your way—you heard a seal bark!" And there was the seal, right above them, you see. And when that was printed, in January 1932, I got a telegram from Bob Benchley. There was nobody whose opinion any American humorist or cartoonist would rather have had, and he said: "Thank you for the funniest drawing caption ever to appear in any magazine!" And when Ross saw that, I became over his dead body an established *New Yorker* artist.

In the end the wonderful thing was that Ross, who had waved these drawings aside as a gag, and then as a passing fancy of the English—he said that with pleasure and faked gruffness because he loved and admired, as I do, the English—could not get enough of them. Ross just went to any length then to make it possible for my drawings to appear though he had once turned them down. Of course, when he turned my first drawings down and they appeared for the first time in a book, he was beside himself. Here was something creative in his own office, something he'd had first shot at, and it had got into the hands of a publisher who published them—and Ross considered publishers a kind of freak. He didn't think they had any intelligence or any sense . . . Then, of course, he kept at me to send him more drawings and finally I did. But I made him wait a year before I turned them in. Then he found out that I had done 307 drawings for *The New Yorker* with captions, 175 of which had appeared in books.

When I began to go blind it finally got so that I couldn't draw even with black grease crayon on sheets of yellow paper 5 by 4—they had to deal with them like blankets at one time—then I got so I couldn't draw at all, so Ross went through all kinds of worry and suffering about that and said: You see, we can arrange all of it. He decided we would reverse cuts and use new captions; we would cut the drawings up and make permutations. He rearranged the figures of men and women, dogs, furniture, bridge lamps, and so on . . . And he'd send me captions himself. We did that for a while, but it seemed to me it was a fake. The first publication to notice it—they were not opposed to it, they just said they detected some of my old drawings with new captions—was the *News Chronicle* of London, England.

Finally I said: Well, if we use captions that you or somebody else devises on drawings that I didn't rearrange, I would have no creative part in it. And then I said: You mustn't think I grieve about not being able to draw. If I couldn't write, I couldn't live, but drawing to me was a little bit more than tossing cards in a hat. I think he needed more cheering up about my blindness than I did, you see. That was Ross. That's why it's so wonderful to write about him because he was such a contradictory personality. I imagine Ross now in heaven pacing the Chalcedonian Halls—complaining to some uninterested angel: "What the hell's the matter with the English? Thurber's drawings are not a passing fancy or a fad—they're here to stay. Don't they know that?" Wonderful man to work with . . .

BRANDON: Did you develop those characters just by chance—inspiration?

THURBER: Yes. They have been called "unconscious drawings"—a great many of them were unconscious—just start drawing, and suddenly you have it. All the best ones started that way with nothing special in mind. And then I would go from the drawing into the caption. If I started with the caption and then drew the picture to fit it, a stiffness was likely to get into the figures, you see. And then the fact that I was not a draftsman—never took a lesson—can't really draw—came out. But if the drawings have any merit, it was that they were—some of them—funny. And that's what they were intended to be. They weren't intended to be a special form of art over which I struggled. Because I don't think any drawing ever took me more than three minutes.

I remember when *Life* magazine sent a man over to interview me, and they had devised a little dial with a hand on it and minutes marked off—ten minutes marked off—and they were going to take pictures of me over the course of ten minutes showing the progress of a drawing, I said: "Well, ten seconds would be better!" And there wasn't a drawing I did for them that day that took more than about a minute and ten seconds.

BRANDON: It's a sort of—something in between a drawing and a doodle, really—

THURBER: Yes, it is that. I never use the word "doodle"—it always reminds me of a housewife at the telephone trying to get the grocery and being unable to reach them—but there definitely is a resemblance to that, yes, since the best ones were more or less unconscious.

The one that caused the most trouble at *The New Yorker*

was the one I described in this new book*, called *The Lady on the Bookcase*. It was a nude woman on all fours on top of the bookcase and a man is saying to a lady visitor: "That's my first wife up there. This is the present Mrs. Harris." And he points to another lady. Well, that upset Ross. He called me on the phone in the country and said: "Is the woman on the bookcase dead or stuffed or alive or what?" And I said: "Well, I'll call you back—I'll have to ask," and hung up. I called him and said: "My doctor says a dead woman couldn't support herself on all fours, and my taxidermist said that you can't stuff a woman—so she must be alive." And Ross roared into the phone: "Then what's she doing in the house of her former husband with his wife—naked?" And I said: "You have me there, Ross, I'm not responsible for the behavior of my characters." But he printed it anyway.

Later I explained to him that I had tried to draw a wife at the head of the stairs—at the head of a flight of stairs waiting for her husband. Having no skill in draftsmanship, I lost perspective and the stairs turned instantly into a bookcase, or what looked like a bookcase, if you made transverse lines—so I made it into a bookcase—and there was this naked lady on top of a bookcase. A great many of the drawings came out accidentally like that—a great many. And it was a great deal of fun not to know what you were going to end up with.

Then, there was the famous incident of Carl Rose's drawing in 1932—very graphic it was, too—of a fencer cutting off his opponent's head and yelling: "Touché!" and the head flies up in the air. Ross thought the Rose drawing—of course, Rose is a fine draftsman and realist—was too bloody and too gruesome. "Let Thurber do it," he said. "Thurber's people don't have blood—you can put their heads right back on, they're as good as new." So I did the drawing and it was run that way and nobody was horrified. But Paul Nash said: "I agree with Ross completely, that this man isn't dead—his head is just off—come off—he's lost his head for the moment."

Nash was extremely anxious to meet Ross. I took him in to see

* *The Years with Ross*

Ross in 1931. I had briefed Ross a little: "You're going to meet a man named Paul Nash—you know nothing about painting— Nash is a distinguished English painter and art critic." Ross said: "Bring him in." So I did. Ross said: "Hi Nash!" That's the way it began—they shook hands— he said again: "Hi Nash!"—there're only two phony arts, painting and music." Nash was delighted. Later, he said: "You know, he's like your skyscrapers—they're un-believable, but there they are." Well, he had a wonderful time.

BRANDON: Considering that you illustrate so much the War of the Sexes, your women particularly, have not much sex or sex appeal.

THURBER: It was Marc Connelly who said: "Well, they have for Thurber's men"—when that question was once brought up. But, I should say there were times when I wanted, really, to get a pretty woman in a drawing, and I had toyed with the idea of having some other artist do it. Then I'd draw the rest of the drawing around it, but Ross didn't go for that one. I mean, a luscious Arno girl, for instance . . . with one of my women.

I haven't sent any captions to *The New Yorker* for years. The last one was illustrated by Whitney Darrow. It showed an ardent young lady talking to a gloomy, intellectual young man and she is saying: "When you say you hate your own species, do you mean everybody?" I think that's the last caption of mine they took.

Once I wanted this Dumb Blonde, as we say in America, sitting in a bar, with a gentleman saying to her: "You complicated little mechanism, you." It seems to me that could be easily done, but . . . again, that was the kind of thing that frightened Ross. He instantly thought of physical or even sexual mechanism, you see. His mind—he was the cleanest-minded man in the world.

He never told a dirty story among men in his life, and he wanted to keep the magazine clean. He *never* went in once in his life for the appeal of sensationalism, or sex stuff. In one case, a series of Arno drawings of a man and a woman supposedly in a compromising situation on a porch swing—the caption was passionless, such as: "Have you read any good books lately?" This still appalled Ross so he made Arno redraw it. Finally I said that the way we ran the series, the man and woman were approximately as sexually involved as the husband and his sister-

265

in-law at a christening. But that was Ross, you see, getting everything as good as possible.

He was afraid of what he called the "functional"—I called him Old-Chief-Afraid-Of-The-Functional. Once Ross brought to me an Arno drawing. It showed one of Arno's distinguished Southern gentlemen of the old school and definitely in his late fifties, dancing with an ardent young woman and saying: "Good God, woman, think of the social structure." Well, that threw Ross—he was afraid of the expression "social structure." "Why, in the name of goodness?" I asked. And he said: "Well, you know, social diseases mean sexual diseases." And I said: "Dismiss it from your mind, Ross." He just questioned everything, you see. He was also afraid that some of *The New Yorker* wits would get things in the magazine that definitely do belong elsewhere.

BRANDON: This idea of a War of Sexes, was that inspired by your mother? From the description that I've heard of her . . .

THURBER: No, my mother was a great person. I owe practically everything to her because she was one of the finest comic talents I think I've ever known—she really was marvelous—she died two years ago within three weeks of ninety years. And up into her late eighties she was still comic and played tricks on the telephone with her friends.

No, I think it's really from having lived two years—1918 and part of '20 in France—and comparing the life of French, English, and other foreigners . . . with family life in America. I could see clearly the domination of the American woman over her man as compared with that of other countries. America is a matriarchy. It always has been, it always will be. It became obvious to me from the time I was a little boy that the American woman was in charge. I didn't really definitely plan to set out to do that War—I just drew on my unconscious, I guess, and my store of observations about that. I think it's one of the weaknesses of America, the great dominance of the American woman. Not because of that fact in itself, but because she is, as a Chinese woman of distinction said to me some twenty years ago, the least interested in national and international affairs and the most ignorant.

266

The Tulle and Taffeta Rut

BRANDON: But there's a lot of talk about the woman's vote nowadays and its influence . . .

THURBER: Yes, of course, there are so many more women than there are men. The League of Women Voters, the last I heard, had only 127,000 members out of 88 million women in this country and it's very hard for them to get members—women care about other things.

BRANDON: But what is different about the American woman, really, from say—

THURBER: I think that Philip Wylie invented the word "Momism." I think that word is a very important word—the mother dominates the son—and every time, I know when he gets home from school in the summertime or wintertime he slams the screen door and says: "Hey—Mom! Can I do this—can I do that?" Permission from "Mom" is the big thing.

BRANDON: I presume you mean that there won't be any revolt by American man against the matriarchy—

THURBER: I don't think there will be. Of course, in the series I did, *The War between Men and Women*, the woman surrenders to the man, but you'll notice in the drawings that each woman has a big rock or club behind her back. In other words, the war is not over, so far as she's concerned.

BRANDON: But, take Washington, for instance; I can't think of a single woman who plays an important political role behind the scenes, like a Madame Pompadour or—

THURBER: No. No—that brings us back to their weakness in interest in politics, economy, in national affairs. I was very much struck by the fact that the average American woman I know hated history in college. They just don't like history; they know nothing about it, either. So I said that the average American woman, when the war broke out, thought that Pearl Harbor was a movie actress. A young man who works in radio was discussing with me and others one day the average woman and one man said: "What do you mean by the 'average woman'? What do you mean, for instance, by the 'average American woman'—who is she?" And he said: "That's easy. The average American woman wishes her husband was dead and she was in the movies." Well, that's carrying it a little far.

BRANDON: I once asked a girl, a married woman in Moscow—where you have so-called equality among the sexes—how she liked that? And she said she'd rather give up her equality . . .

THURBER: You mean she'd rather be the second sex, as the girl in France called it who wrote the book The Second Sex. I do sometimes wish they would.

By the way, the most heartening thing to me that has happened in America for a long time is the Russians getting ahead of us in the Sputniks, because for the first time since the dark ages of McCarthy, the Americans are coming to the realization that God likes other countries as well as this one; that it is possible for American superiority to be exceeded, but once we have to buckle down, we buckle down. I think that has been a very fine thing.

The six or eight years that went by—those terrible years—when all the American Congress seemed to do was to investigate writers, artists, and painters—to me were the dreadful years. All this time Russia was getting ahead of us; all this time we were fighting a new cold civil war—suspecting neighbors, suspecting the very nature of writing, of academic intellectualism, anything—that was a very bad moment in our history—perhaps the darkest we've ever had. But I think we're out of that.

We've always had a belief in push-button superiority and instant lovability—everybody must love us; why shouldn't they, we're Americans! During the darkest years of the McCarthy period, while many writers seemed to be frightened, possibly because they had belonged to some organization when they were in college, they were afraid to write. But I wrote four or five outspoken pieces, because I thought our culture had descended to a pretty low place. Now, when we took the passport away from Arthur Miller—one of the most ridiculous things we ever did, and also one that certainly didn't help our prestige among our allies—I came out, and several of us did, and spoke against that in the New York Times. A Congressman had asked him on the stand: "Do you really believe that the artist is a special person?" Then I wrote in the Times: "A nation in which a Congressman can seriously ask: 'Do you think the artist is a special person?' is a nation living in cultural jeopardy." Well, now I think we get farther and farther out of the dark shadows of that cultural jeopardy—and it's a darned good thing.

Americans pride themselves on being a nation of humorists, but I'm afraid that our sense of humor and comedy—certainly sense of humor—does not go very deep. America is the country of the gag, the hot foot, the pay-off, the belly laugh—and that kind of thing. But a basically, imaginative humorous country could never have overemphasized the way we have overemphasized "Americanism."

I once wrote a small piece about our constant use of "Un-American" when we really mean "patriotic." As if patriotism was a monopoly of the Americans. We would be annoyed and frightened if every time we picked up a foreign paper, there were references to "Englishism"—"Welshism"—"Francism"—"Un-French"—"Un-Belgian."

I have written a little scene in a bar . . . the husband and his wife get into an argument with a man with an accent, and the husband says: "You must be un-American." He says: "I'm a citizen of Oslo" "Then he's un-Swiss," the wife says. "No, I think he's un-Danish." The man finally says: "No, I'm just Norwegian." Well, I wrote that about 1951 and there wasn't anybody who wanted to print that, because we did have the jitters.

Yet, despite the pieces I wrote, nobody ever knocked on my door. Somebody asked a Congressman once—I don't know the Congressman but he's from my state—at a party: "Why have you never investigated Thurber?" And he said—and this is my proudest medal: "Because our wives and daughters wouldn't allow it." I think that's wonderful.

BRANDON: It all means, I suppose, that Americans lack the faculty to laugh at themselves.

THURBER: Yes, they think they can, but they really can't. An old professor of mine at college, Professor Joe Taylor, said: "A thing that cannot endure laughter is not a good thing." There was a period—I wrote about this in some of my pieces—in which we were distinguished for our ability to laugh about ourselves, the days of Mencken, Will Rogers, William Allen White, and many others, with either a broad sword or a slapstick, you know, making fun of Congressmen. But then we got scared of 'em.

And that's a bad thing when we get scared of our Congressmen, because a lot of them are buffoons. When you get right down to it, we're only scared to death in peacetimes—we're wonderful warriors, you know—but it's the jitteriest country in peacetimes.

Put your head out the window and yell: *Here it comes!*—and everybody rushes out on the street. There was actually, some years ago during the dark ages of the McCarthy period, a tremendous hailstorm in Martha's Vineyard—half the size of golf balls—the hail fell on the ancient town of Edgartown which was founded during the reign of King James the First . . . I think—named after his oldest son—I may have the kings wrong . . . but they thought: Here come the bombs—they're now the size of golf balls. Something new. And everybody ran out on the streets and got slugged on the head with these things, in spite of the orders from civilian security to stay indoors. Our desire to take to the open is a panic urge. We're living on the edge of the abyss. As somebody said, the fascination of the edge of the abyss. But I'm very hopeful that America has finally seen that it's got to buckle down and get to work.

Our strength is our weakness and it may get so that we mistake loose talk for free speech and the freedom of liberty for complacency—you see, we don't have to do anything, everything's going to be fine because this is God's country. I did one caption for *The New Yorker* which was printed some years ago. It showed a meeting of representatives of all the nations of the world—just at the opening of the United Nations—and an American saying: "It's a wonderful thing to co-operate with all our friends and allies right here in God's country."

You see, we can't get it out of our minds that this is where God lives—He never even visits any place else. If, as I say, we were a nation of humorists, as we think we are, we would appreciate these things. Actually, during the jitteriest period *The Male Animal*—a play that I wrote with Elliott Nugent in 1940—it ran eight months—was revived in 1952 and ran ten months. It was put on by a company in a small town in California, Laguna Beach. The review was headlined: "Americans attacked at Playhouse!" Well, I had some real fun with that one. I actually laughed him out of existence. I said: "Well, don't you realize

I intended to undermine America in three acts. I also under-mined American womanhood, and wives and football players and everything else—and they ought to come and get me for it." And I said: "After all, when people went to see that play, they joined the party fast—either the Democrats or the Republi-cans or the one going on to Twenty-One after the play." And then I said: "I might as well confess the whole thing—now that they're on to me as an underminer—*The New Yorker* really got its name so that we could change the 'Y' to 'W' overnight and become *The New Worker.*" Well, it turned out the country could—and did—take that as a kind of ridicule of the intimidation and oppression, and it was high time somebody was doing it. I got no bad reactions from it whatever and I got a great many letters from all over the country praising our play. Rather sheepishly the Laguna Beach paper printed an editorial as if *The Male Animal* were an attack on the United States of America . . . Well, it does mention Abraham Lincoln's name in the same breath with Sacco and Vanzetti. My heavens, I also mentioned Herbert Hoover's name in the same breath . . . Of all the people who ever lived, the one who would most have approved of that was one Abraham Lincoln, you know. "If you have enough breath," he once said, "you can mention anybody's name with mine."

BRANDON: In this present generation there are few, if any, humorists, really.

THURBER: It is a curious thing . . . I did some research on that. In the 1920s when Ross said that humorists were a dime a dozen, they practically were. Sally Benson appeared in 1929 and then in 1930, Ogden Nash and S. J. Perelman; after that the pickings have been very few. We've had Peter de Vries, in the last twelve or fourteen years, and John McNulty. But the young people are not funny . . .

I found out in addressing college classes—journalism classes years ago—that since the mental weather of the 1920s there's been a definite decline into grimness. They used to ask me: How old is Peter Arno? What is Dorothy Parker like? And now they ask me what I believe about the future of America—or what is my artistic credo? Everybody is getting very serious. You can just sense that change; the beginning of a kind of a chill.

It is very hard to sustain humor—the desire for humor—in a period when mankind seems to be trying, on the one hand, to invent a pill or miracle drug that will cure us all of everything; with the other hand, it's inventing a machine for instant annihilation—you just light the fuse and *Bang!* Up go all the healthy people. Now that, of course, is part of the dichotomy of the very nature of our species, which makes it interesting and also terrifying.

If there is life on other planets, they must be scared to death of us, sending things up that may finally bring one man of another race to their planet. That would scare me if I lived on Venus, where they must be having a lovely time, if it's anything like its name.

BRANDON: Pity Venus is not within rocket-shot. It sounds much more enticing than the moon. Talking about gadgets, and I mean entirely earthbound ones, an incident comes to my mind which, I think, is perfect Thurberism. It happened at an embassy in Washington the other day. The ambassador or minister or whoever it was had the usual two telephones on his desk, but both suddenly seemed out of order. When the telephone rang and he lifted the receiver, he didn't hear anything and when he lifted the receiver to make a call the second telephone sounded dead. The mechanic came, but he could not find anything wrong with the telephones; it looked like a mischievous mystery until he found that the receivers had been on the wrong telephones. (*Laughter*)

THURBER: Wonderful.

BRANDON: It's as universal as Thurberism. Talking about universal humor—do you understand the humor in *Punch*?

THURBER: I haven't had a chance to see *Punch*, really, I've been so busy just writing about *The New Yorker*, but actually— here I go with my English "actually"—to read *The New Yorker* takes a lot of time. Johnny Miller—John Duncan Miller, the former *Times* of London man in Washington—said to me once: "I used to be able to read *The New Yorker* coming up from Washington to New York. Now if you want to finish it, you have to go at least as far as San Diego." Some 3000 miles . . . We have got into a thing that Ross dreaded all his life—the magazine is turning grim and long. In the early days, he used to pay a premium for stories under 2000 words and even more word-rate if it was under 1000. If you ran past 5000 it was as little as three cents a word extra, you see, which is a valiant but 'fewtle'— 'futile' gesture.

BRANDON: In your earlier days at *The New Yorker* writers with new ideas probably had a much better chance to get a hearing. Now *The New Yorker* has its style—its tradition—its format, and everybody tries to conform to that . . .

THURBER: Yes, yes . . . that's one of the troubles that a magazine is likely to settle into a kind of formula. It's hard . . . It's now a great big business over there—writing and editing—it's terrific. All of us worry about its increase in size, wealth and what I call "matronly girth"—but it lacks comedy. It's very hard to break into *The New Yorker*. They're not really looking for humor—they don't expect it, so they don't really encourage humor. As I said in one piece, Ross used to say: "We're in a velvet rut"—by which I think he meant the stuff is pretty average, but we're making money out of it.

But now we're in a tulle and taffeta rut, 'cause everybody's writing about—and this seems to me a curious escapism—their girlhood, young womanhood, first baby, first year of marriage, and so on. Then *The New Yorker* uses so many women on an island— well, that's a form of escape, too, I think. And then our great love of Westerns—the President reads Westerns—and television is almost dominated by Westerns, you know. Yet if you see those Westerns, they're bloody and cruel and certainly no escape in that sense. *My Fair Lady* was written before the First World War— that is, the Shaw play. There is a return to the past, you see, as a form of escape. It's impossible to analyze it off-hand, but I do feel that people are trying to get away from the terrible pressure of man as a purely political and cold war creature. The strain is terrific.

BRANDON: Also there isn't enough irreverence—there is no magazine or no newspaper, really, where irreverence can find an entry.

THURBER: That's right. You mean as in the days, for instance, of Henry Mencken's *American Mercury*. Yes, we have nothing like that, that's true. There again, the craziness of the 1920s was counterbalanced by its great sense of freedom and liberty of expression—take John Dos Passos' *Three Soldiers*. You could write about anything and nobody was afraid of anybody. Americans were not afraid of Americans. That's the thing that frightens me about America is our tendency to carry on the Civil War in some way.

We've always had this tremendously competitive spirit among Americans, you see. Yesterday, not content with having a football season of professional football, we ended up with a "Bowl" Game in which you select men from the East and the West and then you have them go at each other. And the day before, we had the North and the South—fighting each other in football—in amateur football. In some ways that's healthy, and in some ways it isn't.

BRANDON: How do you feel about the state of American writing?

THURBER: I think it was Edmund Wilson who said that at his age—he's a year younger than I—"You really haven't got time left to spend on contemporary writers because you wouldn't get anything else done." The tendency of a person in his sixties is to go back and read the classics and the great books that you have been putting aside, saying: "I'll take that one with me to Bermuda"—you know—they pile up and you don't get around. So I'm really not competent to judge.

I do have a definite sense that humor and comedy are declining. It shows up in the New York theater. The tendency is to turn to farce rather than high comedy. I was very much impressed when I saw *The Chalk Garden* because that came like a fresh breeze of comedy out of England. I wrote that you felt the girl who wrote this play was writing in a truly free atmosphere, unafraid of criticism or intimidation or of anything else. And it shows up in the ease of writing. Very often the English or foreign play has an effect that we don't have. We seem to have lost respect for comedy in this country. Comedy has declined tremendously on television—to an astonishing and disheartening degree. People get the idea that comedy is easy—comedy is very hard to do right. It is a very important thing, too, and there are not very many holding on. For instance, Sid Perelman* still writes a lot—and I

* S. J.

still get quite a great deal written, but Andy White† and Frank Sullivan don't do very much any more. But there may be, I hope there will be, a renaissance of comedy—good comedy—for the very fact that *My Fair Lady* exhilarated this country beyond belief. There's no parallel. We've finally got back to high comedy —and everybody loved it.

BRANDON: Do you prefer human beings or animals, really?

THURBER: I have my moods. Often I think it would be fine if the French poodle could take over the world because they've certainly been more intelligent in the last few years than the human being, and they have great charm, grace, humor, and intelligence. My old poodle, who died at seventeen, had geniune comic sense . . . But, as I say, when I spoke to the poodle about her species taking over, she said: "The hell with it!" They don't want to get mixed up in it.

But what troubles me most about today are our children. In his recent State of the Union speech two things amused and depressed me that the President said. One was his romantic appeal to the "schoolboy with his bag of books and his homework." Our schoolboys, I am afraid, lack mental discipline. We have a frightened inability to appreciate discipline. We instantly call it, even essential mental discipline, "regimentation," and dismiss it as Communistic. We confuse it with political regimentation. Our kids have given up hard work. Every year, for instance, I get hundreds of letters from English language students from all parts of the United States asking me for biographical material.

Some teachers started a few years ago in what we call junior high school the idea of assigning English classes to write about a given writer—and they said: "Why don't you write to him and ask him a few intelligent questions?" Well, from all over the country came letters . . . Steinbeck was so overwhelmed with letters that he wrote a piece of protest about it in the *Saturday Review of Literature* saying they get peremptory, don't send any. We all had to get up a form letter telling some facts about ourselves. But they don't want that.

I sat down and wrote one boy the other day, named Robert— and their letters are so illiterate and badly spelled—he said:

† E. B.

"My English clarr . . ."—this was how he typed it out—and I said: "How in the world could you do that when the 's' follows the 'a' on the keyboard and the 'r' is on the line above?" And I continued: "You live in New York City—I occasionally help out kids who write me from the small towns, where there's no library available—but you can find out in one afternoon all the 'biographical material' as you call it, about me." He wrote back and said: "If you don't send me some biographical material I'll write to another writer." They don't want biographical material; they want us to do their homework. In one case I wrote back that I spent two years studying the facts about the Loch Ness monster before doing my story about it, but that I never wrote to it.

The other thing that amused and depressed me about the President's speech was his use of the word "finalize." My most intense dedication now is the defense of the English language against the decline it has suffered in this century and particularly since the end of the last war.

My country has always cared little for exactness in language and has always depreciated good English as "book larnin'." Those of us who are dedicated to good English as the very basis of communication and understanding have been called everything from teacher's pet to egghead and nobody is more to blame than members of Congress. They should be regularly punished by fine and one day's confinement in the third grade of grammar school.

In one of the pieces in my book *Alarms and Diversions* called "The Psychosemanticist Will See You Now, Mr. Thurber," there's a complaint about what I call "Congressionalese." It ends up with the story that under President Eisenhower some bureau in Washington sent out to all other bureaus a letter to protest against the use of certain fake words like "finalize." So what does the President do but use "finalize" in his State of the Union address. That awful, fake, synthetic word . . . but now he's finalized "finalize"—so we'll never get rid of finalize. His diction too is careless. He says individual as if it was spelled "individjel." Wendell Willkie too said: "The 'Nine States of Amurica" and "the great resarvar of foreign friendship for us." The very basis of human communication and understanding is language. And when I turn on the radio and listen to discussions at the United Nations, the English representatives speak beautiful English and so do the foreigners, from the Orient, from anywhere. Their English is excellent. The American is likely to be sloppy and full of slang.

I was very much impressed by reading the English papers to see how carefully they write criticism of the theater or books—or of anything else. It's done with loving and painstaking care and we just seem to have thrown English to the wolves. We don't care what we say or how we say it. I'm afraid I'm waging a losing battle trying to do anything about it. I was very pleased to print something by—I can't recall his name right now, an Englishman who told exactly how Americans would say Winston Churchill's great line: "Give us the tools and we will finish the job." "Supply us with the instruments and we will finalize the undertaking." That's *pure* American—pure Congressionalese. If we went out into the streets dressed the way we talk, we would be arrested for indecent exposure.

My basic worry has been the necessity of our understanding each other. For instance, in London I met a girl who, at that time, had lived and worked in New York for nine years. We got to discussing the English language, about which I have written a great many pieces. And when I asked her what word—what American pronunciation annoyed her most, she said: "The way you say 'fewtle' for 'futile.'" And I said: "Well, I'll come back at you, you're right. 'Futile' is a lovely word—the 'ile' is like a chord on a mandolin and must be sounded. If we spelled our word out the way *we* pronounce it, it would be 'fewtle.'" But you people ruin a lovely piano chord when you change 'figure' into 'figger'—so we come out even."

There's another interesting thing—since I have this profound interest in words and speech . . . When I was in England twenty years ago, people were saying "actually"—when they don't always mean it, and also "as a matter of fact." But I was terribly impressed the last time with the fact that almost all Englishmen now use a gesture of speech which has a curious sound—and I started a piece about it called "The Very Best Butter" for *Punch* when Mr. Muggeridge was still editor—I'd even hear it

on the BBC: "Oh yes, I was there but-ta that was years ago . . ."
and then you'd get the real triple effect: "Yes, I've been in
India, it's true but-tmm-ah . . ." you see, then you give it the
three sound—and I noticed it in practically anybody. You haven't
got it, but I noticed it in almost everybody I'd see.

It's a little gesture as of lighting a cigarette or sipping from
a glass while they think of the next phrase, you see. Ours, of
course, is "and-da"—and that's . . . An American woman's
"and-da" comes when she can't actually think what she's going to
say and has lost track. She'll say: "So we went to this party and-
da—and-da . . ." But the English don't lose track of what they're
saying, they just put that lovely coupling as between two cars in
a railroad train—"But-tmm"—and it fascinates me. When the
English say the King's English—now the Queen's English, I
suppose—they really mean something by that. Harold Ross used
to give to each one of us, when we started to work there, a copy
of Fowler's *Modern English Usage*. He knew it by heart—it's a
wonderful book. I did a parody of it called *Our Own Modern
English Usage* and got a very nice letter from Fowler's secretary—
this was way back, thirty years ago. I gave Ross an earlier book
that Fowler had done called *The King's English*. But, you see,
that's a term of vast respect for language—the King's English—we
don't have that. Save us from the President's English!

BRANDON: I feel that I have complete contact with you. Can
you see me?

THURBER: No, I can't see a thing—

BRANDON: But I have a feeling that you can see me, really—

THURBER: I know, I fool people. I have actually sat all evening
with people and they didn't realize that I couldn't see them—at
least, dimly—but that's just what the doctors call "accommodation."

See, I started to go slowly blind in 1940—I lost my left eye
in an accident when I was only six; with glasses I could see very
well until I was forty-five and then the cataract set in and
complications—so that I have every known disease from glaucoma
to Grade A iritis and a thing called "sympathetic ophthalmia."
But what happened was that the sight, which I still have and can't
get at, is covered by what they call "the thickening of the

capsule" from which they take the cataract. I now live in a soft diffusion of light—and it's very pleasant, it's very soft—it's a light without landscape or figures, you see, just a definite diffusion of light.

But I look at voices—people talking—turn my head—because I was always appalled at the blind man who doesn't look at anybody . . . but that's a sheer matter of accommodation. The process started in 1940, very gradually, so that I almost was unaware of it and then it got so I couldn't see.

In 1951, a man who was almost blind, an Englishman living in Manchester, England, sent me what he called a luminous white crayon and dead black paper—all of it by airmail. And with that I could really do some of my last drawings because the white line on the black paper gleamed.

Another thing that is very moving and I like to tell—I don't know if it embarrasses Helen. When she and I both had eye trouble—she was in the hospital with a detached retina—I got letters from ten strangers, two from England, offering to give an eye. They were people with perfect sight, offering to give me or Helen one of their eyes. One of them came from an English gardener in Sussex. He said: "I am thirty-four, married, I have two daughters, seven and four, I have very strong eyes, I am willing to give you one because of the pleasure I've got out of your books."

Well, I had to write to all these ten people saying this: "Since the human being is so ignorant about the eye, the only thing that can be transplanted is the cornea. The cornea is that transparent covering of the whole eyeball, you can get that. But you cannot transplant anything else. Furthermore, no doctor in the world, no ophthalmologist or eye surgeon, would perform what they call a prophylactic operation on a good eye, for the simple reason that they do not know what effect that would have on the other one." But for ten people—strangers to me—to be willing to give up one of their eyes, isn't that wonderful? That's the kind of thing that doesn't get in the papers about human beings, isn't it? We hear all about the ones that gouge eyes out—but we don't hear about the ones who offer their good eyes.

BRANDON: Once I interviewed Axel Munthe, who then was blind. I had the strange experience that when I entered his house, he put both of his hands on my face and he said: "You have a good face—come in."

THURBER: I never tried the sense of touch on friends like that— to see how accurate it would be . . . But it is amazing how you depend more on your ear. For instance, at a party at my house a few years ago, a big party, I said later—after a certain couple had left—"They're going to break up." And they all thought I'd lost my mind. They said: "Why, we have never seen such friendliness and smiling." I said: "Yes, you looked at them—I heard them." And they lasted six months after that.

There's something about voice that is destroyed if you are watching the expression of the face. It will mislead you sometimes. Everybody looks at the eyes and expression, but I concentrate on inflection, intonation, and dropping and raising of the voice—and often surprise people by saying: "What's happened?"—"Well, how do you know that sort of thing?"—"Well, I can tell . . ." Although they're saying something that isn't sorrowful or serious or tragic, you can tell.

A man asked me if I could get my sight back for one day, who would I want to see? Marilyn Monroe? I said: "No, I want to see some old friends of mine. I have a pretty good idea what Marilyn Miller must look like—"

BRANDON: Have you heard the definition of an "egghead"? Someone who calls Marilyn Monroe "Mrs. Arthur Miller."

THURBER: That's very good. Philippa Halsman, the photographer, told me how difficult it was to get different expressions on her face, yet she's a great comic. To get a special new look on her face he said to her: "How old were you when you had your first affair with a man?" And she said: "Seven"—she knew exactly what he was up to—and didn't change at all. When the same photographer was talking to me, he led me over to a chair, an ordinary kitchen chair, cheap, wooden chair, and said: "Lean back on this." I said: "What shall I lean against?" He said: "Against this old-fashioned brick fireplace I've had put in here—nineteenth-century America." And I said: "What's the idea?" "Because I feel you're rugged." I said: "Oh boy, you've found the word that appeals to most American men, but I'm not 'rugged'." Every American, I guess, would love to be thought of as an Abe Lincoln leaning back against the fireplace. That's the old self-made, rugged American type . . . The other type is "Outdoors Western," or "Silent Jim." Helen says I'll never be called "Silent Jim."

BRANDON: I sometimes get the impression from your writings that you really would have preferred to live in a different century.

THURBER: Henry James' great desire, and I don't share this with him, was to have lived in what he called the "Baronic Period"—the English 1820s, around there . . . Of course, I've been considered a great Henry James man and I do admire him as a craftsman very much. But the more I reread Henry James, the more I realize he didn't have a great deal to say except in skill and in the relationships of sensibilities—rather than the clash of anything more important.

My love of London and of England is inherited from somewhere, although my family on both sides have been over here since the eighteenth century. I still feel a sense of "getting home" when I get to London, to England. It is a country where you can hear bells ring. By the way, when we were in London in 1955, we called—as we always do when we're there—on John Hayward who, at that time, was sharing an apartment in Cheney Walk with T. S. Eliot. And Eliot said, pointing to the ceiling above: "I don't want you to think I moved in here for this reason, but I just found out the other day that Henry James died in that room above here."

And he asked me if I knew what his last words were supposed to have been. I said, "No, I hadn't heard that." And he said: "He was supposed to have said: 'The inevitable end—the distinguished thing'." Well I've been thinking about that for two years and while "the inevitable end" anybody might say, "the distinguished thing" sounds exactly like a Henry James title for a short story, such as "The Great Good Place," "The Distinguished Thing," "The Stronger Sense," or anything . . . But I think that his voice was getting low and that what he really said was "the extinguished flame."

I do not believe that Henry James would consider distinguished something that happens to everybody. I want to see what his reaction to that would be.

But I'm satisfied living in this century. If you lived in any other century, you would miss some of the greatest and most appalling things . . . Well, to use the phrase of the greatest phrasemaker of our time, Sir Winston Churchill: "The awful and the magnificent." He was speaking of the A-bomb—that awful and magnificent weapon. Well, this is an awful and magnificent century to live in, and I wouldn't miss that.

C 2